The ART of CREATIVE ADVERTISING

A VISUAL/VERBAL PROBLEM-SOLVING APPROACH

MICHAEL ANTEBI

The ART of CREATIVE ADVERTISING

MICHAEL ANTEBI

A VISUAL/VERBAL PROBLEM-SOLVING APPROACH

REINHOLD BOOK CORPORATION
New York   London   Amsterdam

For B.S.D.

© 1968, Reinhold Book Corporation
All rights reserved
Printed in the United States of America
Library of Congress Catalog Card Number 68-16025

Edited by Mary Lyon
Printed by Mutual Lithographers, Inc.
Bound by Van Rees Book Binding Corp.
Published by Reinhold Book Corporation
430 Park Avenue, New York, N.Y. 10022

CONTENTS

PREFACE

When first I started this project, more than ten years ago, I had no idea of formulating a method for classifying all forms of print advertising, much less of putting them together in a book. This book grew, spontaneously, out of my collections. Just as others collect stamps or coins, I collected significant advertisements.

☐ I spent long hours looking through hundreds of magazines and newspapers, collecting thousands of examples of creative advertisements. As my files grew more and more complex, I tried to simplify the method of retrieval so that I could quickly find specific ads I was looking up. I was seeking underlying similarities, ideas susceptible of correlation. But as it stood, this mass of material was intermixed, indiscriminately, in folders under every product category.

☐ When I abandoned the standard ways of classifying advertisements, I went on collecting and filing in a more or less intuitive fashion, but with an undefined feeling that there was probably a better way. However, no alternative method occurred to me immediately. I simply brought my files up to date from time to time, putting into the same folders those ads which, I felt, had some relation to each other.

☐ Following this system for some months, I finally paused to look back. I was astonished at what had happened. Almost automatically, it seemed, the hundreds of diverse ads had been sifted out, then drawn together into coherent categories. All I had to do was to label the individual folders.

☐ The classification structure in this book is the refinement of what, I believe, is a unique approach to creative Problem-Solving in Advertising.

■ Michael Antebi

INTRODUCTION

Ideas don't occur on demand. Usually, long hours of research are required to find even the germ of an idea that will prove helpful in solving a client's problem. Used as a working tool in solving day-to-day problems, this book can be invaluable. Its chief purpose is to release the creative person from countless hours spent in the elusive pursuit of an idea.

☐ This is not an Art Directors Annual. Award-winning ads are here in plenty, but very many more ads were chosen on the basis of how skillfully they solved problems.

☐ To use the book most effectively, the reader is advised first to skim through it, not excluding the Contents and Index; then to settle down with the table of Classifications which follows, to absorb its structure, from a practical standpoint, and the philosophy which underlies it.

☐ In the Bibliography is a listing of books covering sources of creativity, the value of exhaustive research, the practical aspects of preparing good copy, effective layout, choice of media. These books were written by the best minds in the advertising industry about how they conceive of and practice their art.

The PSA Method of Classification.

This is a convenient arrangement of all types of print advertising. Classification can do more than eliminate chaos; it can supply information we should not otherwise have had access to. It enables us to evaluate, to compare, and in some measure to predict, the validity of our solutions.

☐ The classifications are: Animation ■ Analogy ■ Contrast ■ Diagrams ■ The Familiar ■ The Incongruous ■ Nostalgia ■ Personalizing ■ Participation ■ Sequences ■ Symbolism
☐ Small ads, coupons, and posters are grouped together irrespective of the Classifications.

Flexibility of PSA.

The classifications presented here are based on logical appraisal arrived at over a long period of study. Some ads do overlap one or more classifications. The decision to put these into one group or another might sometimes have been decided by the toss of a coin.
☐ Hence, the method is really a flexible one. The reader, professional or student, is free to arrange the ads into categories according to his own logic or a need, perhaps, for an off-beat solution. Creative people in particular shy away from dogmatic limitations. This aversion is clearly justified. Indeed, any rigid formula can cripple the problem-solving propensities of the individual and kill his originality.
☐ At first glance, one method of classification may seem about as feasible as another, provided the premise it is based on is made clear.

The original intent here, as already explained, was to find the underlying relationship between ads, dissimilar as they might appear on the surface. The PSA classification system soon emerged as the one that best related ads in several ways, with the promise that they might prove to be related in still other ways.

How To Make Use of PSA. Faced with a client's problem, the reader might leaf through the pages of this book, trying to relate any of several ideas to the problem of the moment. He might find part of an ad he can build on to evolve a fresh concept. Or he may simply hunt for an example of something he has a 'feel' for but can't quite bring to the surface of his mind.

☐ If the problem seems to lead in a specific direction, or if the reader has already decided on a particular approach—for example, to animate the product, or to dream up a symbol for it—he can simply refer to the appropriate section (Animation, Symbolism), where he should find several applicable ideas.

☐ If he is boxed in by a stereotyped approach, let him refer to the Index for a fresh start, see if other products comparable to his are listed there. Then let him turn to the appropriate section, see what particular devices have been successful, and take off from there.

☐ The reader might find an interesting layout, a bit of typography, a special kind of photograph, or a fresh copy approach—any one of which might suggest to him a novel solution. The re-working of successful ads

stimulates the imagination and puts intuition to work. It is actually a deterrent to copying since it can only provide the mind with a springboard for reaching new — and different — plateaus. The result, it is hoped, will be higher standards of advertising.
□ Using this book as a reference work, a teacher might assign to students the problem of devising new solutions alternative to those presented here, thus further attesting the flexibility of PSA.
□ The majority of ads in the book can be projected with an overhead projector. The various ads can be shown consistently large without adjusting the placement or focus of the projector. If need be, projection slides can be made at low cost; they can be made on a production line basis since the ads are almost all of the same proportions.
□ As many ads as possible are included, and they are shown as large and as legible as possible. Some ads are shown full page to duplicate the impact of the originals. The surprises of ads in sequence, on two or more pages, are duplicated in quarter-page reproductions. If an ad was in two units, back to back, it will be found so placed in this book.

Problem-Solving. The number one problem in advertising is to get an ad read. According to top advertising men — and the research pollsters — something like 85% of all advertising is ignored, merely passed over by the reading public. Virtually every advertising agency has evolved a system of rules for copywriters and art directors in aid of creating good ads.

☐ In *Principles in Advertising* (1925), Daniel Starch sets down these objectives for a successful ad: "1. Must be seen. 2. Must be read. 3. Must be believed. 4. Must be remembered. 5. Must be acted upon."

Readability. Since getting an ad read takes priority over many other challenging considerations that tax the best brains in the advertising industry, it follows that the requirement of readability is axiomatic. In order for an advertisement to arrest and hold the reader, it must be easy to read. Obviously, copy, illustration, layout and type all contribute to readability. Following are some examples of what can be done visually to make an ad easy to read.

1   KLM

This ad is a classic. All the elements are correctly in place. The picture is at the top, the headline at the center, and the copy at bottom. If you are selling a Tiffany image, the fewer elements in the ad the better. This might be a reason for abandoning the picture caption. But the reader is more likely to read the one-line caption than he is a block of copy. For busy readers, the caption can be a second headline, echoing it; or it can sum up what is in the body copy. It is an important point in any layout, not to be discarded without due consideration.

The bold Gothic headline says a lot in two lines without being crowded. The subhead, in italics, contrasts well with it. Type designers and new photographic methods have helped the art director in condensing the type he wants to use if he lacks the width for his headline.

However, extremely condensed type is hard to read. The extra condensed headline may seem merely compact; for readability, it would be better to set a four-line headline of normal face type than to set one short sentence in extra condensed type. The KLM body copy is broken up into three visually acceptable columns rather than in two wide columns or, worse, set in a single full-width column. The enlarged initial is a good lead-in; numbering each copy block obviates the use of bold headings.

The Acropolis at sundown. A new KLM tour plan lets you visit Athens for only $5 a day. See details below.

Fly to Athens with reliable KLM—every KLM jet gets a 1000-mile test flight after every major overhaul

(For more news about reliable KLM and the careful, punctual Dutch—read on)

THE facts below can help you with two decisions you have to make before touring Europe. Which cities to visit. Which airline to fly with.

They also explain why so many experienced travelers say that KLM is the most *reliable* airline to Europe.

1. KLM engineers baby their jets. They strip down every jet as soon as it completes a thousand hours of flying. They also insist on hangar doors being closed to keep out dirt and dust.

The jet is then taken up for a special 1000-mile test flight to make sure every-

KLM technician uses endoscope to check engine. Device lets him see round corners, to make sure all parts run smoothly.

thing works impeccably. This typically Dutch thoroughness has a lot to do with KLM's reputation for punctuality.

2. The flight engineer on your KLM jet checks 369 points before every take-off. Diligent fellow. He even checks the coffee machines. Until he is satisfied that the entire plane is in tip-top condition, KLM will not allow it to leave.

3. Even the crew is tested before take-off. While you're checking in at the airport, the crew of your KLM jet is being re-examined on routine flight procedures. They've been through all this time and time again. But KLM leaves nothing to chance.

4. The captain of a KLM jet has four crews—one in the air, and three on the ground. On a flight to Europe, KLM flightwatch crews in New York, Montreal and Amsterdam track long-range weather conditions, and keep your jet flying on *schedule.*

$5 for bed, breakfast and sightseeing in Athens

If our photograph makes you want to see Athens, here's good

news. You can now visit the capital cities of Europe without spending more than $5 a day on bed, breakfast *and* sightseeing. Before fixing your tour, look into KLM's surprising new "$5-a-day Plan." You may save yourself a lot of money.

You can also visit Athens on one of KLM's air-land-sea cruises. Prices are from $998 for 19 days, and include your round-trip jet economy fare from New York.

You can get all the facts on KLM tours and air-sea cruises from your travel agent. Or clip the coupon below for a free 20-page booklet about KLM tours.

For information, see your travel agent, call KLM, or mail coupon

KLM Royal Dutch Airlines
609 Fifth Ave., New York 17. Tel: PLaza 9-3600

Please send me KLM's new booklet of tours, called "Gateway to Travel Enchantment"

Mr./Mrs./Miss _____

Address _____

City _____ Zone ____ State _____

(Name of your travel agent)

Unusual sights to see while soaking up sunshine in Southern California

(the vacation at hometown prices)

Sea secrets. An ocean-floor world long hidden from humans is open to view aboard the glass-bottom boat at Santa Catalina Island. Buried canyons; kelp jungles; odd creatures from starfish to stingrays.

The lush desert. Think it's all bone-dry sand? Our new desert cities are man-made *oases*. Golf courses, pools and patios everywhere. Gardens exploding with color. And the people? Colorful, too, soaking up sunshine!

Land of long ago. A startling contrast in ultramodern Southern California: our lovely, legendary Spanish missions. One has adobe walls seven feet thick; another, an altar light that has never gone out in 180 years.

What holds our prices down?
We're not crowded with visitors one month and deserted the next. Southern California's year-around good weather keeps people coming year-around. With no slack season to make up for, most prices don't zoom up or down. Lodging, meals and other expenses average about the same as at home.

The Far East. Winding paths and tiny red bridges take you there in the Oriental Garden at Huntington Library. A Japanese teahouse features shoji screens, authentic carvings, and exotic flower arrangements.

Our winter landscape. Warming it up (and you) are geranium lawns, acres of camellias, 10-foot-tall poinsettia hedges. Front-yard orange trees are heavy with fruit. And homeowners, instead of shoveling snow, are pruning ivy.

A movie studio. Now you can tour a giant studio: inspect a sound stage crammed with lights, cameras, props; view outdoor sets that recreate Paris, Africa and the Old West; take in filming of actual scenes. All without knowing a studio tycoon!

3-level sailing. There's a regatta most any weekend at Pacific harbors. Also *below* sea level at our big desert sea. Also a mile high on a sparkling lake surrounded by snowy mountains and pine forests.

Old gold mines. They're thick in certain desert regions, and just as colorful as their names. Like Rainy Day, Burning Moscow, Red Raven and Sidewinder. (One mine now conducts regular tours.)

Forest without trees. The Joshua tree (above) actually is a weird desert lily, often centuries old and 40 feet high with bristly arms sticking out in all directions. Eerie Joshua forests stretching for miles seem as strange as the Land of Oz.

Lake without water. Going out to see desert sand dunes, date groves or painted canyons, you may notice an inviting blue lake ahead. Coming closer, the lake suddenly dries up! It's a desert mirage, just like the ones that fooled early explorers.

Parading whales. Not hundreds but *thousands* of whales migrate south in winter along our Pacific seacoast. See these 45-foot-long monarchs from shore—spouting and thrashing mighty flukes.

Los Angeles: early look. In the shadows of City Hall is the Plaza, where the tiny pueblo of Los Angeles was born (1781). Nearby are Old Plaza Church (museum, early paintings); Avila Adobe (city's oldest residence); and an authentic Mexican marketplace (silver, leather goods).

Los Angeles: new look. Joining the skyscrapers now shooting up everywhere, the new County Art Museum and Music Center Pavilion have won national attention. Plazas, pools, and acres of parkland set off the striking Art Museum. And the handsome hilltop Music Center—a part of Los Angeles Civic Center—makes music appealing to the eye *and* ear.

Enjoy all this...and the U.S.A. on the way! When you get here, visit the All-Year Club Information Center at 705 W. 7th St., Los Angeles, for free official vacation-planning help.

FREE! OFFICIAL VACATION GUIDE. Color pictures, sightseeing map, dozens of Southern California attractions. Mail the coupon today.

Please send me your free Official Vacation Guide.

All-Year Club, Div. 2F-24
705 W. 7th St., Los Angeles, Calif. 90017

NAME _____
PLEASE PRINT

ADDRESS _____

All-Year Club of Southern California. This advertisement sponsored by the Los Angeles County Board of Supervisors for citizens of Glendale, Hollywood, Inglewood, Long Beach, Pasadena, Los Angeles, Pomona, Santa Monica, Torrance and 181 other communities.

2 Southern California

This ad appeared in a full-size newspaper on approximately one-third of a page. It is shown here in full. It demonstrates that readability consists in part of clear copy, in part of well-executed layout. The copy was carefully researched. It comes through well in an apparently simple presentation of copy blocks.

Art work also can be readable. These pen-and-ink sketches came across, fresh and clear, on a newspaper page full of smudged-looking photographs and washed-out halftones. The art director who designs an ad without considering the medium in which it will appear probably deserves the indifferent communication he projects.

The coupon is in the lower right-hand corner, easy to tear off.

3 Arnold Firehouse Coffee

This Arnold coffee ad opens up easily for the reader, with the product shown below the copy, the headline above. White space around the headline makes it easy to read, at the same time expanding the allotted space.

The body copy is broken into two columns with indents which sum up the main points for the busy reader. Indents could be used, also, for brief testimonials alongside informative copy.

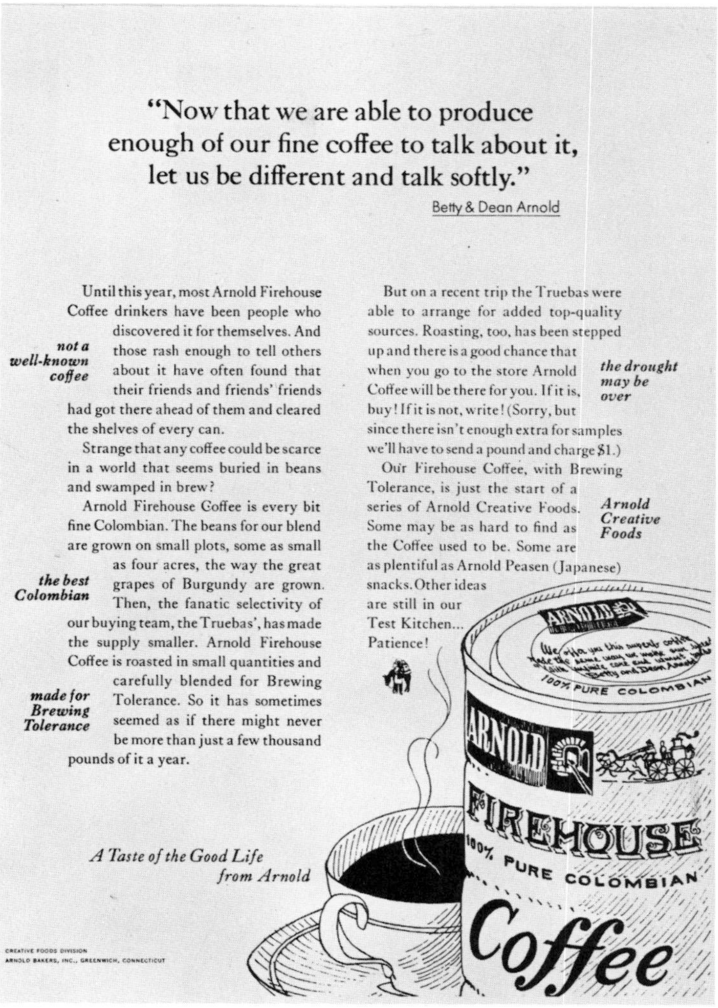

4 Golden Magazine

A way to steal space that is not paid for is by not filling the space that is paid for. This may seem contradictory, but giving the headline white space all around it automatically annexes the space at the top of the page. Again, if the advertiser has bought a seven-inch width, columns of copy need not hit the edge of the paid space; copy can fall a half-inch short of it without harming the layout. Thus, again, all the white margin becomes his.

Paragraph spacing is too subtle an announcement for the eye in two columns of tight copy. Enlarged indented numerals act as signposts for the eye before it crosses the long desert of copy.

Type usually runs beneath a picture. Here, however, type straddles a number of pictures to allow room for the blocks of informative copy. Rather than being separated, the photos were artfully combined to form a unified element in the layout as a whole. Although the pictures are butted together, the copy has ample space between blocks to make it easy to read.

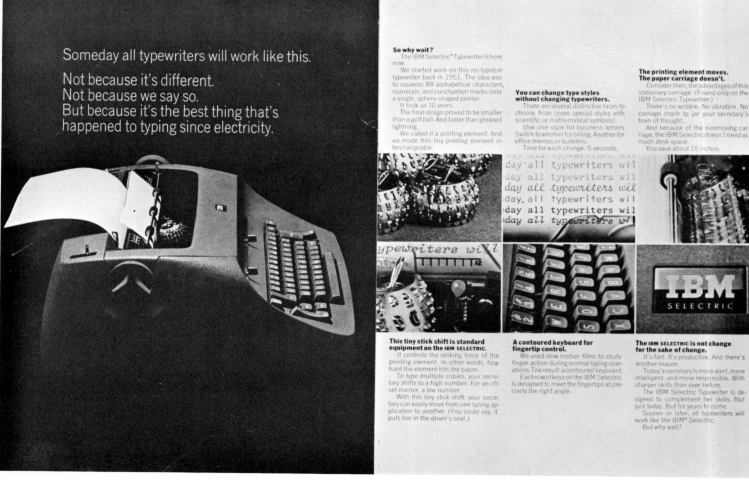

Someday all typewriters will work like this.

Not because it's different.
Not because we say so.
But because it's the best thing that's happened to typing since electricity.

So why wait?
The IBM Selectric* Typewriter is here now.
We started work on this no-typebar typewriter back in 1951. The idea was to squeeze 88 alphabetical characters, numerals, and punctuation marks onto a single, sphere-shaped printer.
It took us 10 years.
The final design proved to be smaller than a golf ball. And faster than greased lightning.
We called it a printing element. And we made this tiny printing element interchangeable.

You can change type styles without changing typewriters.
There are several distinctive faces to choose from (even special styles with scientific or mathematical symbols).
Use one style for business letters. Switch to another for billing. Another for office memos or bulletins.
Time for each change: 5 seconds.

The printing element moves. The paper carriage doesn't.
Consider then, the advantages of this stationary carriage. (Found only on the IBM Selectric Typewriter.)
There's no wobble. No vibration. No carriage crash to jar your secretary's train of thought.
And because of the nonmoving carriage, the IBM Selectric doesn't need as much desk space.
You save about 15 inches.

This tiny stick shift is standard equipment on the IBM SELECTRIC.
It controls the striking force of the printing element. In other words, how hard the element hits the paper.
To type multiple copies, your secretary shifts to a high number. For an offset master, a low number.
With this tiny stick shift, your secretary can easily move from one typing application to another. (You could say, it puts her in the driver's seat.)

A contoured keyboard for fingertip control.
We used slow motion films to study finger action during normal typing operations. The result: a contoured keyboard. Each row of keys on the IBM Selectric is designed to meet the fingertips at precisely the right angle.

The IBM SELECTRIC is not change for the sake of change.
It's fast. It's productive. And there's another reason.
Today's secretary is more alert, more intelligent, and more responsible. With sharper skills than ever before.
The IBM Selectric Typewriter is designed to complement her skills. Not just today. But for years to come.
Sooner or later, all typewriters will work like the IBM* Selectric.
But why wait?

ANIMATION

You're at home anywhere in Dan River Sheets

Dan River sheets change even a tent on the sand into the most beautiful bedroom in the world. This dream is "Staccato," our luxury Dan River muslin in exquisite shades of Daybreak Pink, and four other fashion colors. Beautifully gift-boxed. At fine stores.

6

Please do pick the flowers.
Who else but Cannon could bring you
so many lovely towel colors to bloom in your bath!

7

Your company's ready for a new-generation computer? And some of the executives are still on the fence — don't know which way to jump?

Well, you know what's best for your company. And you know the longer a decision is put off, the longer you're without the modern data processing capabilities you need.

So here are a couple of points to help you support your choice:

Money is a good place to start.

Naturally, your choice is a computer that'll give you as much power as possible for every dollar you invest. And you can point out that your computer will be designed to do only what you want it to do. So there'll be no wasted speed, capacity or capability.

Next, show your colleagues the advantage of being able to choose from the industry's widest range of rental and purchase plans.

Then, stress the importance of on-time delivery — software as well

as hardware. And how you need proven, easy-running software, including the best COBOL compilers in the business.

They'll understand. And when your Honeywell Series 200 computer arrives, you'll have their wholehearted support.

And a reputation as a pretty smart cat.

Honeywell
ELECTRONIC DATA PROCESSING

Picking a computer is no time for pussyfooting.

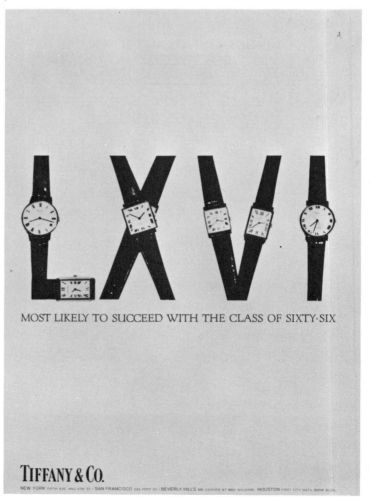

8

MOST LIKELY TO SUCCEED WITH THE CLASS OF SIXTY-SIX

TIFFANY & CO.

9

6 Dan River Mills

Product advantages may be emphasized by showing the product used in an unusual way. This beach scene conveys the idea of durability by using the sheets as tent material. The encroachments of TV (note the antenna) and the Dalmatian with his own "pup" tent add a note of gentle humor. The copy points out that the product can "change even a tent on the sand into the most beautiful bedroom in the world."

7 Cannon Mills

This ad was in full color, with forty-two towel colors making up the floral bouquet and the butterflies. The cast shadow helps bring some dimension to the bunch of flowers, and the butterflies add a touch of nature to the composition.

8 Honeywell

Who would have thought that a mess of wires and transistors could have been conducted into a harmonious picture? No matter how "ugly" the product, it can be shown effectively if done in an imaginative way.

The headline is a fair one; a less imaginative art director might have shown a cat, wonderfully photographed or painted. But he could have used that same approach for a hundred other products. By taking the computer (which is what Honeywell is selling) as a starting point, he has married the picture to the headline, and there is no mistake as to what kind of product is being advertised. Other ads in the series showed a lion, an elephant, and others, all made up of the guts of a computer.

10 Nabisco

Cookies can talk and, although these haven't much to say, what they do say is important.

These cookies are to be cut away (see following right-hand page) to show what is inside them, and are reproduced about actual size in the ad. On the inside of the fold-out flap, the package each kind of cookie comes in is shown with descriptive copy.

The danger of an ad this simple lies in the temptation to fill the white space.

©Nabisco

9 Tiffany & Co.

Animated lettering can serve a purpose. Here it says that watches are good graduation gifts for the class of '66. The Roman numerals are easily made because they are composed of the straight lines of the watches and the wristbands.

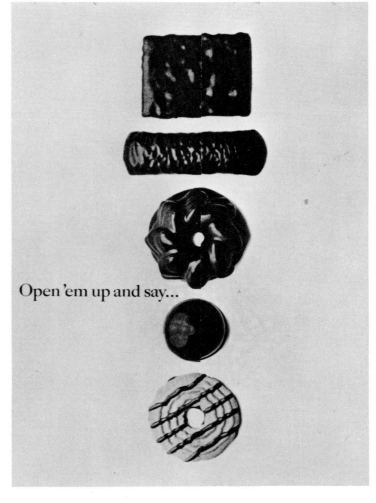

Open 'em up and say...

There's only one Kool-Aid. The smile on the pitcher tells you it's delicious. The name on the package says—here is America's best-loved instant soft drink. You get so much more with Kool-Aid. Fun. Flavor. Pure, wholesome refreshment. One package makes two full quarts, still costs only five cents.

11 Kool-Aid

By itself, the glass pitcher remains merely a cold object. An animated face could have been painted superficially on the pitcher but, etched into the frost, it gives this frosty drink a motivating, animated-product appeal.

© General Foods

Sandwich in Krispy Crackers and soup around the clock!

Lunchtime, munchtime, anytime — Krispy Cracker sandwiches are so easy to fix and so nourishing with good hot soup. Make sure they're Krispy Crackers — twice wrapped for twice the freshness.

12 Sunshine Krispy Saltine Crackers

No matter how clever an idea is, it must be related to the product's advantages if it is to succeed in selling the product and not merely attracting attention to itself. In this case, the versatility of the product for snacks is emphasized by the clever use of the clock motif.

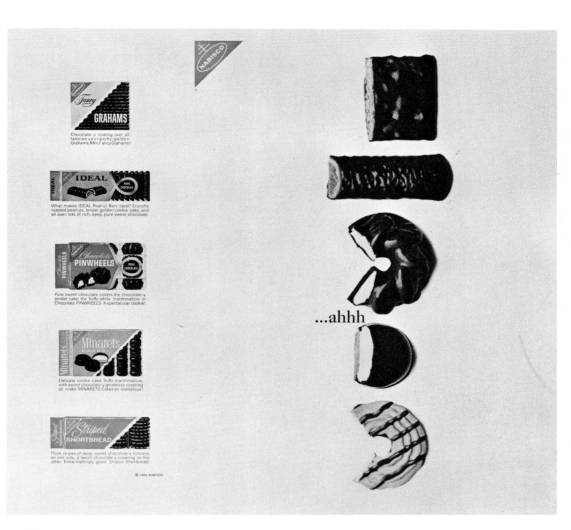

"My name is Buster Brown. I live in a shoe.
This is my dog, Tige. He lives there, too."

More kids have worn Buster Brown Shoes than any other shoes. For a lot of reasons.
■ Buster Brown stands for more styles of shoes for boys and girls 3 to 12 years old than any other brand.
■ Buster Brown stands for unqualified fit that helps young feet run and jump and grow. And stay healthy.
■ Buster Brown stands for the kind of fashion the kids call "neat." And "cool."

■ And Buster Brown stands for quality. PVC soles that are guaranteed to outlast the uppers. Uppers made of fine, pliable leathers that wear and wear. And wear.
Millions of kids grew up with Buster and Tige, and millions still do.
Buster Brown Shoes. Get them at better stores everywhere. They're priced a little higher. But in the long run, you'll find they cost a lot less.

Buster Brown Shoes
BROWN SHOE COMPANY, ST. LOUIS

Meet new Mr. Clean. He's mean.
He hates dirt.

What made new Mr. Clean so mean?
Dirt. He hates dirt. Wherever he finds it.
Walls, halls, floors, stove tops, cabinets,
refrigerators, bathtubs, tile, outdoor furniture,
painted woodwork, countertops, even in the laundry.
No other kind of cleaner on the face of the
earth cleans like new mean Mr. Clean.
No liquid. No powder.
No cleanser. No detergent.
No soap. Nothing.
Try new mean Mr. Clean.
You'll love him.

you'll love him

is Tweed tame?

Yes, but only on tame people.

Tweed Perfume, cologne, mist, bath powder from $1.50 to $14.00. **Tweed** by **Lenthéric**

"Are you trying to say
I'm a slacker?" gasped Elsie

Harumph!" snorted Elmer, the bull. "Then, how do you explain this shortage of milk products that everyone's talking about?"

"Why, we cows aren't to blame at all," retorted Elsie, the Borden Cow. "We're giving more milk than ever before. The shortage is due to the war."

"Sounds pretty thin to me," jeered Elmer. "You can't blame the war for everything."

"I'm not blaming," smiled Elsie. "I'm explaining. You see, it's hard for farmers to increase milk production, because so many dairy hands have gone to war. On top of that, the men in our armed forces drink more milk now than they ever did as civilians. The way things are, it takes one quart of milk out of every four to supply our armed forces and Allies."

"That's all very well," bellowed Elmer, "but war or no war, children must have

milk. You cows will just have to work another shift."

"That's been suggested and we'll try to do it," laughed Elsie. "But it isn't like making bullets. Every drop of milk requires the personal attention of a cow and the man who milks her. But don't worry. Children will get first call on all the pure, wholesome Borden's Milk that's available."

"What about grownups?" roared Elmer. "Are they supposed to chew milkweed?"

"Of course not," replied Elsie. "There'll be some milk for grownups although they may have to get along with less than they're using now in some sections. Of course, there won't be any milk to waste anywhere."

"In that case," said Elmer, "it looks like we grownups will just have to do without. Oh well, if there's not enough

milk, there's always ice cream."

"Oh, but there isn't," explained Elsie. "Due to the milk shortage, we can't make nearly as much Borden's Ice Cream as we used to. That means folks ought to use ice cream like any other nutritious food. For example, when ice cream is served for dessert, it should take the place of another milk dish in the meal."

"Cut it out," growled Elmer. "Dawgonnit, can't you say anything encouraging?"

"Of course, silly," giggled Elsie. "I think it's terribly encouraging to know that milk producers and distributors are doing everything possible to see that people get the dairy products they really need. And I'm sure my friends will do their part by using dairy products carefully. I'll do my part, too. Every Borden product available will still be the kind that makes people say: If it's Borden's, it's got to be good!'"

13 Buster Brown

The Buster Brown trademark goes back to 1840 when it was licensed to the Brown Shoe Company and later to a cigar and whiskey producer at the Saint Louis World's Fair in 1904. Buster Brown was the Charlie Brown of his day - an engaging and irrepressible symbol of youth.

Recently, the old Buster Brown comic strip was temporarily revived in full-page ads. It was used to sell kids on buying their shoes at a local dealer and getting a premium with each purchase.

A prime requisite of a trademark which is used over a long period of time is that it convey the same memorable meaning to the current generation as when it first appeared, or have a genuine nostalgic value, as in the case of Buster Brown.

Brown Shoe Co.

14 Mr. Clean

Sometimes even the product can be humanized. While other companies were playing around with feminine help (see Mary Mild, the maid, and Josephine, the plumber, numbers 22 and 26) along comes a strongman who can really clean up for the bedeviled housewife. Not even the strongest of females could ever bring to bear on household chores the muscle of a Mr. Clean.

The problem of finding a model to fit the characterization was left to the resourcefulness of his creator. The result is a tough but approachable he-man who can't stand dirt.

15 Tweed

The name of a product can often be made a tangible thing. The Tweed name is simple and tweed fabric has been used to make up the stuffed lion. In this same campaign, other stuffed tweed animals have been used.

Lentheric

16 Borden Co.

Since there is little difference in the standard quality of milk, as between one dairy and another, it's difficult to appeal to either retailer or consumer to buy a special brand of milk.

Creating an animated character, Elsie the cow, identifies Borden's product with a warm company image. This ran during World War II when there was a milk shortage. At that time, Macy's staged a promotion, actually presenting Elsie in the flesh with her new-born calf, fenced in beside a cottage.

© Borden Co.

17 M. C. Schrank

There is usually reason behind rhyme, and a good ad rarely uses a gimmick for the gimmick's sake. It can and does use a gimmick literally only when it fits like a glove, as it does here.

The picture word, STRETCH, is made up of photographs of the same girl shown in the large photo above. She does not go through contortions, as is often done, to fit in and form the exact shapes of the letters.

The dark gray background she was posed against holds the shape of the letters well enough. To insure meaning to the word, the girl in the big picture is modeling one of the S-T-R-E-T-C-H Jamas.

18 Rheingold

For years, the Miss Rheingold election drew more ballots than any other American election except the Presidency. Depositing their ballots at places where Rheingold was sold, beer-drinkers and non-drinkers alike chose each year the face to launch a thousand kegs in one of the most successful sales promotions of modern times.

© Liebmann Breweries

17

18

Please
turn around.

Why, it's
Harvey Probber!

Who but Harvey Probber would bring this kind of elegance and comfort to architectural furniture? This new and complete series of chairs, benches, cabinets, sofas, desks and tables, designed with classic simplicity for executive offices and public areas, is (we think) unique. The materials are posh: mirror-polished (#7) stainless steel, selected woods (walnut, rosewood, teakwood, ebony and the like). The chair shown takes 54 sq. ft. of black Himalayan goat skin. Upholstered. Comfortable. For photographs and specifications, write Department A

HARVEY PROBBER, INC., FALL RIVER, MASS. New York, 41 E. 57th St. / Boston, 475 Commonwealth Blvd. / Chicago, 638 Merchandise Mart / Dallas, 230 Decorative Center / Denver / Milwaukee / Nashville / Pittsburgh / St. Louis.

19

Our first anniversary Married one week. Skål! *Snowed in. Nothing but steak and Carlsberg. Skål!* *First place! Bring on Goren. Skål!*

Our very own sailboat. Christen it with Carlsberg. Skål! *Twins! A boy for you, a girl for me. Skål!*

Carlsberg—the celebrated beer of Copenhagen

Whatever the celebration—big or little—Carlsberg helps.
That's because Carlsberg is an extraordinary beer; a mellow, flavorful beer. Part of its secret is in the brewing. Carlsberg is slow-brewed for a minimum of solids and a lighter-brighter flavor.
It takes at least four months to create Carlsberg. That's longer than it takes to make most of the beers you used to drink—before you tried Carlsberg.
Carlsberg is especially appropriate for celebrations now, in its graceful new sculptured bottle. Ask for it at good hotels, restaurants and fine stores in 159 countries and at the New York World's Fair. Insist on Carlsberg—the glorious beer of Copenhagen. Each time you drink it—it's a celebration.

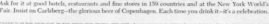

20

19 Harvey Probber Inc.

The product does not even have to be adapted graphically, here, in order to turn it into a living being. All that need be done is to address it as a live person. The ad does just that and shows both front and back of the chair which answers to its name.

The fact that it does what is asked of it in the headline strengthens the idea that the chair is a responsive being — Harvey Probber, in fact.

20 Carlsberg Breweries

A few simple props and a bit of imagination can convert humdrum human experience into an occasion, one that can animate your product. It can also say that Carlsberg, the celebrated beer, is a beer to celebrate with.

The essential symbols of such human occasions were chosen here and used as background for the product shot. The copy explains each occasion in very personal terms: "Our first anniversary/Married one week. Skål!" A hatchet and logs by a lodge: "Snowed in/Nothing but steak and Carlsberg. Skål!" Two ribbons for "Twins! A boy for you, a girl for me. Skål!" Carlsberg becomes part of happy times.

21 F. J. Cooper

When products are themselves animated, little need be done other than to refer to them in living terms and, in so doing, invest their sentient personalities with added value and charm. This copy does an excellent job of light-hearted appraisal of Mr. Cooper's little animals, shown actual size. Read it!

"Show us all your little animals or else,"
customers have growled at Mr. Cooper.
"Which animals and or else what?" replied Mr. Cooper.

It's bad enough when you (our customers) write in and tell us what to advertise. Now you're even threatening us. Well, we can't show you all the denizens of our zoo. There's not enough room. But this is a pretty fair sample. Good hunting.

Hiccupping Hippo can't stop. Only by taking him in and giving him a good home will his psychosomatic hiccups stop. 18 karat gold with ruby eye, $120.

Snail is a most delightful fellow. He goes his own pace (and a pox on anyone who tries to hurry him). 14 karat gold, $65.

Angel Fish will swim away if you don't catch her. Can also be used as bait to catch bigger fish (if that's your sport). 18 karat gold with sapphire eye, $90.

A very wise and worldly owl sees all, knows all, but tells nothing. 14 karat gold with peridot eyes. $60.

Devilish Dragon Fly loves to flutter flirtatiously about. If you catch her she'll bring you good luck. 18 karat gold with onyx eyes; $145.

We had a little gold canary here somewhere, but you-know-who must have polished him off. You-know-who is 14 karat gold with rubies in his collar and sapphire eyes, $65.

Foxy Fox is very loyal. Can be trusted with any secret. (Just like your best friend.) 14 karat gold, $90.

Silly, seasick Sea Horse can't stand the sight of water. Likes to cruise about on black cocktail dresses. Ruby eye watches hungrily for hors d'oeuvre tray. 14 karat gold, $55.

Non-biting Spider is 14 karat gold with a black star sapphire body, $18. Mouse squeaks when you pull her tail, but you can't hear her. (Which is just as well.) 18 karat gold with a diamond eye, $70.

F·J·COOPER INC.

jewelers by birth...since 1883
1416 Chestnut Street, Philadelphia, Pa.
F. J. Cooper International Co.,
2 Orange St. at Union, Montego Bay, Jamaica,
W. I., and F. R. Cooper, Colchester, England.

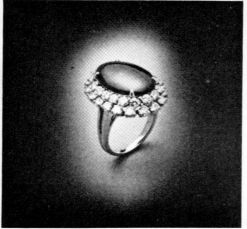

Contented Koala Bear just downed a delicious luncheon of white gold leaves. Tree limbs are white gold, too. (But he's saving them for dinner.) 18 karat gold, $195.

Dieting Crab has a dreadful weight problem. She'll remind you to watch your diet if you remind her to watch hers. 14 karat gold with ruby eye, $95.

Or else. You wanted to see our little animals "or else." Here's a superb "or else" —a magnificent diamond-tiered Jade ring. Three thousand three hundred dollars. P.S. The little Happy Bug way up top is 18 karat gold with a green chalcedony body. Guaranteed to cheer you up, $26.

Mail address: 1406 Chestnut Street. Add 5% for Pennsylvania delivery.
Jewelry shown actual size.

21

COPPERTONE®
guarantees* the fastest tan
with maximum sunburn protection!

Don't be a paleface!

Tan, don't burn . . . use Coppertone! There's nothing like a Coppertone *suntan* . . . so smooth, sleek, rich, deep . . . so flattering! Coppertone's special balanced *sunscreen* scientifically blocks out burning rays. Its special *beauty cream ingredients* moisturize and condition your skin so it "takes" a tan better, responds to the sun's tanning rays with a softer, more youthful tan.

*That's why with Coppertone, you get the best looking tan possible . . . guaranteed fastest, longest-lasting with maximum sunburn protection . . . or money back from Coppertone. America's favorite—*far outsells all others!*

Winner in Greatest Suntan Test! Two week Florida test conducted by a noted skin specialist proved Coppertone gave faster, deeper tans than the next two widely advertised suntan products . . . scored highest in test on combination of qualities people want.

NEW! *Royal Blend* World's most luxurious suntan body lotion. 7 special beauty benefits! Tan like a sun goddess.

Coppertone is a Reg. T. M. of Plough, Inc.   Also available in Canada   •   Visit Coppertone exhibit in Florida Bldg. at N. Y. World's Fair!

23

Greetings from **PHILIP MORRIS**

Yours for a Happy Holiday!

PHILIP MORRIS
America's Finest Cigarette
ALWAYS BETTER .... BETTER ALL WAYS

TIME, DECEMBER 16, 1946   5

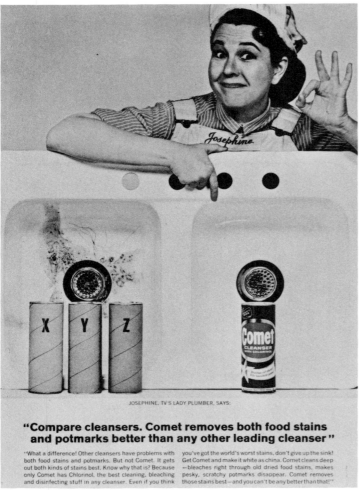

JOSEPHINE, TV'S LADY PLUMBER, SAYS:

"Compare cleansers. Comet removes both food stains and potmarks better than any other leading cleanser"

"What a difference! Other cleansers have problems with both food stains and potmarks. But not Comet. It gets out both kinds of stains best. Know why that is? Because only Comet has Chlorinol, the best cleaning, bleaching and disinfecting stuff in any cleanser. Even if you think you've got the world's worst stains, don't give up the sink! Get Comet and make it white as china. Comet cleans deep—bleaches right through old dried food stains, makes pesky, scratchy potmarks disappear. Comet removes those stains best—and you can't be any better than that!"

22

I dreamed
I lived
in a castle in
Spain . . .
in my
maidenform
bra

Brief, bare and beautiful! This bra is just one of six from the fabulous new "Dream-Aire" collection. Pared-down to a minimum, with plenty of hold and mold . . . and straps that stretch without rippling. A, B, C cups. 3.95. Reg. U.S. Pat. Off. 1965 by Maidenform, Inc., makers of bras, girdles, active sportswear

24

25

22 Comet Cleanser

Joe the plumber has finally met his match: Josephine. A woman plumber. Unbelievable? Sure, but nevertheless an effective saleswoman.

Once a fictional character has been created, the choice of the right model to represent that character becomes of the greatest importance. Be sure to pick a model who is believable, since she already presents an incongruity in everyday life.

26 Ivory

Mary Mild, the maid, helps to convey the idea that Ivory liquid soap with its "Young-Hands Formula" can rejuvenate your hands. Mary Mild says Ivory is "kinda like you had a maid, like me, to do your dishes!" There have been a few ads in this series that showed a happy couple, with Mary Mild as Mrs. Cupid in the background.

Procter & Gamble

23 Coppertone

Here is an honest way to show the effectiveness of a suntan lotion. The little girl, with the mischievous puppy tugging away at her last remnant of cover from the sun, makes a cute and corny picture — easily remembered and, with its appropriate slogan, "Don't be a pale-face," instantly recognizable on displays, posters and billboards, where brevity is essential.

Plough, Inc.

24 Maidenform

A bit of whimsey conjures up various backgrounds for the girl who dreams in her Maidenform bra.

This campaign has been running for many years. It can because, while it has used a live model throughout the series, it is not dependent upon any *one* model. The two constants in the ads are "I dreamed I ... in my Maidenform bra" and the half-clad model. The copy bears out the headline idea, adding that the bra shown is one of six styles from the current "Dream-Aire" collection.

27 Schweppes

The president of a company can be most interesting to meet if he has a strong, attractive personality, as does Commander Edward Whitehead of Schweppes. He's not behind a stuffy old desk, but on a boat, very casually at ease, telling the reader how Schweppes discovered America.

The Americans have tasted, and accepted, "Schweppervescence — those exuberant little bubbles that tickle the palate and delight the soul." So entrenched has Schweppes become that it is "practically *unconstitutional* to mix a Gin-and-Tonic *without* Schweppes." Also, new drinks are appearing, such as Vodka, Rum, and Bourbon — mixed with Schweppes.

In a postscript, the Commander advises that if your storekeeper or favorite bar has not yet received Schweppes, "drop us a card and we'll take the necessary steps."

25 Philip Morris

Johnny, the famous Philip Morris symbol, originally worked as a hotel bellhop. Hearing his dramatic voice one day, an advertising man had an idea, paged him and told him that there was a phone call for a "Philip Morris." The celebrated "Call for Philip Mor-ris!" ensued, and from that emerged a famous campaign, featuring the original Johnny. It was used extensively on radio and was revived, years later, on TV.

26

Special offer for boys and girls who eat their vegetables

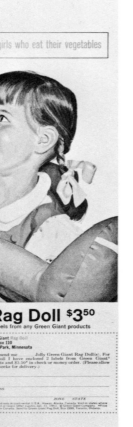

4-foot Jolly Green Giant Rag Doll $3.50

with 2 labels from any Green Giant products

Maybe this is just the fellow you need at your house to help get the children going on their vegetables. He's a soft, cuddly 4-foot version of the Green Giant. And he's stuffed with lightweight styrene fluffing so he won't lose his shape.

Actually, the Green Giant puts up vegetables so good that children go for them

as much as grownups. And the two cans you buy to get this doll will be gone before you know it. Order your Green Giant Rag Doll today. It's an ideal Christmas gift.

GREEN GIANT®
Good things from the garden

Green Giant Rag Doll
P. O. Box 110
Spring Park, Minnesota

Please send me _____ Jolly Green Giant Rag Doll(s). For each doll I have enclosed 2 labels from Green Giant® products and $3.50* in check or money order. (Please allow three weeks for delivery.)

NAME
ADDRESS
CITY   ZONE   STATE

How many roles will your telephone play today?

Want to arrange an appointment?
Presto, your phone is a secretary.

Forget a few items at the grocer's?
Zip, it's an errand boy.

Plain lonesome?
Whoosh, it's a friend.

Need help in an emergency?
G-r-r-r, it's a watchdog.

P. S. Your telephone's 1001 roles are always at your service...that's one of its great enduring values!

Bell System
American Telephone and Telegraph
and Associated Companies

Most tape recorders are toys:

The AMPEX 861 is a musical instrument. □ And yet, despite its technical perfection, the Ampex is one of the simplest tape recorders in the world to use. It offers uncomplicated straight line threading, versatile 3-speed operation (7½, 3¾, and 1⅞ i.p.s.), and accurate record level VU meters. And, of course, our exclusive dual capstan drive insures constant tape tension for perfect flutter-free recording and playback. Two microphones and two slide-on stereo speakers are included. This neat package proves once again that when you want to record and playback sound beautifully you need something better than a plaything. You need Ampex. Only $299.95—complete.

AUDIO AND VIDEO RECORDERS   /   SPEAKERS   /   MICROPHONES   /   VIDEO CAMERAS   /   TAPES   /   ACCESSORIES
ask anyone who knows
AMPEX CORPORATION, 2201 LUNT AVENUE, ELK GROVE VILLAGE, ILLINOIS 60007

AMPEX

You'll want everyone to know...

New Parliament award for horsemanship? Neigh! The medallion's just a gentle reminder that horsemen (like other smart Parliament smokers) want everyone to know *their cigarette* is special. And you, too, will appreciate the crush-proof cigarette case . . . the superb tobaccos . . . the luxurious flavor . . . and above all, the exclusive Mouthpiece that keeps the filter deeply recessed away from your lips. With Parliaments, *only the flavor touches your lips!*

You're so smart to smoke **Parliaments**

ONLY THE FLAVOR . . . . TOUCHES YOUR LIPS

28 Green Giant

This animated premium idea pleased both the purchaser and the company. The consumer got the Jolly Green Giant rag doll for only $3.50 and two labels from one of the products.

The company thereby sold at least two cans of the product to each customer and had a wide distribution of a familiar animated representative.

The premium had a direct relation to the company; indeed, it was an animated representative that would serve as a mnemonic for the company in every household that ordered it.

32 Talon

A product may be animated out of relation to its actual size, either larger or smaller. Here, few props are needed to mock-up a construction worker out of a zipper wearing a helmet, gloves, and heavy-duty boots. He is posed with his hands on his hips. The picture supports the copy, which says that Talon zippers "are built to work for a living."

29 Bell System

Showing situation shots of the various ways in which a phone can be of service is probably less convincing than showing the product animated to depict those situations.

The cartoons in this ad, painted directly over the telephone instruments, do not adhere rigidly to the outline of the photographs. The copy follows style, thus: "Want to arrange an appointment?/Presto, your phone is a secretary./Forget a few items at the grocer's?/Zip, it's an errand boy./Plain lonesome?/Whoosh, it' a friend/Need help in an emergency? G-r-r-r,/it's a watchdog."

American Telephone & Telegraph

30 Ampex

If you want to transmogrify an object, do it literally. The tape recorder might have been turned into a trick projector, or a face, but that would involve altering the unit artificially.

By using the reels for a start, turning the recorder upside down to show a wind-up key in the rear, and putting in the doll, you have quite simply transformed it into a toy. The unit in the right-hand corner below looks like the face of a robot animal, with the two reels for eyes, the recording head unit as muzzle, the gray panel as a mouth and the two speakers behind the unit for ears.

The copy points out that "despite its technical perfection, the Ampex is one of the simplest tape recorders in the world to use."

33 Better Vision Institute

A fascinating machine, the Refractor, is made to look more so by showing it in use, with a face peering at us from behind it — it might even be a mechanical monster from the moon. The big, bold capital letters complement the headline idea. Here, the normal viewpoint has been switched. If the copywriter had thought only in terms of the patient, he might have ended up with an old eye-chart cliche.

31 Parliament

One way of drawing attention to a product is to use it in forming another inanimate object, in this case the medallion for the winning horse's ribbon.

The copy stresses the crush-proof cigarette case, superb tobacco and above all, the exclusive Mouthpiece that keeps the filter... away from your lips. With Parliaments, *only the flavor touches your lips!*"

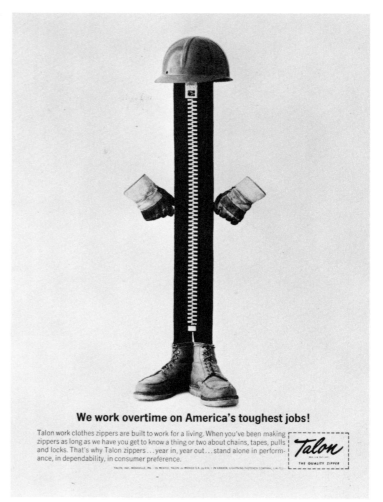

We work overtime on America's toughest jobs!

Talon work clothes zippers are built to work for a living. When you've been making zippers as long as we have you get to know a thing or two about chains, tapes, pulls and locks. That's why Talon zippers...year in, year out...stand alone in performance, in dependability, in consumer preference.

Talon THE QUALITY ZIPPER

32

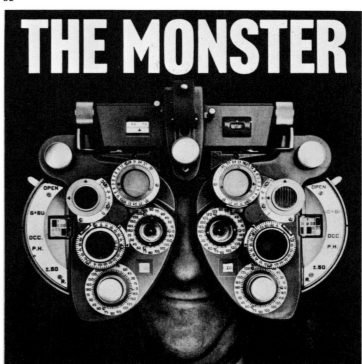

THE MONSTER

Ah, eye examinations. So relaxing. And you meet such nice—er, machines. Like the Monster.

You just look him in the eye. He won't bite. People are his best friends. He'll just check to see if you have any errors in refraction. And what the corrections should be.

The Monster is only one of many devices used to determine how well you're seeing. And how much better you might see—with the remarkable help available now. For instance: 2 or 3 different lens focuses, for different needs, in *one* pair of glasses. Lenses coated to reduce glare. Lenses that resist impact. Plastic lenses. Prescription sunglasses.

Speaking of the Monster, if you run into him at your next eye examination, don't call him that. His real name is the Refractor. Nice and dull and reassuring. With a face like his, it's just as well. **Better Vision Institute.**

34 Scotch Tape

If a brand name can be converted into a character whose name has a mnemonic ring to it, it can give the product a fresh individuality, particularly if similar products have entered the field. The client, 3M Company, created an amusing character, Scotty McTape, to imply thriftiness in the use of Scotch Tape.

The ad induces a child to cut out the mask according to the instructions and then, presumably, ask his mother for Scotch Tape to hold the mask in place.

Scotch-brand cellophane tape was the successful innovator in developing this type of tape and had a legitimate advantage. This became somewhat watered down when other cellophane tapes were referred to as "scotch tape." The conversion of a brand name into a generic term should always be guarded against. Any threat of infringement, such as the use of a similar logo by other companies, should be dealt with immediately.

3M

35 Movado

Your ad idea need not be revolutionary to be a stopper. The reader's double-take is due simply to the perception that a small something is wrong with the centerpiece.

Radical, attention-getting gimmicks, such as showing a picture upside down, or a person with a face painted green, are most likely to be passed up. We know immediately that they are gimmicks.

Here we sense something odd about the centerpiece on the cake, and we have to look again to catch it. We look back because our feeling for the conventional piques us. We see that the bride and groom are looking away from each other and at their wrists.

ANALOGY

**All the ingredients for
a summer cocktail party
should be refreshingly different.** **So should the drinks.**

Move the party outside. Serve crisp cold
canapés and chilled relishes.
 Be sure you have a supply of Seagram's
Extra Dry Gin on hand. It's the smoothest, dryest gin you can buy anywhere.
 Seagram's Extra Dry: the gin no party
can be without—Summer or Winter.

ORANGE BLOSSOM COCKTAIL: Shake hard: 1 jigger
Seagram's Gin, 1 jigger orange juice (fresh, if possible), cracked ice. Strain, serve, savor.
TOM COLLINS: Try summer's greatest thirst quencher.
GIN JULEP: Strip leaves from 3-4 sprigs fresh mint and
crush in small glass with ½ tsp. sugar and 2 oz.
Seagram's Gin. Strain into tall glass or silver tumbler
with cracked ice. Fill to the top with chilled pineapple
juice. Stir. Delicious!
MARTINI ON-THE-ROCKS: A great summer version
of a winter classic.

SEAGRAM-DISTILLERS COMPANY, N.Y.C. 90 PROOF. DISTILLED DRY GIN. DISTILLED FROM AMERICAN GRAIN.

36

Use one of our systems analysts.
(All or any part of him.)

If you want paperwork systems help,
Standard Register is a good place to go.
We'll let you use our experts. And what's more,
we'll let you call the shots on how you use them.
For instance, you can use one of our men to supplement your own staff. Or you
can call him in on a special job. Or you can simply ask him for his advice.
No matter how you use him, a Standard Register systems
man brings two important assets to every problem he tackles.
First, his experience with all kinds of forms,
systems, and equipment. Second, honest objectivity that results in
honest advice. No prejudices. No axes to grind.
To get this kind of help, call our local representative.
Or write us at Dayton, Ohio 45401.
The great thing about this offer? You pull the strings.

MACHINE MATED® FORMS BY STANDARD REGISTER

Circle No. 2 on Reader Inquiry Card)

36 Seagram

The animation process can be reversed, and
living things turned into cardboard cutouts.
Putting a shallow shadow to the left of the sil-
houetted objects flattens the three-dimensional
effect of the photographs so that the forms re-
semble cutouts.

38 Helene Curtis

Taking off from the "classic look," a classic
type of face was used for the model. It was
sculptured in black and white with real hair of
reddish-gold.
 The copy was institutional, in a way, because
it was soft selling women on the idea that even
"casual" hair styles cannot be properly managed
without a "casual" permanent, given by a trained
expert like their regular hairdresser.
 Of course the copy mentions that today's hair
styles have Helene Curtis permanents designed
for these hairdos. The newest is called Change
of Pace.

39 Enro Shirt Co.

A vintage store dummy can serve as an animated
model at little cost to the advertiser, with the
extra bonus of being able to pose him exactly
as needed. The pipe in the manikin's hand helps
the illusion that this man is not entirely imaginary.

37 Standard Register

Of the animated body forms, only the face and
the hands are human. The copy explains that the
businessman can use Standard Register experts
either to supplement his staff, for a special
job, or simply for advice.
 The parts idea (systems analyst) relates well
to the picture and the final sentence ties up the
relationship neatly when it says that Standard
Register can be objective about what system is
needed; they have a complete line to choose
from, and "You pull the strings."

40 Librium

A formidable "anxiety-ridden" machine is made
more so by showing it with tormented eyes
peering out at us. The bold capital letters complement the headline idea.
 Built up of small metallic parts — screws, cogs,
compass, springs, wheels, it bears a frightening
resemblance to a human head and face, rivetted
in position over the headline, "for The Age of
Anxiety," and the name of the product, Librium.
The message seems to be that even this hard
impregnable monster can relax with Librium.

Roche Laboratories

41 Dimetapp Extentabs

Although the art director may get the praise,
picture-evoking copy frequently serves as the
spark for his fire. The simple headline provides
a verbal starting point which the artist graphically extends.
 We can see the word "drip" extended to the
familiar faucet, but it is imagination that turns
it into a face.

A. H. Robins Co.

Does the classic look need a hairdresser?

The classic, uncomplicated look of new hair styles has created the impression that all a woman needs is a brush. Nothing could be further from the truth.

Never have hair styles needed a hairdresser more.

Let us draw an analogy for you. The simplest dress is the hardest to make. The cut must be perfect, the line immaculate, the fabric absolutely right. It needs a great designer. So do hair styles. They stand or fall on the expertise of your hairdresser and her knowledge of permanent wave techniques.

Yes, you understood correctly! These styles need a permanent. A professional permanent.

A permanent is the beginning of every great hair style. The simple, uncomplicated styles are no excep-

tion. They require unobvious-looking permanents. And that kind of permanent demands the deftness and experience only a professional hairdresser has.

Your hairdresser doesn't *just* give you a permanent. Before she puts in the first rod she has many important decisions to make about the characteristics of your hair. Then she must decide what kind of permanent to give you, how to wrap it, when to neutralize it. These are things you couldn't possibly determine yourself unless you had her kind of training.

She also knows that the right permanent makes all the difference. It makes a hair style easier to set and easier for you to maintain.

Not only have the hair styles changed, permanents have changed

along with them. For example, today's hair styles have permanent waves designed just for them. The newest is called Change of Pace by Helene Curtis. With Change of Pace as a beginning your hairdresser can set dozens of different hair styles. Each one will look "natural," yet last longer.

Can you have today's new look without a permanent? It's possible, but hardly practical considering the amount of time you'll have to spend every day.

So put your hair in the hands of the one person who makes a full time job of it. Your hairdresser. Let her give you the change you've been looking for. Chances are she'll begin your transformation with Change of Pace permanent by Helene Curtis. Available only at salons.

HELENE CURTIS

Button yourself into Darcura*, a sumptuously substantial sport shirting blended of the very finest cotton and worsted. Darcura* is woven exclusively for us in Bangalore, India, where weaving has been a fine art since the days of Alexander's invasion in 327 B.C. Elwood wears the Dress Barclay tartan here, but with our usual habit of perfection, we also do it in a complete collection of plaids, glens and tattersalls. About $17 at the finest stores here and abroad.

Enro

The Enro Shirt Company • Louisville, Kentucky

---

for The Age of Anxiety   **LIBRIUM** (chlordiazepoxide HCl)
PLEASE SEE "COMPLETE PRESCRIPTION INFORMATION" ON PAGE 35.

"eased up nasal drip"*
Dimetapp® Extentabs®

(Dimetane® [brompheniramine maleate], 12 mg.; Phenylephrine HCl, 15 mg.; Phenylpropanolamine HCl, 15 mg.)

In sinusitis, colds, U.R.I., Dimetapp lets your "stuffed-up" patients *breathe easy again*. Each long-acting Extentab provides clear relief for up to 10-12 hours, yet seldom causes drowsiness or overstimulation. (The balanced Dimetapp formula is *the* key to success.)

BRIEF SUMMARY: Indications: Dimetapp reduces nasal secretions, congestion, and postnasal drip for symptomatic relief of colds, U.R.I., sinusitis, and rhinitis. **Side Effects:** In high dosages, occasional drowsiness due to the antihistamine or CNS stimulation due to the sympathomimetics may be observed. **Precautions:** Administer with caution in the presence of cardiac or peripheral vascular diseases and hypertension. **Contraindications:** Antihistamine sensitivity. Not recommended for use during pregnancy.

*Clinical report on file, Medical Department, A. H. Robins Co., Inc.

A. H. ROBINS CO., INC., RICHMOND, VA.

GALLI-CURCI   GRACE MOORE   CARUSO   TETRAZZINI   PINZA

Imagine one voice with the range of all these. That's what we did with a Scotch.

We must have auditioned a thousand whiskies to get the Scotch we were after.

We wanted the Balmenachs, the Strathislas, the Macallans and a handful of others.

The rare key whiskies that form the base of Scotland's greatest Scotches.

Most distillers are happy to have one or two of these key whiskies in their Scotch.

We wanted to take the whole lot and combine them into one. (At a reasonable but commensurate price.)

For years we searched the Highlands and the Lowlands collecting

the whiskies we were after.

In fact, it took more than 20 years and 530 combinations to get these individual key whiskies all in one bottle.

And if you thought they were great individually, you should try them in perfect harmony.

EVERY DROP BOTTLED IN SCOTLAND · SELECTED AND IMPORTED BY SEAGRAM-DISTILLERS COMPANY, N.Y.C. BLENDED SCOTCH WHISKY · 86 PROOF

100 Pipers Scotch by Seagram

ARMSTRONG
THE SAFE TIRE

Grips the road to save your life as no other tire can!

This "Ounce of Prevention" can save your life.

Only Armstrong Tires have patented Safety Discs between the tread ribs. No matter how hard you brake, these discs keep the tread open — always ready to *grip* the road to help prevent deadly skids. You can't buy a better tire, to save your life. And it costs no more! So get Armstrong, The Safe Tire. See your Armstrong dealer, listed in the Yellow Pages.

The Armstrong Rubber Company, West Haven, Conn. · Des Moines, Iowa · Natchez, Miss. · Hanford, Calif.

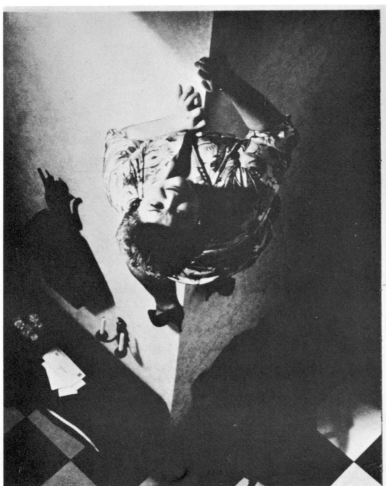

IF
AMPHETAMINE
PUTS
HER
ON
EDGE,
PUT
HER
ON
DESBUTAL
GRADUMET

She's the overweight patient who's edgy, nervous, a compulsive eater—the type who may overreact to plain amphetamine—yet fails to respond at all to less potent drugs.

TWOFOLD THERAPY: Visualize two tablet sections, back to back—each with its own release rate. One section contains Desoxyn* (methamphetamine) to curb the appetite and lift the mood. The other contains Nembutal* (pentobarbital) to calm her and counteract any excessive stimulation. The release rates are designed to make the drugs available in an optimal dosage ratio, *minute by minute throughout the day.*

REMARKABLE RELEASE: The release action relies on only one factor found in every patient: gastrointestinal fluid. There is no dependence on enteric coatings, enzymes, motility, or "an ideal" ion concentration in the gastrointestinal tract. *The Gradumet release rate is precise and constant throughout the body.*

PATIENT BENEFITS: With peaks and valleys of drug release eliminated, she feels more comfortable and confident of success. And she won't forget to take Desbutal Gradumet because *dosage is just once a day.*

PRECAUTIONS: Use with caution in patients with hypertension, cardiovascular disease, hyperthyroidism or those who are sensitive to ephedrine and its derivatives. Careful supervision is advisable with maladjusted individuals.

DESBUTAL GRADUMET

Brand of Methamphetamine Hydrochloride and Pentobarbital Sodium in Long Release Dose Form. Desbutal 10—15 mg. Methamphetamine, 60 mg. Pentobarbital. Desbutal 15—15 mg. Methamphetamine, 90 mg. Pentobarbital. Gradumet—Long Release Form. Abbott, U. S. Pat. No. 2,987,445.

Calms her anxieties even as it controls her compulsive urge to eat

42   43   44

42 100 Pipers

The monetary advantage of using portraits-of-
the-past is that there are no models to pay
(though there might be a number of legal fees).
And you have faces of the famous to escort your
product to market.

The copy does not abandon the operatic
theme. "We must have auditioned a thousand
whiskies to get the Scotch we were after...
you should try them in perfect harmony."

Seagram Distillers Co.

45 Band-Aid

The band-aid has been improved upon by al-
lowing taped-up skin to "breathe." The air-vents
over the pad are for faster healing and to reduce
whitening of the skin under the adhesive which
holds the band-aid on. A great idea was the use
of a screen as background to give the concept
of air going through! A band-aid taped over a
screen, with a hand behind it, shows exactly
how the band-aid fits over a cut.

The headline says "Now air goes through,"
with the last letters of "through" surprinted
by the screen. The package is large and can be
easily identified with the idea, since the words
of the ad are repeated diagonally across it.

Johnson & Johnson

43 Armstrong Rubber

We can create a humanized analogy so the
reader can better grasp the idea we are trying
to get across.

Out of the tire comes a gigantic hand with
disks between the fingers to keep them apart.
The tire is similarly constructed: the disks keep
the treads open, always ready to grip the road.
In the TV commercial, the hand comes slamming
down hard into clay as the headline announces,
"Grips the road!" The slogan is: "This Ounce
of Prevention can save your life."

44 Desbutal Gradumet

In a medical magazine filled with monotonous
advertising, this dramatic photograph jumps
right out of the page. The acute camera angle
and the literal application of the headline, putting
this miserable, overweight woman on the edge
of a wall, make for a real attention-getter.

The woman's flowered dress serves as contrast to the blank walls; the checkerboard floor
supplies a patterned frame of reference for the
eye.

The copy explains that this drug will at once
curb appetite and relieve tension. Because it
contains two ingredients — methamphetamine
and pentobarbital — a visualization is suggested
in the copy to convey the purpose of combining them: "Visualize two tablet sections,
back to back, each with its own release rate."
The slogan is "Calms her anxieties even as it
controls her compulsive urge to eat."

Abbott

46 Volkswagen

The copy suggests that you "Ask any hen./You
just can't design a more functional shape for
an egg./And we figure the same is true of the
Volkswagen Sedan.../Like the egg, it's the right
kind of package for what goes inside."

The copy further asserts that in arriving at
that shape nearly 3,000 changes were made,
and closes with a punchline: "push-button door-
knobs. Which is one up on the egg."

©Volkswagen of America, Inc.

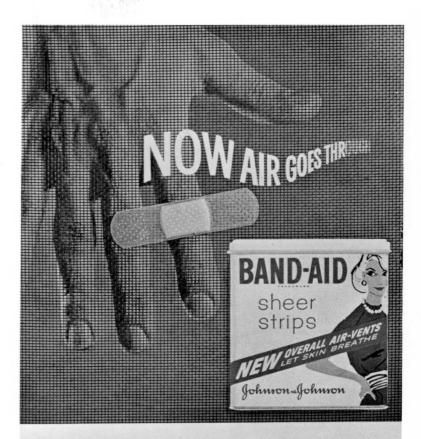

New Air-Vents over the pad for faster healing...new Air-Vents
over the tape to reduce skin whitening...and with Super-Stick

Exclusively Johnson & Johnson

45

Some shapes are hard to improve on.

NATURE'S PROTECTIVE BLENDING PROTECTS THE POLAR BEAR

CLARK: What's wrong with this picture?
MARK: The dark background. Mother bear is too wise to expose her fleecy white cubs like that.

CLARK: Right! She's careful to keep them against a light background of snow or ice.
MARK: Makes them hard to see. Shields them from the hunter.

CALVERT'S PROTECTIVE BLENDING
protects the flavor and good taste of Calvert Whiskey

CLARK: Here's another fine example of Protective Blending. This exclusive Calvert method certainly *does* something for this mellow whiskey.
MARK: Sure adds a lot of enjoyment to this whiskey collins. Do you blame me for recommending it to my friends?

RICHER   LIGHTER

Calvert RESERVE   **Calvert** SPECIAL

BUY BETTER WHISKEY — BUY CALVERT

"RESERVE": Millions gladly pay a little more for this *richer* premium blend.
"SPECIAL": Favorite of millions who prefer a *lighter* whiskey. Costs a little less.

CLEAR HEADS (CLEAR-HEADED BUYERS) CALL FOR Calvert

BLENDED WHISKEY Calvert "Reserve": 90 Proof — 65% Grain Neutral Spirits... Calvert "Special": 90 Proof — 72½% Grain Neutral Spirits. Copyright 1940, Calvert Distillers Corp., New York City.

47

Weary from shopping all over town for what you want? Take the trudgery out of shopping! Before you take another step...

Let your fingers do the walking!

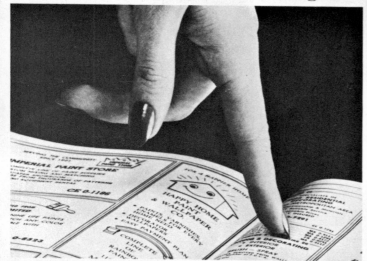

Today's Yellow Pages — America's handiest shopping guide

You'll find every product and service you want—from appliances to zippers—listed under the handy Yellow Pages headings. Read the ads under the heading you want for valuable information on

Yellow Pages

brands, special features, store locations and hours. Why not see how easy it is to find what you need today? Save time, temper and your feet—let your fingers do the walking through the Yellow Pages.

47 Calvert

There are three ads in one, here, each with its own headline. In the first, dialogue between Mark and Clark concerns the hazard for the cubs exposed against a dark background as opposed to a snowy white one. Instead of the phrase "protective coloring" used by animal-watchers, they call it "protective blending," to tie in with the blended product; but without a word about the product.

In the second ad Mark and Clark discuss the relative merits of blends. Headline and subhead: "Calvert's Protective Blending protects the flavor and good taste of Calvert Whiskey." The third ad concentrates strictly on the product. "'Reserve': Millions gladly pay a little more for this *richer* premium blend. 'Special': Favorite of millions who prefer a *lighter* whisky. Costs a little less."

The headline is the slogan: "Clear Heads (Clear-Headed Buyers) Call for Calvert."

49 Volkswagen

Starting with a familiar, commonplace item, the reader is led through the steps of thought which produced this automotive body design. What seemed like a curious design at first is revealed as a perfectly logical one. The copy illuminates each step as the "box" evolves:

"Now add a few seats. Say 8. Make an aisle so you can walk to the back. Cut a hole in the roof to let the sun in. Windows? At least 21. Doors? 5 should do. Paint it up and what have you got? The whole idea behind the Volkswagen Station Wagon."

©Volkswagen of America, Inc.

50 Esso

A product difference (when almost imperceptible) must be visually dramatized. The analogy between power and the tiger does this admirably.

"New power-formula Esso Extra gasoline boosts power three ways: 1. Cleansing Power!... 2. Firing Power!... 3. Octane Power!..." Power is a welcome word to most people and the nth degree of gasoline's power is visible in the giant tiger.

When Humble, makers of Esso, manufactured stuffed cotton tiger tails, thousands of motorists hooked them onto the gas cap so that they seemed, literally, to have a tiger in their tank.

Humble Oil & Refining

48 Yellow Pages

Did you ever see finger shadow-play? Here is an analogy easily identifiable because the reader sees in a new light something he has always known about. Another ad in this series showed the fingers of a giant hand walking down a shopping street.

Feet suggest the same idea. But this copy suggests you rest your feet. "Weary from shopping all over town for what you want? Take the trudgery out of shopping!" And the subhead: "Today's Yellow Pages — America's handiest shopping guide."

51 Chevrolet

How does riding a car on crumpled paper sound to you? The reader can readily sense crumpled paper becoming a solid road and can imagine what it would be to ride over it without Chevy's softened shock absorbers.

The girl with the ice cream cone lends credibility to a smooth ride. Imagine the bumps transferred from the road to the cone, without those shock absorbers. The car was photographed standing still, but clues in the photo give us a sense of movement: the perspective of the road dividers, the rear view shot of the car picking up speed; also the close attention the driver is giving the road, not the girl.

General Motors

Got a lot to carry? Get a box.

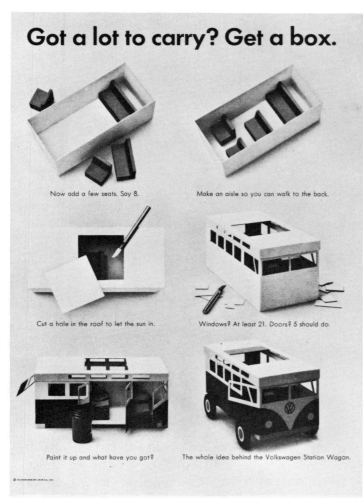

Now add a few seats. Say 8.

Make an aisle so you can walk to the back.

Cut a hole in the roof to let the sun in.

Windows? At least 21. Doors? 5 should do.

Paint it up and what have you got?

The whole idea behind the Volkswagen Station Wagon.

PUT A TIGER IN YOUR TANK!

FIRST WE START WITH THE TAIL...

NEW POWER-FORMULA ESSO EXTRA GASOLINE BOOSTS POWER THREE WAYS:

1 **Cleaning Power!** Dirt can clog even a new carburetor in a few months of normal operation—causing hard starting and rough idling. Your very first tankful of New Esso Extra will start to clear away these deposits—in new engines or old—to improve power and mileage.

2 **Firing Power!** Spark plug and cylinder deposits can cause misfiring, pre-ignition and hot spots. New Esso Extra neutralizes these harmful deposits—to help your engine fire smoothly, to help preserve the power of new cars and restore lost power to many older cars.

3 **Octane Power!** New Esso Extra has the high octane that most cars now need for full smooth performance without knocking. You'll get all these extras with New Power-formula Esso Extra gasoline—it puts a tiger in your tank! *Happy Motoring!*

HUMBLE OIL & REFINING COMPANY   AMERICA'S LEADING ENERGY COMPANY   MAKERS OF ESSO PRODUCTS   **(Esso)**

1. Tear off this road.
2. Crumple it up.
3. Now put it under a Chevrolet

and watch it flatten out again.

Impala SS Convertible with 8 new safety features, including outside rearview mirror. Check it before passing.

We softened shock absorbers. Now they absorb bumps better. We softened bushings and rearranged body mounts. Now they isolate vibrations better. We again matched the coil springs to the different weights of each body style. We made available a Turbo-Jet V8 to give you as much as 425 smooth horsepower, an AM-FM Multiplex Stereo radio to entertain you, Tilt-telescopic steering to let you adjust the wheel up, down, in or out. And we put soft Strato-bucket front seats in Impala Super Sport models, so now you can relax and enjoy the ride completely.

CHEVROLET | **GM**

Impala: Jet-smoother the Chevrolet Way

Originality Can Not Be Copied

WE ARE FULLY AWARE of the fact that Rambler will soon have new competitors.

It has always been true that when any new idea or product promises to serve mankind in a better way, it is at first deprecated and ridiculed by its competitors but when it wins outstanding public acclaim it is imitated.

This has been true in art and literature and science, ever since time began.

Only twice before in its sixty years has the automobile industry been so completely shaken by a fundamentally new and different concept as it is today by the Compact* Rambler.

The overwhelming public approval of this car is confirmation of our correct interpretation of public demand. That will always be our goal.

Today's Rambler is not merely an annual model. It is a new standard of basic excellence, a new measure of balanced value by which cars of the future will be judged.

The senseless competition for ornate design, with its attendant fast depreciation, *for excessive size*, for unusable power, for wasteful operating expense, is coming to an end.

Dependability in performance, economy in operation, ease of handling, *durability*, and adaptability to the needs of today are and should be the new goals of automotive design.

We of American Motors welcome all other manufacturers to this area which has been pioneered and exclusively promoted by Rambler.

It is our belief that at least half of all the automobiles built in the years to come will follow the Rambler pattern. But it will take time.

A good new car cannot be built in a year *or two*, no matter who tries.

A GREAT new car can never be built *without* the *conviction*, the singleness of purpose, the drive and devotion that are the ingredients of creative achievement.

The automobile industry knows a great deal about Rambler. They have seen us raise our production schedules ten times this year. They saw

Rambler move to third place among all cars in retail sales in June. They are fully aware that never before in automotive history has an "independent" sold as many cars in any year.

They know of our pioneering in every phase of design and production.

Their work will be aided and accelerated by what we have done.

Their cars will have the benefit of our research in design and construction.

Our Single Unit Construction* is essentially that of the airplane and the streamlined train. It is far stronger. *It is safer*. It eliminates squeaks and rattles. It provides more usable space for passengers and luggage. It is the very essence of compact design—and we have *twenty years of experience* with this advanced type of body construction.

Our competitors know that Rambler bodies are submerged in a rust-proofing solution and that their own manufacturing layouts will have to be changed if their new cars are to approach Rambler in long life and durability.

They know of Rambler pioneering in engine design and carburetion that has resulted in smooth operation and lasting economy.

They know of Rambler research in air-conditioning, in springing, in the conservation of usable space without excessive bulk and weight.

Because of its public approval, Rambler will be copied.

Over a period of years, all cars will be better

because of Rambler pioneering.

We of American Motors will never cease in our efforts to set new patterns for the industry to follow. We are dedicated to the concept that our cars must provide the utmost in usefulness, comfort, safety, beauty and balanced value.

They must continue to be the standard of basic excellence.

We will not deliberately make exterior changes just to obsolete owners' earlier models. We will avoid the extreme, the radical, the gross and the tiny.

We will strive always for the lowest possible price and the highest resale value, for exceptional gas mileage and good performance.

How large a share of the total automobile industry volume American Motors will account for when more than half the cars are the Rambler type, will be determined by car buyers.

We believe in what we have done.

We are devoted to the idea and ideal of ever-increasing usefulness to all who drive automobiles.

We have come so far because we have dared to be original.

An Original is of great worth.

It is never quite equalled by a copy.

And Originality itself cannot be copied.

AMERICAN MOTORS CORPORATION

RAMBLER • KELVINATOR • METROPOLITAN

Trademark American Motors.

RAMBLER...The New Standard of Basic Excellence

52 Rambler

In this ad, American Motors stresses in detail the features which made their new Compact Rambler an immediate success, and points out to the reader that other manufacturers are apt to produce similar models — as later proved to be the case.

The comparison with DaVinci's familiar masterpiece is intended to imply the inherent superiority of the original conception and the inferiority of subsequent imitations.

American Motors

53 Xerox

Can you get more ordinary (or literal) than a brown paper bag? The paper bag was shown in brown tones, and the copy was Xeroxed onto the bag itself. It is difficult reading but sharp enough to read.

The copy says, "This is a permanent copy. Xerox copies last as long as the paper lasts." It ends with "if you like this paper bag trick, wait'll you see what can be done with your own letterhead."

The reader is left with no second guesses about this ad idea. The copy below the bag says: "This is an actual photograph of a memorandum copied on the side of a brown paper bag...It proves a point: the Xerox 914 Copier makes copies on ordinary paper."

54 Victor Comptometer

The strip of calculator paper coming out of the abacus and a touch of Chinese-English lingo keep the idea in this ad analogous to the main concept. It is not enough to imply a relationship between the abacus and a comptometer. So the copy says in the very first sentence "Victor printing calculators reduce errors with abacus-like simplicity." And, again, in the last line: "Velly wise thing to do."

53

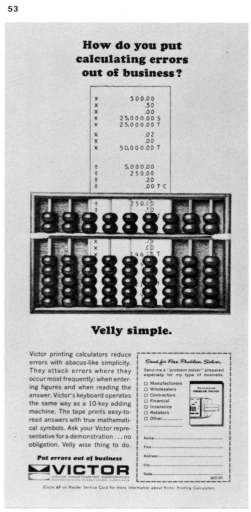

54

little girls...

grow up!

Thank heavens. And thank Trifari for the bewitching bow pin. Pavé jewels are sparked with dazzle and set into golden-toned Trifanium. This bow is the place-it-where-you-please kind; pin it wherever you want to make a point. But don't stop there. Make a point of seeing our entire Petit Point Collection of pins, bracelets, necklaces, and earrings, priced to $50 plus tax. The pin shown (actual size) is $25 plus tax.

Jewels by TRIFARI

Jewelry Designs Copyrighted. Trifari, Krussman and Fishel, Inc.

55

© 1966 P. Lorillard Co.

To a trainer, it's to win first prize...

To an angler, it's a fish this size...

To a lady, it's a gallant gent... To a smoker, it's a KENT

More taste...fine tobacco

KENT puts the flavor of the world's finest tobaccos through the KENT filter—for the most satisfying taste in filter smoking today.

56

Man... that took muscle!

Woman...that took Brillo!
SAYS ARNOLD STANG

Brillo soap pads

Other pads are puffed with air... pull them apart and see. Brillo is packed with *muscle* because there's practically no air in Brillo...just extra soap and extra metal fiber. That's what it takes to clean and shine pans. Buy the soap pad that's made better to work harder. That's Brillo.

You'll find the Woman's Touch in every Purex Product.

BRILLO MFG. CO. DIV. OF PUREX CORP. LTD.

57

There's a big difference between a

possum...and a...blossom

—and there is a powerful difference, too, between gasoline and "ETHYL" gasoline!

On a trip to the country ...or around the town... you'll appreciate the extra power of "ETHYL" gasoline

When you see the familiar yellow-and-black "Ethyl" emblem on a pump, you know you are getting this better gasoline. "Ethyl" antiknock fluid is the famous ingredient that steps up power and performance. Ethyl Corporation, New York 17, N. Y.

Other products sold under the "Ethyl" trade-mark: salt cake...ethylene dichloride...sodium metallic...chlorine (liquid)...oil soluble dye...benzene hexachloride (technical)

58

55 Trifari

The blue ribbon bow symbolizes the tender age of childhood. The child grows up and the ribbon does too, by analogy, becoming a lasting, fine piece of jewelry.

The copy comments on the headline, then says: "This bow is the place-it-where-you-please kind; pin it wherever you want to make-a point." The pin was shown actual size, in about a two-inch square area.

Trifari, Krussman & Fishel, Inc.

59 Wurlitzer

As simple a device as the pose of the model can point up an analogy with clarity. In this case it involves the dexterity of a child engaged in two different but exacting activities.

The ads appeared on facing pages, surrounded by editorial matter. The relationship between them was easily seen because of the similarity of the pose and the same striped T-shirt. The analogy goes for a little girl, too. "If she can handle a jump rope."

"Will your child practice? Yes, if you give encouragement, keep practice periods short, hold out a reward for progress, and be an appreciative audience." This part of the copy is concerned not with selling a product but with resolving some of the doubts a parent might have about successful use of the product. "Wurlitzer means Music to millions."

56 Kent

This analogy campaign is a refreshing break from the mass of cliché-ridden cigarette advertising The problem of appealing to a young audience was solved in this ad by the use of a cartoon character of indeterminate age, instead of a photograph.

Kent was really in, with the gay singing commercials used on radio and TV. When a popular marimba band made a recording of the tune, Kent had it made.

"More taste...fine tobacco" is the slogan.

© P. Lorillard Co.

57 Brillo

The exclamations in the headline size up the achievement — and the analogy — with conviction and punch. The copy gives a less dramatic explanation of Brillo's "muscle." "Other pads are puffed with air...pull them apart and see. Brillo is packed with *muscle* because there's practically no air in Brillo."

© Purex Corp.

58 Ethyl

Gasolines may all seem alike, but here is visual indication that what may seem alike can be, in fact, radically different.

This whole campaign had illustrations painted to look alike at first glance. But on closer inspection, they proved to be decidedly different. Ethyl gasoline was in this way distinguished from other brands. The copy gives a mnemonic for identification, the familiar yellow and black "Ethyl" emblem.

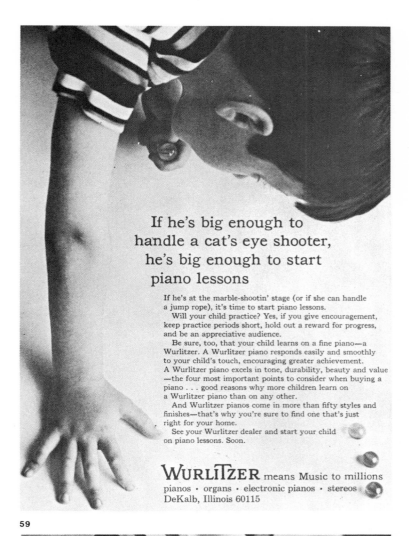

59

Harvesting Jersey Belles — photo by Mark Shaw

Unshackle yourself. You have a friend
at Chase Manhattan to help you care for
your nest egg and <u>act as your trustee</u>.
Delegate us at your convenience.

THE CHASE MANHATTAN BANK
NATIONAL ASSOCIATION / Head Office: 1 Chase Manhattan Plaza, New York, N.Y. 10015

new **SUNSHINE**
RINSO
WITH SUNSHINE WHITENERS

You'll love washing with sunshine...

New sunshine Rinso with "sunshine whiteners" really <u>does</u>
act new! It makes your clothes so fresh and sunny
they <u>glow</u>—like drying them outdoors!

Fair Warning: Get out your sunglasses and
be ready for that wild sunshine Rinso glow!

60 Chase Manhattan

Take a familiar idea literally and you can come
up with a pretty ludicrous picture; enough to
make you laugh at your money anxieties. Why
carry around your worry about your savings?
Simply contact your friend at Chase Manhattan.

In this series, various situation shots showed
a middle-aged or elderly person with chains,
forged through life, linked to a nest egg. Let
Chase Manhattan do the worrying.

62 El Al Israel Airlines

This full-page newspaper ad interprets the headline literally. It communicates in a dramatic way
the concept of a shorter way across the Atlantic
by air.

A three-dimensional ocean suddenly becomes
two-dimensional by the simple device of turning
it into a flat sheet of paper. Tearing it part way
down one side demonstrates to the startled
reader how easily the vast Atlantic can be rolled
up, made smaller in fact. Shadows at the curled-
up edges of the paper, lower right, add a convincing Q. E. D. to the trick.

The only line of copy is: "Watch for the inauguration of the first jet-prop service across the
Atlantic, introducing the Bristol Britannia, starting Dec. 23 EL AL Israel Airlines."

© El Al Israel Airlines

61 Rinso

Chemicals were developed that really brightened
the clothes washed with them. Picking on the
brightest object known to man — the sun — the
name of the product was changed to Sunshine
Rinso. The tag, "with sunshine whiteners," was
added to it, in case the reader doesn't get the
idea the first time.

The strong glow coming from the package is,
of course, from those tiny sunshine whiteners
throwing off their strong little bursts of light.
This obliged the model to put on a pair of sunglasses. The bright reflections on her glasses
also show the brilliance of what is in the package.

The copy below says "Fair Warning: Get out
your sunglasses and be ready for that wild sunshine Rinso glow!" The package with the sym-
bolic sunburst was dark blue with "Rinso" in
orange and the center of the sun in vibrant
orange and yellow. It is nice to see harmony in
all the aspects of marketing a product - idea, art,
copy, packaging.

Starting
Dec. 23
the
Atlantic
Ocean
will be
20%
smaller

Watch for the inauguration of the first jet-prop service across the Atlantic, introducing the Bristol Britannia, starting Dec. 23. **EL AL**
ISRAEL AIRLINES

See your travel agent or: El Al Israel Airlines, 610 Fifth Avenue, New York 20, N. Y., PLaza 1-3400

You can't get the whole picture in just a day or two.

What national monument is 14 feet wide, 10 miles long, and moves at nine miles an hour? The answer is San Francisco's cable car system — and it can show you a lot of the city for 15 cents.

Some other surprising things about San Francisco: A street that changes direction ten times in one block. A night club that presents grand opera. Italian restaurants that serve the best French bread in the country. Grant Avenue — main street for the largest Chinese community outside the Orient. A modern pharmacy that sells charms to ward off dragons. A bridge that crosses the Pacific. A temperature that can change 20° in 20 miles.

Of course it takes more than one or two cable car rides to learn all there is to know about this surprising city. So may we make two suggestions? When you come to San Francisco (1) bring some small change, and (2) *plan to spend a week.*

SAN FRANCISCO
CONVENTION & VISITORS BUREAU

For a free illustrated guide write to
San Francisco Convention & Visitors Bureau · Dept. NY4
1375 Market Street · San Francisco, California 94103

63

Most girls swear by only one sock—
Bonnie Doon

What's so exciting about socks? Plenty. When they're by Bonnie Doon. Brand-new styles. Striking new colors. Original new patterns. And all for the same old price—of a pair of socks!

Shown: Highland. nylon. 12 colors. 9½–11. Only $3. Bonnie Doon of New York, Inc., 11 East 36th Street, New York, New York 10016.

tycora

64

COME OUT OF YOUR SHELL...TRY SMIRNOFF

Everyone else is enjoying these smart new Smirnoff drinks. Why not you? Smirnoff Screwdrivers with orange juice. Smirnoff Bloody Marys with tomato juice. The Smirnoff Mule made with 7-Up®. The dryest Martinis. The smoothest drink on-the-rocks. Only crystal clear Smirnoff, filtered through 14,000 pounds of activated charcoal, makes so many drinks so well. Come out where the sun and the Smirnoff shine. It's a *delicious* world!

Get acquainted offer: Try the delicious drinks you've been missing with this new half quart sampler bottle. Now available in most states.

Always ask for *Smirnoff* VODKA *It leaves you breathless®*

65

...those heavenly carpets by Lees

When you buy fine carpet look for seven things: The color you've dreamed of, the price you can afford, rich, resilient texture, fine imported wool, long wear, proper width and ease in decoration. You'll find all of these in a Lees. Carpet is Bramble in Biscayne Blue.

Lees CARPETS

66

63 San Francisco Convention & Visitors Bureau

Now that travelers are coming to your town, how do you make them stay longer? The reason they're coming, to begin with, is that they expect to find it interesting. Convince them that there is even more to your city than they had thought, and they may stay long enough to get the whole picture.

The copy further piques curiosity by posing an odd question at the very beginning: "What national monument is 14 feet wide, 10 miles long, and moves at nine miles an hour?" "The answer," obviously, "is San Francisco's cable car system."

Other intriguing tidbits are offered: "A street that changes direction ten times in one block. A night club that presents grand opera...A bridge that crosses the Pacific. A temperature that can change 20° in 20 miles."

64 Bonnie Doon

Just because people wear socks in pairs, there's no need to show both. This pose is clearly bent on hiding the bare foot so that the pattern of the sock has no competition from the model.

65 Smirnoff

Take it literally. A man might come out of his shell with Smirnoff. The many other ads in this long-running campaign have been consistent, sticking to the same basic layout and typography, as well as interpreting the headlines literally. Other ads were headlined: "Get your party off the ground," showing Sid Caesar being carried aloft on a steel beam to a party on an unfinished skyscraper, and "I'd ride a mile for a Smirnoff martini," showing a camel sitting in the middle of a New York street — Fifth Avenue — with a model leaning over his back.

Smirnoff has also introduced new drinks. One concoction, the "Smirnoff Mule," was well supported by advertising. The slogan following the logo is a play on words, explaining what is unique about vodka: "It leaves you breathless."

66 Lees

Most extraneous objects have been left out of the picture for Lees carpets, while it tells the story. The artist has taken literal advantage of his opportunity by featuring only the carpet. The scene is a room floating somewhere in the heavens.

The copy tells the reader seven things to look for: color, price, resilient texture, imported wool, long wear, proper width, ease in decoration. The carpet name is shown for those who may want to order it.

James Lees & Sons (Burlington Industries)

67 Hertz

This dashing young man floats down to earth with ease, proving that the Hertz system is so widespread that "Wherever you land / there's a pretty Hertz girl / waiting to meet you." His faked shadow, touching the shadow of the car, lends credibility to the act.

There is, in addition, "Certified Service" which guarantees $50 in car rental certificates in case Hertz fails to arrive. The copy advises, "So don't settle for second best." (Avis, the competitor?) The slogan is: "Let Hertz put *you* in the driver's seat."

©Hertz System

68 Clairol

Selling the product indirectly, this ad convinces the customer that local hairdressers who buy Clairol products for their salons are the ones who can bring out her loveliest look.

If the reader is not so lovely, the copy has something for her, too: "Besides, it's fun to be fussed over, and the luxury and relaxation of a salon treatment works wonders for the morale."

©Clairol Inc.

Wherever you land
there's a pretty Hertz girl
waiting to meet you

Who else but Hertz is big enough to greet you at every airport you are likely to land at?

And only Hertz can offer you this assurance of satisfaction: Certified Service...the plan that pays you $50 in car rental certificates in the unlikely event that Hertz should fail you.

So don't settle for second best.

One local call makes a Hertz reservation anywhere in the world. And when you land, a pretty Hertz girl will be waiting with a key to a shiny Chevrolet or other fine car. A lordly feeling.

Let Hertz put *you* in the driver's seat.   HERTZ RENT A CAR

67

Whenever you need a lift, get your hair done.

That
magic touch
can send you
flying—

With a cut, a set, a little color, your hairdresser brings out your loveliest look. Besides, it's fun to be fussed over, and the luxury and relaxation of a salon treatment works wonders for the morale.

Hairdressers—who know best how to make the most of a woman's looks—use more Clairol than all other haircolorings combined.

69 Herald Tribune — WPAT

This ad brings the reader an announcement about the news in a visual-verbal way. The message is given for the eye, literally showing the interruption in the music running down the staffs on the sheet music. In actual fact, it is the ear that will receive both the announcer's message and the break in the music.

©Herald Tribune — WPAT

71 Klopman Mills

This concept has been used with hundreds of different models leaning backwards on Klopman Mills for Dacron/cotton fabrics.

One good aspect of the approach is that these ads work equally well for consumer, retailer, or manufacturer; it saves time, money, and effort in dreaming up a separate appeal to each. The copy describes this custom-made coat (not available anywhere) to show that the fabrics are great fashion innovators.

Burlington Industries, Inc.

72 Frojen Advertising

A creative idea must be tempered by the results of its effect on the reader. If the readers are real swingers, they will go along with a way-out idea in an ad. The realistic question arises as to whether a businessman, when it comes to his own business, will trust his account to fun people or give it to an agency that thinks more conservatively.

73 Land-Rover

If imitation is flattery, then this copy is a sincere example of it. Light-hearted in layout, photography, and wording, it is a take-off on a Rolls-Royce ad (see number 185). It's fun to read. All the "bad" features are satirized and turned into comfortable assets endorsed by John Steinbeck, who says: "Except for rattles, I am against silence in a car."

The copy is catchy throughout: the car's "throaty authority is assuring in times of stress; which nowadays is usually...The Land-Rover is built to resist the charge of a bull rhinoceros; or a bull Lincoln for that matter...The after compartment has facing seats. This arrangement, although somewhat reminiscent of riding in a paddy-wagon, is extremely sociable. Late at night, it is hilarious."

This is one of the few ads — if not the only one — that signs off: "Thank you."

©Rover Motor Co. of North America

70 Kelvinator

This arresting photo, in full color with pervading reddish glow, sells the concept of Kelvinator. Paradoxical phrasing, and the fantasy of denizens from the torrid nether regions enjoying ice-cold drinks in the kitchen, tell the story visually better than dull product shots.

However, the body copy is packed with detailed information about the refrigerator. The slogan: "Kelvinator, the uncommon cold."

American Motors

look before you lean

make sure it's a fabric you can lean on by Klopman

Klopman is not only the world's fussiest maker of Dacron/cotton fabrics they're great fashion innovators as well. As you can see in this "wherever coat" made from Klopman heavy-weight twill with striped lapels, lining and pants of poplin. Both fabrics are 65% Dacron® polyester/35% combed cotton. Designed for illustration only—to show some of the wonderful ways Klopman fabrics work for fashion and you. Klopman Mills, Inc. A division of Burlington Industries, Inc.

71

You can draw upon a lot of talented people at Frojen Advertising. Help yourself.

▶F

Frojen Advertising Inc.
3600 Wilshire Boulevard, Los Angeles
DUnkirk 6-8600

72

Land-Rover 109 Station Wagon with Heat Shield Roof.

"At 60 miles an hour the loudest noise in this new Land-Rover comes from the roar of the engine"

What makes Land-Rover the most conspicuous car in the world? "There is really no secret," says an eminent Land-Rover enthusiast.

1. "Except for rattles, I am against silence in a car," writes John Steinbeck, a Land-Rover enthusiast, "and I don't know a driver who doesn't want to hear his engine."

2. If this is so, then you may like the Land-Rover very much indeed.

3. Our 4-wheel drive (8 speeds for-

© 1965 Rover Motor Co. of North America Ltd.

ward, 2 in reverse) masterpiece is not mousey. Its throaty authority is assuring in times of stress; which nowadays is usually.

4. Nor is this claim true only at 60 miles an hour. A Land-Rover is more conspicuous even when it is standing still. With the ignition off.

5. The Land-Rover stands nearly seven feet tall. All its features tend to heroic proportion.

6. Therefore, when driving, you will simply loom over traffic which previously had scared the devil out of you.

7. This is not only safe and enjoy-

able, but you will exult to observe how other drivers, awe-inspired by the Land-Rover's casual might, yield in deference.

8. (Small wonder that women are enormously fond of driving Land-Rovers. The easy command of such massive, maneuverable masculinity is heady stuff.)

9. You may have read of tests where "imported cars" fared badly in collisions? It's a pity we weren't in there to help out the side. The Land-Rover is built to resist the charge of a bull rhinoceros; or a bull Lincoln for that matter.

10. The Land-Rover's sturdiness of construction (the under-frame resembles a reinforced section of railway track) makes it ideal for trackless wastes, car pools of small children, wretched ordeals, etcetera.

11. There are perhaps 14 Land-Rover hardy perennials ranging from safari cars and campers to police vans and getaway cars. Our most popular passenger models are the 7-seater Model 88 and the 10-seater Model 109 Station Wagons.

11-A. An attractive feature of the '65 Land-Rover is that it is precisely as attractive as the '64.

12. Both of these have capacious rear doors for unloading bulk or people. The unathletic may use the fold-down step.

13. The after compartment has facing seats. This arrangement, although somewhat reminiscent of riding in a paddy-wagon, is extremely sociable. Late at night, it is hilarious.

14. The Land-Rover is available with a spare tire either mounted on the rear door or on top of the hood. The tires are identical in every respect save that it costs $7.40 more to have one on the hood.

LAND-ROVER WITH & WITHOUT TIRE ON HOOD

15. People who feel diffident about driving a Land-Rover with the spare tire on the hood can buy the conventional Land-Rover and save $7.40.

PRICE: The Model 109 Station Wagon illustrated in this advertisement costs **$3,906** on the Atlantic Coast, **$4,092** on the Pacific Coast; at places in between, it costs in between. The Model 88 Station Wagon (shorter by 1 door) costs about **$600** less.

If you would like to listen to the Land-Rover, or to the embarrassingly quiet Mark II Rover Sedan, or to the Rover 2000 Sports Sedan (which has "a little panty mutter when idling that rises to a whispering roar in the lower gears," according to Mr. Steinbeck), please ask any dealer here listed.

(LR) signifies a Land-Rover dealer; (R), a Rover dealer; (R & L R), both.

Thank you.

73

CONTRAST

74 Davidow

Next time the client wants his name as large as possible, feature it!

The colored label, in the same warm, bright red-white-and-green as the Italian flag, is featured in contrast with the black-and-white photo of two models traveling in Davidow clothes. The copy is plain and simple. The texture makes the label more interesting than if the words had been set in type on a white background.

74

75 Boris Kroll

Contrast often is supplied by distinctive textures. The background here is a close-up shot of the same fabric used to upholster the armchair.

The word fabric (difficult to read even in the original ad) is in big black letters behind the logo, Boris Kroll.

75

Inside your obese patient a slim one signals to be freed

Release her with

Preludin® brand of phenmetrazine hydrochloride

Geigy

76

76 Preludin

This two-color ad, one of a series, was a line mezzotint made from a photograph and shown against a solid yellow page. The original figure was distorted and screened to show, by contrast, her obese caricature.

Geigy

78 Simmons

Things can materialize right in front of the reader's eyes, even mattresses and families; just flip the flap and see! (See following right-hand page.)

Poppa, nonchalantly dead to the world, with his unhappy wife, is seen — two kids and a 6-1/2-foot-wide mattress later — serenely uncomplicated on a Simmons Beautyrest. The contrast in size of the two mattresses registers immediately, and the idea is underlined by the small photo of Mommy sitting up in the baby's crib (which is shorter too, of course).

The first photo shows how ordinary mattresses are constructed, with interlinked springs, forcing the sleepers to roll together; while the next photo shows that Simmons has independent coil springs which let each person sleep on his own part of the mattress. The sales clincher is the 15-year guarantee in case the mattress proves structurally defective.

©Simmons Co.

77 Bell System

A dramatic stopper can be the result of a simple affirmation of something that becomes quickly obvious to any reader. The headline is starkly presented against a background of minimum complexity. With teeming rain driving hard against the window pane, it obviously is *not* outdoor shopping weather. The white, all-capital-letter headline stands out boldly against the dreadful bleakness outside.

American Telephone & Telegraph

IT'S A PERFECT DAY TO SHOP BY PHONE.

BELL SYSTEM
American Telephone & Telegraph Co. and Associated Companies

79 Remington

The use of fold-outs first must be justified as essential to expression of the idea; second, must persuade the reader to open the flap, and third, should surprise the reader. This ad (see following right-hand page) qualifies in every way: the headline has an arrow pointing to the fold-in, expressing the picture idea while leaving the denouement to the inside fold.

The inside picture surprises us by the change of expression from a doubtful frown to a smile, and the half-shaven face as contrasted to the growth of stubble.

The full-page photo of a half-doubting Dad helps make for an attention-getter closely related to the product. The role of the little shaver trying to convince his Dad that the electric shaver outshaves the razor is a tactful way for an advertiser to knock old-fashioned ideas without causing offense.

78 a

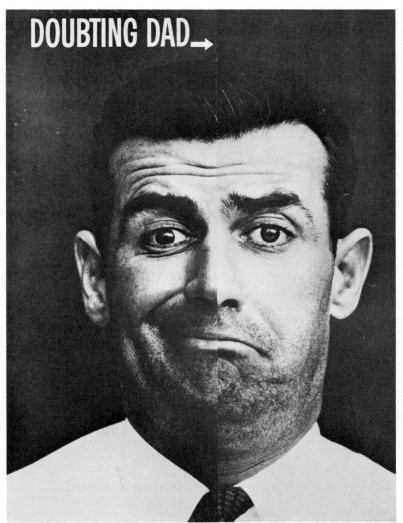

79 a

80 Ambush

The contrast in this ad lies in the art work: the marked difference between the delicate line drawing and the bold halftone of the bottle. The ink drawing symbolically illustrates the name of the perfume, Ambush.

This contrast might not work well if techniques were reversed.

Dana

80

81 Marvella

The range of contrast shown in this back-lit photograph establishes a background (the beach), a middle ground (the pearl diver), and a foreground (his palm).

The small insert of a two-strand necklace shown close-up is photographed against a sand background in keeping with the setting of the main photograph.

A pearl diver _can_ tell. But your catty friends can't and your best friends won't. Marvella simulated pearls deceive everyone but the pros. marvella.

81

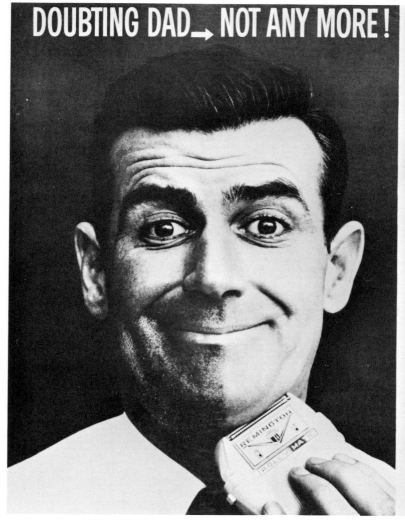

Ever notice how when products compete with each other,

they get better.

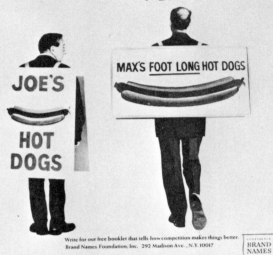

JOE'S HOT DOGS

MAX'S FOOT LONG HOT DOGS

are you a Springmaid?

You can see for yourself in Muriel Ryan's pin-stitched dress. It's Springmaid Gambit oxford cotton. Neat. Crisp. Tireless. The cotton that makes you a Springmaid. Navy, red, black, light blue or white. Sizes 5 to 15. About $15. Best & Co., New York; Bullock's, California; L. S. Ayres & Company, Indianapolis; John Wanamaker, Philadelphia; Miller & Rhoads, Richmond. Fabric by Springmaid Cottons, 104 West 40th St., N.Y.

82

83

An unfair comparison between the VW and the Rambler American.

The Volkswagen on the left gives you the advantages of a little economy car.

The Rambler American on the right gives you the advantages of an economy car without being little.

It lists for $1,946, scrimps on gas, and doesn't change styles from year to year.

Yet it seats six comfortably, and gives you more than twice the horsepower and trunk space of the VW. It also offers you the choice of four doors. The VW 1500 doesn't.

The American gives you a bigger battery, wider tires, bigger brakes, and bigger fuel tank than the Volkswagen. It outweighs the VW by 800 pounds.

Still, with all its extra size, the American has exactly the same 36-foot turning diameter as the Volkswagen. For easy parking and handling.

And the American has more than twice as many factory-authorized service centers in the U.S. as the VW.

On American roads you need power, comfort, and service as well as economy.

Which is the nicest thing about the American.

It's American.

American Motors
Ambassador · Rebel · Rambler American · And the new Javelin

The Volkswagen 1500

The Rambler American 220

84

82 Brand Names Foundation

Basically, this ad puts over the idea well. There is no point in belaboring the message; the visual contrast between the two frankfurters is effective enough.

Nevertheless, upon further investigation certain questions nag. Does a longer frankfurter mean a better one? Might the foot-long hot dog be made of cheaper meat on inferior bread? Could it be that they are sold in a grubby shack at the edge of town instead of Joe's sanitary kitchens a block from where you work? And what about price?

These quite reasonable questions could have been forestalled by a simple footnote on each sign: "All beef — only 25¢." The Brand Names Foundation invites the reader to "Write for our free booklet that tells how competition makes things better."

85 Cover Girl

Real cover girl models were used to exemplify the product name. On TV, the cover of an actual magazine was shown and then opened up onto a live-action situation shot.

The layout of this ad reinforces the idea by imitating a magazine cover. The lines of copy are written and set up as though they were titles of articles. A few related cosmetics are set in, at lower right, and there is an insert, lower left, of the cover girl as she appeared on an actual magazine cover.

©Noxzema Chemical Co.

83 Springmaid Fabrics

What's a Springmaid? It's a girl dressed in Springmaid Gambit oxford cotton.

This contrast picture idea is good for showing two styles on the same girl. The type, upside down and in reverse, gives you a subtle visual hint that the model in the bathing suit is reflected from a spring.

86 Fraser's

This mellow, full-color photograph rather suggests a still life by Vermeer in its handling of light. The matte burlap background contrasts with the hard, fine stainless flatware. The orange dominates, with the knife cutting into it at the angle of brightest reflection. Blueberries in the spoon and the fork with a strawberry delicately poised are carefully planned. In the background, the fruit bowl, emerging from the shadows, serves to highlight the knife even more. The delicacy of the shadows helps to give a three-dimensional quality to this composition. Finesse is one of many patterns minted of Cromargan steel.

84 Rambler

Advertisers usually hold to the principle of not mentioning a competitor by name, to say nothing of showing his product. This very successful ad is one of a series which struck at its competitors head on, making deadly visual/verbal comparisons, always favorable to the Rambler.

Visually, the Volkswagen is dark, contrasting with the light-colored Rambler (the bad guys and the good guys). Although the wheel bases are the same and are shown at about the same angle, the VW is higher on the page than the Rambler making the VW look shorter than it is.

American Motors

85

86

82

BEFORE

AFTER

A Coty Cremestick turned Alice Pearce.. into Joey Heatherton.

And you thought lipsticks weren't important, eh?
Another Cremestick trick: they're moisturizing,
but they're never greasy.
And zip! They're on in a stroke.
Ask Alice Pearce.

POPPY LOVE
Wear it.
But watch it!

PINK ME UP
That's what it's called.
That's what it does.

WET APRICOT
Much nicer than
dry apricot. "

SUN SHIMMER GLOSSER
For come-hither
highlights.

Some luscious Cremestick colors: And:

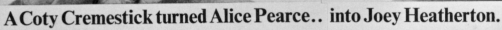

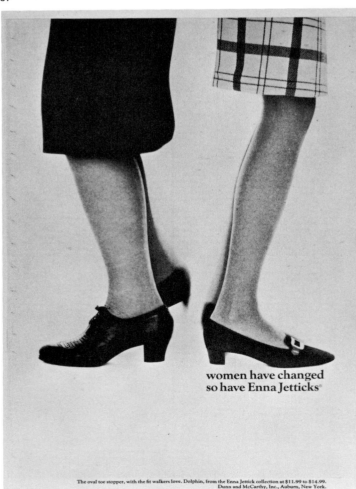

women have changed
so have Enna Jetticks®

The oval toe stopper, with the fit walkers love. Dolphin, from the Enna Jettick collection at $11.99 to $14.99.
Dunn and McCarthy, Inc., Auburn, New York.

Now, enjoy all the excitement of color in the brightest,
most true-to-life RCA Victor Color TV ever...from $399.95 *

Lifelike natural color. New Vista® Color
TV for 1965 gives you the most true-to-
life RCA Victor Color ever . . . with better
color purity, greater contrast than ever
before. Color is so bright, so lifelike, you
have to see it to believe it! Crisp, clear
black and white pictures, too. Automatic
Scene Control for balanced brightness and
contrast.

Most widely proved—dependable.
RCA pioneered and developed Color
TV—made it a reality—proved it in
homes like yours across the country.
It's the most widely proved Color TV
you can buy. Today, it's America's
first choice—more people own RCA
Victor than any other TV—black and
white or color.

***New low price.** Now only $399.95
for the *Darcy*, not shown. Manufacturer's nationally advertised price,
optional with dealer. All prices, specifications subject to change.

 The Most Trusted Name in Television

87 Coty

In a light-hearted manner the Before-and-After ad is reduced *ad absurdum*.

The idea is simple and involves real, live people. The names of the lipsticks are followed up by zany explanations of what they do to a girl. For instance: "Poppy Love/Wear it. But watch it!"

90 Breck

The Caucasian girl with blonde hair is contrasted with the Tahitian girl and her jet-black hair. The copy explains that "For centuries Tahitian girls have possessed the secret that keeps hair from snarling and tangling."

Another ad showed the Tahitian girl alone, full face, the right half of her hair with a comb in it dividing off a third of the page. The ad used an excerpt from the original theme: "Your comb seems to float through your hair."

©John H. Breck, Inc. Reproduced by permission.

88 Enna Jetticks

A short skirt, slender legs, and slim shoes, that's what little girls are made of — in this mod generation, anyway.

The styles of two different periods are contrasted here, expressing the concept of the headline.

Dunn and McCarthy, Inc.

91 Emeraude

Here the contrast is between the sexes. The idea is that men will respond to feminine allure in a more masculine way if women become by contrast more feminine. The headline allows each reader to apply it to her personal situation.

©Coty

89 RCA Victor

This classic series of ads set off a whole epidemic of ads featuring the product in full color against a black-and-white photograph. RCA was selling not only a console model, but also the idea of accepting color TV as a radical change from the black-and-white picture.

92

DIAGRAMS

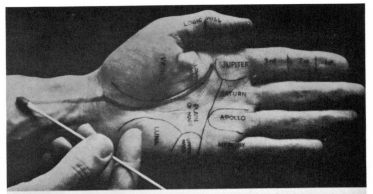

WHAT'S HAPPENING TO MAN'S LIFELINE?

It's lengthening—figuratively—because of the cooperative probing by many different scientists into problems once faced exclusively by medical researchers.

Fever, the great warning symptom that may first have been measured by Galileo, is now being located exactly instead of generally, by infrared detection. Even soft tissue and fluids are being "photographed." Strep throat and certain other infections can be diagnosed in hours instead of days by utilizing a fluorescent antibody testing technique developed by optics and electronics engineers, physi-

cians, and biochemists. The fluoroscopic light microscope used in this technique is also of value in research.

It is not surprising that Avco people should also apply electronics, physics, chemistry, engineering—their fund of knowledge—to medicine.

Thus, to permit examinations the physician never could make before, techniques of television and fibre optics are being combined at Avco for use in internal observation. Avco has developed a timesaving intubation system to open the pyloric valve between the stomach and

intestines. Avco is also producing a surgical bridge that greatly strengthens the hold of deep sutures by optimizing stress-strain ratios.

The interplay of the physical sciences and engineering with medicine is developing many new products. The benefits to mankind promise to be immeasurable.

If you are interested in joining Avco—an Equal Opportunity Employer—please write. *Avco—leadership in broadcasting; aircraft engines; farm equipment; space and defense research, development and production.*

Avco

Avco Corporation, 750 Third Avenue, New York 17, N.Y.

Detroit has used up all the words for a new car introduction, except these:

Jaguar XK-E 2+2

2" higher than the XK-E for added headroom.

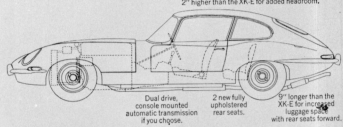

Dual drive, console mounted automatic transmission if you choose.

2 new fully upholstered rear seats.

9" longer than the XK-E for increased luggage space with rear seats forward.

It has the XK-E 4.2 litre double overhead camshaft engine, XK-E 4-speed synchromesh gearbox with diaphragm clutch, XK-E aerodynamic styling, XK-E lightweight all-steel monocoque body, XK-E dual hydraulic braking systems, XK-E power-assisted 4-wheel disc brakes, XK-E independent suspension on all 4 wheels, XK-E fine grain leather bucket seats, XK-E wood-rimmed racing-type telescopic steering wheel, XK-E positive rack-and-pinion steering, XK-E Powr-Lok limited slip differential. If you don't need back seats, buy the 2-seater roadster or coupe.

Jaguar: A different breed of cat.

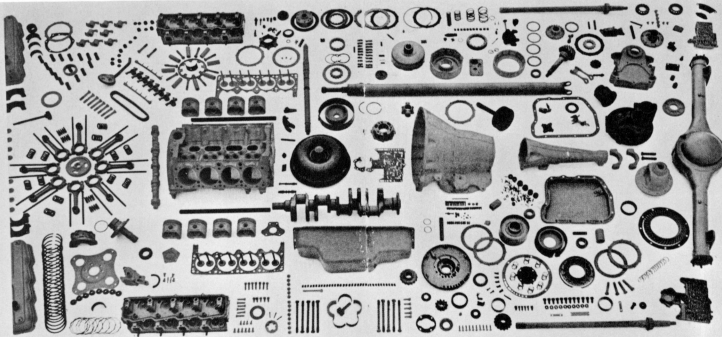

SEE BOB HOPE AND THE CHRYSLER THEATRE, NBC-TV, FRIDAYS

Every part shown here is protected by the 1964   Chrysler Corporation 5-year or 50,000-mile warranty

Every new 1964 Chrysler Corporation car carries this warranty* that made automotive history. This warranty comes with 1964 Plymouth, Valiant, Dodge, Dart, Chrysler and the Imperial.

It protects you against big repair bills resulting from defects in engine, transmission and other expensive power-train components.

It lasts for 5 years or 50,000 miles. And it can be transferred, adding extra value to your car when you trade or sell (as some '63 owners are already discovering).

All you have to do is have your car serviced regularly (you'd probably follow the schedule shown here anyway) to keep in effect the strongest protection your car investment ever had.

*Chrysler Corporation warrants for 5 years or 50,000 miles, whichever comes first, against defects in materials and workmanship and will replace or repair at a Chrysler Motors Corporation Authorized Dealer's place of business, the engine block, head and internal parts, intake manifold, water pump, transmission case and internal parts, (excluding manual clutch), torque converter, drive shaft, universal joints, rear axle and differential, and rear wheel bearings of its 1964 automobiles, provided the owner has the engine oil changed every 3 months or 4,000 miles, whichever comes first, the oil filter replaced every second oil change and the carburetor air filter cleaned every 6 months and replaced every 2 years, and every 6 months furnishes to such a dealer evidence of performance of the required service, and requests the dealer to certify (1) receipt of such evidence and (2) the car's then current mileage.

Plymouth • Chrysler • Imperial • Dodge

 **CHRYSLER CORPORATION**

94 Avco

In this unusual application of diagramming, the hand is depicted as fortune tellers might see it.

At first glance, it might remind the reader of a space program, since the markings are the names of heavenly bodies; it's only when he reads the body copy that he realizes Avco is involved with electronics, physics, biochemistry, medicine and engineering.

97 Bulova Watch

This full-color explosion of a Bulova watch shows all the little parts that make up a Bulova, each one tagged "Bulova made." The parts are carefully laid out, the spring unwound.

The sum of the parts equals the whole Bulova. There's no problem of identification with the parts of a watch, but if a product is to be shown dismantled, it should also be shown assembled, or identified, so that the reader can readily recognize the parts taken out of normal context.

The copy explains that "It's not the easiest way, nor the cheapest, but it makes it very unlikely that anything will go wrong with a Bulova. If it does, we'll have no one to blame but ourselves."

95 Jaguar

Rather than mar the beauty of the car by showing cut-away sections, the diagram is shown the same size as the photograph, except that it's in outline, with dotted lines to show the inside.

A repetition of the photograph in line is possible when one has the space for it, but if there are six different models to show and volumes of copy, it's probably better to revert to a surprint diagram or cut-away.

98 Western Electric

Since few people know anything about the production of an intricate mechanism, it's smart for a company to demonstrate the great pains they take to please the consumer. Western Electric has done so here with a specially constructed transparent instrument.

The copy explains how dificult an engineering job it was to squeeze a dial, dial light, and button into the "Trimline" phone that fits in the palm of a hand. For extra convenience — a new dial tone without hanging up. Below is the instrument with opaque covering. The slogan: "How handy!"

Bell System

96 Chrysler

Everything is methodically laid out. The only thing one might ask is whether the car parts are grouped with appropriate pieces near each other, or if they are simply set down at random to make a nice layout.

This is an ad that gained in effectiveness when it was seen in magazines of large format.

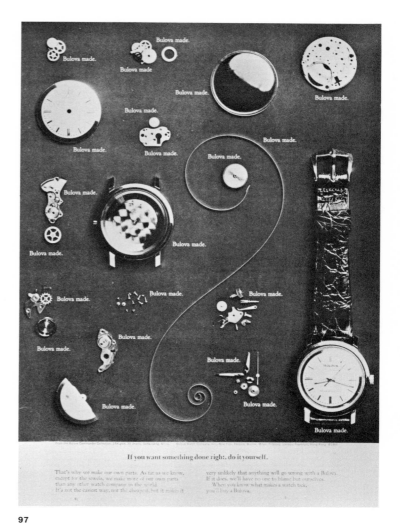

97

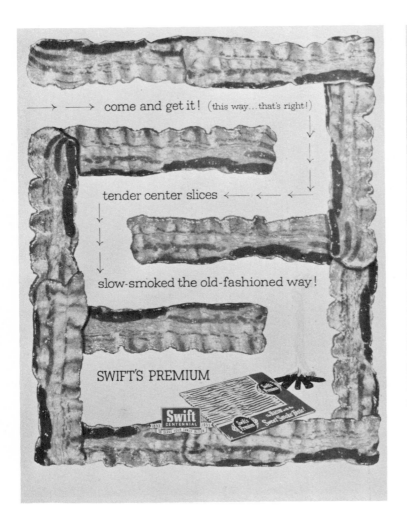
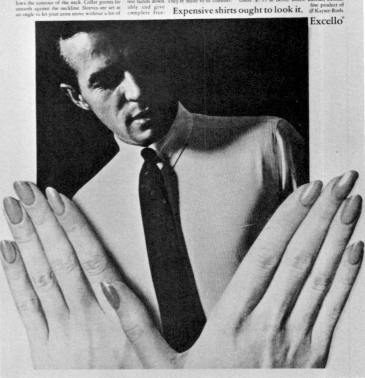

99 Swift's Premium

Although artificial, this use of a diagram is valid. By using the slices of fried bacon to simulate a maze, the product is favorably shown. The arrows point their way into the maze, a device for getting the copy read. Where the copy ends, the smoke from the log fire continues to lead the eye down the page.

102 Imperial '400' Motels

Without props of any kind, the model is ensconced in a comfortable background — asleep in his bed, his swimming pool at hand, with every convenience a traveler might wish for at his fingertips. All these invisible things are evoked simply by the copywriter's skillful, leading headline.

A bigger problem has been solved by this approach. All the motels in the chain have the same standards, although they may not look alike. Showing photos of representative Imperial '400' motels would give only a sampling, with no guarantee that the one you chanced upon would look anything like the photographs. By concentrating on the idea of convenience, the ad has made a better selling point. Here's the follow-up copy: "Most motels are out-of-town... Most motels are tip, tip, tip all the time...And listen to this. When's the last time you found a brightly-lit table with plenty of space to work on and leg room, too?"

100 Excello

A most ingenious way of measuring off that "Tell-tale Triangle" has been found in this ad. Laying together a pair of well-groomed, feminine hands and opening them out to form a V makes a perfect frame for the area in question. However, the hands are so out of scale that we soon perceive that they are lying on a flat photograph, despite the shadows that make them look normally three-dimensional.

The copy explains the special features of the product: "the collar follows the contour of the neck. Collar points lie smooth against the neckline. Sleeves are set at an angle to let your arms move without a lot of extra material. A uniquely tailored curved yoke eliminates unsightly pleats and gathers..." The slogan is, "Expensive shirts ought to look it."

Kayser-Roth

103 Clorox

A tough situation for any laundry. The team has the legend "Clorox needed here" spotting the extra-dirty places on their football togs.

Other Clorox ads showed how tough it might be to get the dirt out of a bowling team's toggery. The diagramming captions are varied. For example: "Too tough for detergents" "No job for weak bleach," "See sock test below" (shower before and after shot).

© Clorox Co. (Procter & Gamble)

101 Old Crow

Diagrammed maps can lead not only to sunken treasures but to greater readership. The dotted line in the path of the ship is lashed tight to the Old Crow theme: "Yo-ho-ho and a bottle of Crow!" Repetition of the ghost of the ship leaves no doubt as to which direction the eye should follow.

The copy continues the treasure theme throughout: "All paths lead to profits on the Old Crow route. These new display pieces will be 'pieces of great' appeal....They'll make your store a Treasure Island. This local stop will help you line your treasure chest with extra sales and profit." At the end, Mr. Old Crow himself uses a paraphrase of the slogan for the trade: "Yo-ho-ho and a bundle of DOUGH!"

102

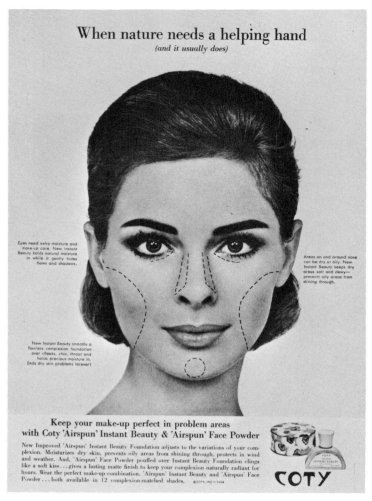

104

105

104 Coty

In searching for product concepts, an ad man should make a point of finding out beforehand where the ad will appear. He can find out a lot about the prospective customer by studying the publication, its editorial matter as well as its advertising. In doing this he will also find out what the competition is doing. He may even pick up an idea for the very ad he is working on.

Beauty articles in women's magazines quite often use diagrams to show the reader how to apply cosmetics. This Coty ad is one of the first in which dotted lines actually were used on the face of the photograph to spot the problem areas. These are wisely accompanied by blocks of copy telling how the product solves the problems.

©Coty

106 American Enka Corp.

This black-and-white ad, borrowing an idea from the paint-by-number sets, says more eloquently than could any color print ad that this blouse is too bright for a color ad to do it justice.

The use of black-and-white rather than four-color has also saved a considerable sum of money. The numbers are not just thrown in for effect; the color values are labeled accurately with the same number wherever they appear on the blouse. The copy explains why you must see the actual fabrics. "Enkalure gives a silken sheen to the colors...Go see the colors. Go feel the fabric."

107 Tigan

When dealing with products that have to do with the vital processes of the human body, the most logical diagram is an anatomical one. A cut-away of a live person is not practical, of course, but, with a competent artist and retoucher, one may cut away on paper to his heart's content.

When a photo of a human being is shown, the cut-away becomes less macabre if only the areas referred to are highlighted. Clothing the figure also helps.

Roche Laboratories

105 McCall's Magazine

The headline in this ad, "If your 3 year old grandchild has suffered any of these, check if the loving parents are so loving," is deeply disturbing. It refers to the X rays, identified in six-point type as "fractured skull...broken leg... broken wrist...cracked rib." The copy implies that quite possibly the parents, or one of them, may be deeply disturbed.

108 Kinsey

Help the reader complete the ad. With his eye, he will pick up the pieces of the puzzle to see which one fits where.

109 Gold Bond

Sound-deadening board placed between walls and floors, with acoustical tile for ceilings, are shown in their natural relationship, demonstrating how they would help in providing peace and privacy within the home. The cut-away house is borrowed from Hollywood; even the logo (unintentionally?) looks like a scene marker. Usually ads show an entire room of a house but here the cut-away diagram has been carried out cleverly to show three varied activities at several levels, each demanding peace and quiet from the others.

It might have been more dramatic if the boy had been shown sleeping instead of doing homework. But with the camera at the angle required to show the acoustical ceiling, you wouldn't have seen the small sleeping boy. Much thought went into the planning of this shot.

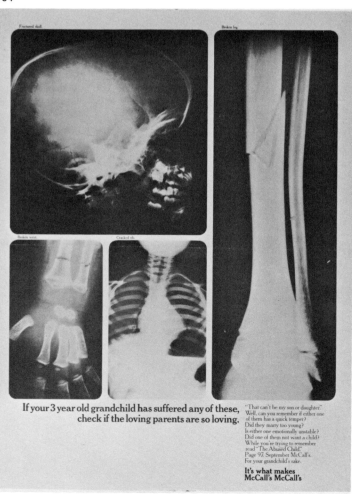

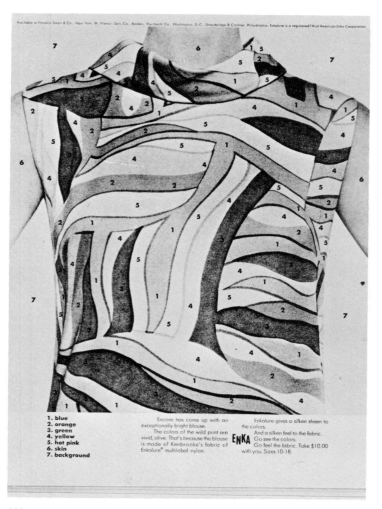

1. blue
2. orange
3. green
4. yellow
5. hot pink
6. skin
7. background

Encore has come up with an exceptionally bright blouse. The colors of the wild print are vivid, alive. That's because the blouse is made of Kenbrooke's fabric of Enkalure® multilobal nylon.

Enkalure gives a silken sheen to the colors. And a silken feel to the fabric. Go see the colors. Go feel the fabric. Take $10.00 with you. Sizes 10-18.

ENKA

The clinical benefit provided by Tigan (trimethobenzamide HCl) is the prompt and effective control of nausea and vomiting. Its specific and selective action suppresses emetic impulses from the chemoreceptor trigger zone (CTZ) to the vomiting center. It has no other demonstrable therapeutic action. Well tolerated by patients of all ages, it can be used with confidence in most conditions accompanied by emesis. It is highly effective in preventing nausea and vomiting as well.

In prescribing: Dosage – Adults: one 250-mg capsule t.i.d. or q.i.d.; in pregnancy, one 250-mg capsule at bedtime and on arising; up to 4 capsules daily. Children: 30 to 90 lbs, one or two 100-mg capsules t.i.d. or q.i.d.
Caution – If drowsiness, dizziness, headache, blurring of vision, depression of mood or diarrhea occurs, consider reduction or discontinuance of medication. If sensitization occurs, discontinue drug and, if indicated, initiate symptomatic treatment. Since drowsiness may occur, patients should not drive or operate machinery until response is determined. Antiemetic effects may render diagnosis difficult in certain conditions. As with any therapeutic agent, caution should be exercised in prescribing this drug for pregnant patients, and before doing so, the package insert, particularly the section Drug Administration During Pregnancy, should be consulted.
Supplied – Capsules, 250 mg, bottles of 50 and 500; Capsules, 100 mg, bottles of 100.
Roche Laboratories,
Division of Hoffmann-La Roche Inc.
Nutley, N.J. 07110.

Tigan® 250 mg
(trimethobenzamide HCl)
acts at the CTZ to promptly control nausea and vomiting

How to complete your Thanksgiving picture

1. You start by placing a bottle of Kinsey on the table. This superb whiskey is so light and mellow, so pleasing to the taste, that it goes a long way toward solving your holiday entertainment problem.

2. For the guest who likes highballs, you just add ice and soda to a couple of ounces of full-bodied Kinsey, and place the amber-colored nectar into the waiting hand.

3. Manhattan-fanciers are usually fussy. So make your Manhattans with smooth, rich Kinsey Whiskey... and complete the picture of Thanksgiving contentment.

KINSEY
BLENDED WHISKEY
the unhurried whiskey for unhurried moments
Since 1892

86.8 Proof. 65% Grain Neutral Spirits.
Kinsey Distilling Corp., Linfield, Pa.

The Gold Bond difference: Walls and ceilings that keep hootenannies from spreading

It's simple. Put Deciban — Gold Bond's new wood-fiber sound-deadening board — between the walls and between the floors. And add Gold Bond Silentex acoustical tile to the ceiling. (Silentex® absorbs up to 80% of noise.) Then let the gang whoop it up to their hearts' content. You won't give a hoot!

Like to know more about these remarkable new noise controllers? See your nearest Gold Bond® Building Products Dealer, or write to Department T-64, National Gypsum Company, Buffalo, New York 14225.

Gold Bond
DECIBAN

Gold Bond materials and methods make the difference in modern building

110 Chanel

Our minds react to the suggestion of relationship. If we are given a hint as to how shapes relate to one another, we can work them into a coherent whole.

Here the photograph of the model, with background, is divided into nine squares, with Chanel products shown in four of them. The human shapes within the other spaces are meaningless if isolated, but taken together they give us the figure of the model, leaning diagonally across the layout.

©Chanel, Inc.

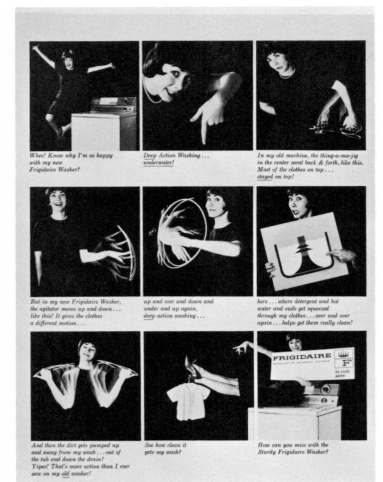

111 Frigidaire

Stroboscopic photographs (in which movement is frozen at separate stages on one print) give action to the demonstration of various types of motion used for effective laundering. A light source at the tip of the model's fingers helps to emphasize some of the actions.

This is a picture-and-caption ad and copy quotes might have been appropriate since the model is discussing the product. One picture makes use of a painted cut-away of the inside of the machine. The last two pictures are one, interestingly divided, with a caption under each part.

General Motors

THE FAMILIAR

Big, vine ripened tomatoes...

plus seven spices from around the world...

make Hunt's the catsup with the Big Tomato Taste

Lees "Island Park" carpet wasn't made to take this kind of punishment. But it can.

We actually made "Island Park" into a trampoline and let six kids and one dog go to work on it.

Now, "Island Park" wasn't really made for this sort of thing. It was made to take only common everyday mayhem. And look great while doing it.

Which is why Lees made it of tough heavy filament nylon. Packed good and thick to give "Island Park" a deep dense pile.

We inspected it 27 times to make sure there were no skips, flaws, ravels or misweaves.

We even inspected our inspections. When we were finished, "Island Park" was stain-resistant. Spill-resistant. Feet-resistant. Roller skate-resistant. Just about everything-resistant.

Including trampoline-resistant.

After hours of jumping and tumbling on our trampoline, the kids and the dog pooped out.

"Island Park" didn't. Even after this uncommon mayhem, it still looked great.

You'll probably never use "Island Park" on your trampoline.

But if you have one of those bouncy families, shouldn't you have it on your floor?

You can, for less than $9 a square yard.

For a lot of good, down-to-earth reasons, "those heavenly carpets by Lees."

©James Lees & Sons Co., Bridgeport, Pa. A Division of Burlington Industries.

WHEN IT LOOKS LIKE RAIN, BELIEVE IN LONDON FOG.

On Noah's Ark or the Staten Island Ferry, in foul weather or fair, people go in London Fogs two by two.

London Fog

112 Hunt's Tomato Catsup

The bottle shape is repeated, but it contains a new element each time. The tomato follows the ship-in-the-bottle idea.

If a product name is difficult to read (as it is when shown on its side), be sure the name is repeated in the headline.

Hunt Foods, Inc.

115 Fundador Brandy

The legendary story of the Dutch boy who saved a town by plugging a leak in a dike with his thumb lends itself well to this ad.

The headline is necessary to steer us away from any quick conclusion that some child is getting at the brandy, or has his finger stuck in the bottle. It leads us to the correct interpretation of the picture.

The copy explains that Pedro Domecq received an order from a Dutch firm for 312 butts of brandy made precisely thus and so. But the order turned out to be too expensive and was canceled. What to do with a quantity of costly brandy in a sherry-drinking country? For a long time it lay forgotten. When rediscovered, it had aged, becoming "delicately dry with a rare bouquet." The Domecq family decided to go on making it and called it Fundador.

113 Lees

A durability demonstration need not be drab. And in isolating the idea of "toughness," we need not show the entire room. Take the familiar trampoline and add six children and a dog to the free-for-all. About the carpet, the copy says: "It was made to take only common everyday mayhem...We inspected it 27 times...We even inspected our inspections...After hours of jumping and tumbling on our trampoline, the kids and the dog pooped out."

The logo on a folded-back carpet is a recurrent element in Lees ads and serves as a mnemonic (just like Kodak's turned-up page corner).

©James Lees & Sons (Burlington Industries)

116 Gamins

One chair and a bit of imaginative copy take this leg shot out of pedestrian advertising and open up a world of fashion. "With dramatic little flourishes it kept on its toes, and by discreetly revealing its charms at the end, It soon had twelve friendly men at its feet." The typewritten copy sums up: "Obviously, an open-and-shut case — just pure fashion."

114 London Fog

Noah's ark, with the creatures going in two by two, is a bit of Biblical lore with universal human appeal.

Since the zebra has the most attention-getting epidermis aboard the ark, the two models in London Fog coats are posed against its stripes to hold the spotlight.

Don't leave the whole idea to the headline. When you write body copy remember that, as with sports, there must be follow-through, as here: "On Noah's Ark or the Staten Island Ferry, in foul weather or fair, people go in London Fogs two by two." This is an arresting ad with only one line of copy.

You can thank the Dutch for this 110-year-old Spanish accident

Purely by accident, Pedro Domecq, who was famous for sherry, created Fundador Brandy. This is how it happened. In 1853, an order arrived from a Dutch firm for 312 butts—not of sherry, but of brandy. It was to be distilled "just so." Señor Domecq accepted the order and produced the brandy, but at such a high price the Dutch order was withdrawn. What to do with 312 butts of very expensive brandy in a sherry-drinking land? They found a forgotten corner, and there the butts lay for a long time. When rediscovered, the brandy had become delicately dry with a rare bouquet. "Soft and mellow," one could say. Why not make more the same way and call it Fundador? The Domecq family did. And today, for $6.94 a bottle in New York (slightly more or less in other States), you can enjoy the premium brandy with the regal Spanish accent that has earned all the world's acclaim. Favor yourself with **FUNDADOR**, the classic brandy of Spain.

80 PROOF. IMPORTED BY CANADA DRY CORPORATION, NEW YORK, N.Y.

115

This is a Gamin that was found 'NOT GUILTY.
With dramatic little flourishes it kept on its toes, and by discreetly revealing its charms at the end, it soon had twelve friendly men at its feet.
Obviously, an open-and-shut case—just pure fashion.
For $20, you can get away with it, too, at Andrew Geller stores. GAMINS*

MOM ART

Any contemporary collection of the creative masterpieces mother cooks up in the kitchen will no doubt include a can of Campbell's Tomato Soup. That red and white can is a model of practicality. Here's a rough outline of the clever things mother can do with it: **1** Serve it hot and buttered in cups or mugs. **2** Top hamburgers with it. **3** Slice yesterday's roast and reheat the slices in it. **4** Serve it in bowls garnished with parsley or a dollop of sour cream. **5** Paint pork chops delicious with it. **6** Bake fish fillets in Campbell's Tomato Soup. However Mom does it, it's an art. Ask Pop.

They always eat better when you remember the soup

117

He loves me.....
He loves me not
He loves me.....
He loves me not

carven

He loves me
He loves me
He loves me
He loves me

carven parfums—high fashion in fragrance from France. ma griffe... robe d'un soir... vert et blanc. — from $4 to $125 (plus Fed. tax)

117 Campbell's

Since Pop art uses famous products such as Campbell soup cans as subject matter, it seems only fitting that Campbell's use Pop art in their advertising.

The colors used in the paintings are vibrant and the six winners are keyed to the copy by numbered stickers.

"Any contemporary collection of the creative masterpieces mother cooks up in the kitchen will no doubt include a can of Campbell's Tomato Soup...Paint pork chops delicious with it...However Mom does it, it's an art. Ask Pop."

The generic slogan is an easy problem-solving mnemonic for mother: "They always eat better when you remember the soup."

119 Corn Flakes

Kellogg's psychologist can tell a lot about you by the way you pair up words. "Word-association" is the name of the game: "If he says 'Kellogg's' and you say 'Who?' — he's apt to raise an eyebrow. He finds your answer a bit more significant if you say 'Battle Creek.' But if you say 'Corn Flakes!' he grants that your reflexes are perfect."

This ad is daring because it hides the name of the product. This represents a growing trend; without official logos, ads are coming to look more and more like reading matter.

©Kellog Co.

120 Chun King

Using a time-honored American phrase but applying it to a foreign situation makes for an ad stopper. The sweet old lady we are used to seeing is there all right, but instead of baking apple pies she is making egg foo young.

Foods of the Chun King line are spread out, in full color, just as they might be served up, with delicious sauces waiting to be eaten. A package is shown at lower right, encased in a block of ice.

Bits of caption strewn about give the American equivalent of the Chinese food: "Egg foo young is an omelette...fried rice...may put potatoes out of business!" About chicken chow mein, "Serve it over waffles or spaghetti," and egg rolls are suggested as a hot appetizer with cocktails.

The slogan is: "Keep a great Chinese chef in your freezer." Another ad in this series showed literally that.

118 Carven

Starting with a familiar saying, this advertisement shows the product making a wish come true.

The picture of the product between the two rhymes gives pause to the eye before it transforms the doubts of a lovelorn lass into joyous affirmation. Using the top rhyme in white on black and the bottom one in black on white serves to emphasize the change of heart.

121 U. S. Keds

The visual analogy seems to be that just as the child cannot be separated from his bunny so, too, he cannot be separated from his Keds. The bunny is a nice break from the Teddy Bear cliché.

The copy carries on the headline idea, "Don't let anything separate you and Keds, either." The mnemonic, "Look for the blue label," makes sure that the customer won't switch to another brand.

United States Rubber (UniRoyal)

122 World Carpets

What good is a carpet if you have to preserve it as though it were in a museum? The heavy velvet rope is typical of a roped-off area in a museum, where you may look but not touch. Simple props and a related headline are all that is needed to create this setting.

"Word-association" is his name for the game

Our psychologist says he can tell a lot about you, simply by the way you pair up words.

For instance, if he says "Kellogg's" and you say "Who?"—he's apt to raise an eyebrow. He finds your answer a bit more significant if you say, "Battle Creek." That's where we live.

But if he says "Kellogg's" and you come right back with "Corn Flakes!"—that's when he snaps his notebook shut. Reflexes perfect. You're A-Okay. All systems, GO!

We tried saying "Corn Flakes" to *him*. His rabbit-quick reply was "Conquerable Resistance!" Turns out he's discovered that when you crunch down on those crackling flakes, they crunch back—gently—then let you bite on through.

Let you feel like you've *won*. And you leave the table with the nice conviction that you'll be a winner all day.

When we said "Nourishment," he sort of got carried away. "Vitamins and such!" he shouted. "About as much as any well-adjusted Corn Flake could have, and still taste like a Corn Flake!"

How about *that*, now?

Just like Grandma used to make

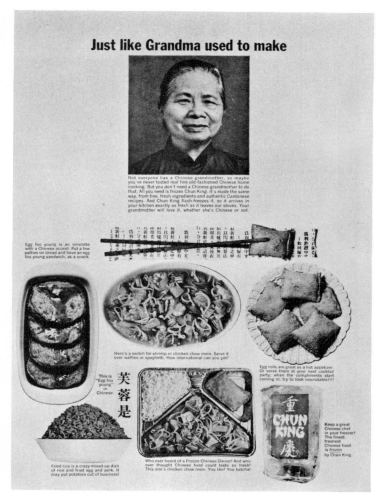

Not everyone has a Chinese grandmother, so maybe you've never tasted real fine old-fashioned Chinese home cooking. But you don't need a Chinese grandmother to do that. All you need is frozen Chun King. It's made the same way, from fine, fresh ingredients and authentic Cantonese recipes. And Chun King flash-freezes it, so it arrives in your kitchen exactly as fresh as it leaves our stoves. Your grandmother will love it, whether she's Chinese or not.

Egg foo young is an omelette with a Chinese accent. Put a few patties on bread and have an egg foo young sandwich, as a snack.

Here's a switch for shrimp or chicken chow mein. Serve it over waffles or spaghetti. How international can you get?

This is "Egg foo young" in Chinese. 芙蓉是

Egg rolls are great as a hot appetizer. Or serve them at your next cocktail party; when the compliments start coming in, try to look inscrutable!!!!

Fried rice is a crazy-mixed-up dish of rice and fried egg and pork. It may put potatoes out of business!

Who ever heard of a Frozen Chinese Dinner? And who ever thought Chinese food could taste so fresh! This one's chicken chow mein. You like? You betcha!

Keep a great Chinese chef in your freezer! The finest, freshest Chinese food is frozen by Chun King.

It's hard to separate a boy and his Keds

Look for the blue label

U.S. Keds

Don't let anything separate you and Keds, either. Because there's absolutely no substitute for Keds fit, Keds wear and Keds comfort—for everybody in your family.

United States Rubber

Rockefeller Center, New York 20, N.Y. • In Canada: Dominion Rubber Company, Ltd.

Do you have a museum where your living room should be?

KEEP OFF THE CARPET

You can make a room beautiful to look at but impossible to live in.

How? By putting in the wrong kind of carpet. When a carpet wears and stains easily, you shudder every time somebody walks on it.

You pick on the kids for dropping cookie crumbs. You nag your husband about his cigar ashes. In short, you make your living room a place where nobody can do any living.

Is it possible to have a living room that's both a joy to live in and beautiful to look at? It is with World Carpets.

They're created by America's most gifted designers. And made from the most modern, tough, stain-resistant, wear-resistant fibers. That's why the luxurious pile—so deep, so lush, so resilient—keeps its good looks so long.

The next time you buy carpet buy it from World. It will look handsomer, last longer. And because you don't have to worry about it, you will, too.

WORLD
CARPETS/DALTON, GEORGIA

We built the Rolex Explorer because there isn't any watch repair shop on top of the Matterhorn.

This is the watch we engineered for the lonely places.

We carve its case out of a single block of Swedish steel so there are no seams to come apart.

We test it at minus 50° and plus 150°F. We subject it to an underwater pressure of 330 feet.

We then have an official Swiss Institute for Chronometer Tests double-check the accuracy of its 26-jewel movement for 15 days and 15 nights.

If it passes, the institute gives it a certificate guaranteeing "especially good results."

Then, and only then, do we sell it.

The Explorer sells for $180 (with authentic Rolex bracelet, $195) at fine jewelry shops. Other waterproof*, self-winding chronometers from $175. **ROLEX**

AMERICAN ROLEX WATCH CORPORATION, 580 FIFTH AVENUE, NEW YORK 10036.
ALSO AVAILABLE IN CANADA.
WRITE FOR FULL-COLOR CATALOG. *WHEN CASE, CROWN AND CRYSTAL ARE INTACT.

123 American Rolex Watch Corp.

The props are few in this ad: the rugged rock face, a rope and climbing gear, the grip of a hand — and we're on top of the Matterhorn.

Slightly larger than life-size, this hand is shown on a full page, so close up that it gives the reader the full impact of witnessing the actual scaling of the Matterhorn. The copy tells of the critical tests made on the watch before it is guaranteed for "especially good results" — it is subjected to temperatures of minus 50 and plus 150 degrees, and underwater pressure of 330 feet, and a two-week accuracy test.

124 Sussex Clothes Ltd.

A good ad need not have elaborate props to interest the reader. As in this ad, a single symbol may be more than enough to catch his attention. All it took was the badge of a plainclothes police detective.

When the detective-model turns back his coat to reveal his badge, he exposes the Sussex label at the same time. The copy follows suit, "We always get our man. We get him around the shoulders and behind the neck...We listen to his complaints about the way his suits fall apart at the cleaner's. Then we get him in front of a mirror in a Sussex...We see him surrender when he turns around. It happens every time." The copy tells of a booklet the reader can send for: "Better still, you can be captured physically by Sussex..." and there follows a list of smart men's shops across the country.

125 Palizzio

This is a shoe ad? It is, indeed. Like many other ads that allow readers to use imagination, it's first of all intriguing. Then, when the reader realizes that Palizzio is "shoes and handbags for swooning," the photograph makes sense.

Let readers put their imagination to work, but make sure there is enough information in art work and copy to help them complete the picture. The picture could have been shot showing the entire figure of the girl. But then it wouldn't have gripped the reader's attention in the same way or forced him to study the copy.

WE always get our man. We get him around the shoulders and behind the neck. We get him with a mirror and a few brief words. We let him do all the talking. We let him tell us how he's strictly a natural shoulder man, but there isn't a suit made that fits right. We listen to his complaints about the way his suits fall apart at the cleaner's.

Then we get him in front of a mirror in a Sussex.

When he sees how he looks, he's ours. We see him surrender when he turns around. It happens every time.

We could go into a long song and dance about our hand-basted canvasses, hand-finished linings, hand-basted armholes, and how they keep a Sussex suit looking and feeling like new. But he's not even listening. It's all written down in a booklet you can send for. Better still, you can be captured physically by Sussex, in a crisp finish striped imported fabric, like this one at Walker, Ltd., and The Finchley Est., in New York City; Al Berman, Inc., Phil., Pa.: Farnsworth Reed, Ltd., Wash., D.C.: Mr. Guy in Los Angeles, Calif.; Hoffman's Mens Wear, Dallas, Tex. or for another store nearer you, please write to Sussex Clothes Ltd., 120 5th Ave., N.Y.

124

Any Palizzio is better than no Palizzio

SHOES & HANDBAGS FOR SWOONING

SPRAY ME

Spray any leading hair spray (except Breck) here for 3 seconds. You'll see how wet and runny it is. How it can soak your hair, drag out the curl and look stiff and sticky.

SPRAY ME

Spray New Breck Hair Set Mist here for 3 seconds. And you will see why it holds best. No sticky puddle and drip. New Breck starts holding before the others even get dry.

Beautiful Hair
BRECK

126

Send a monstrous shiver up his spine

Make his blood run hot & cold

Bewitch him by day

Make him mad for you under the moon

These are the shades to haunt him with. Be warned. Be wary. But wear them! DARE YOU!

KiLLER-DiLLER COLORS by CUTEX

Bewitch Him Bronze Come Mad Mauve Turn Pale Pink One Step Beyond Beige Wicked White Stock Racing Pink

Also available in nail polish coordinated to these lipstick shades

127

126 Breck

This newspaper ad ran in two quarter-page parts, on two facing pages. It is a take-off on the famous headline of a long-running correspondence art school campaign, titled "Draw Me."

The girl in the first part of the ad has been sprayed for three seconds by Brand X, which is shown dripping down to her neck. The copy says "You'll see how wet and runny it is." Using the same outline drawing on a following page, the ad says "Spray New Breck Hair Set Mist here for three seconds. And you will see why it holds best. No sticky puddle and drip. New Breck starts holding before the others even get dry." The second half of the ad includes the Breck hair spray package.

©John H. Breck, Inc. Reproduced by permission.

128 Bates

Photographs, although good in concept, cannot stand up without support from both headline and body copy. What would happen if the headline were changed to imply that this bedspread is so fabulous in itself that it could be mistaken for a fashionable dress?

The model is well posed, and the extra care that has gone into setting her up is obvious, especially in the draping of the material and the use of the Imperial Crown lent by Van Cleef and Arpels.

127 Cutex

Frankenstein, Dracula, the Mummy, and the Werewolf welcome you — a fine theme for a new group of lipsticks. The horrors are tossed off light-heartedly; we can tell by their faint, enigmatic smiles that these girls are not in any real trouble. Dracula's light-hearted expression is the only monster one to match the girls'.

The backgrounds are simple — the woods, rocks and marsh are the natural habitats of these creatures; the velvet drapery and crystal chandelier make a fit setting for Count Dracula. Each picture is captioned to suit the monster shown.

The subhead says, "These are the shades to haunt him with. Be warned. Be wary. But wear them! DARE YOU!"

The odd hand lettering of the headline, each word in a bright color with a drop shadow, lends itself to the theme, as do the names of the lipsticks.

129 Mona Lisa Wigs

The ad has taken full advantage of the company's name by using a mock-up of the Da Vinci painting in a photograph.

The curled edge of the canvas reveals the copy, which tells a woman she can fix her hair in a jiffy after stepping out of a pool or wrestling "a couple of spirited kids into bed," just by putting on a wig.

The sign-off, slightly rewritten, might have been even better as a headline: "Now you know what's behind that Mona Lisa smile."

Fashion Industries Inc.

128

129

130 Coca-Cola

Some advertising men look with mistrust at ads that have no headlines or body copy. But until the validity of their viewpoint is proved, it remains merely their personal opinion.

Santa and his elves are a pleasant seasonal change from the groups of people usually shown drinking some beverage or other. In those ads you could probably interchange any bottled beverage and the photographs need not change one iota.

This painting is unusually realistic, with the green of the sofa and Santa's red vest and trousers providing the colors associated with Christmas. All this illustration needs is the sign-off, "The pause that refreshes."

©The Coca-Cola Company, 1960. Coca-Cola and Coke are the registered trademarks which identify only the product of The Coca-Cola Company.

THE PAUSE THAT REFRESHES

130

131 Parker 61

"Holy Smokes! Is it? Wait, let me look at the bottom of the ad...No credit line. Nothing! Guess I'll have to read the copy to find out if it is.

"Gee Whiz! It probably is former President Hoover. Imagine a President of the United States in an ad. That Parker must be some pen!"

Other famous people have been shown looking at the capillary pen filling itself, without the ad giving the slightest hint as to their identity.

©Parker Pen Co.

132 Old Crow

Guessing games are always popular and become especially interesting here because the personalities — Daniel Webster, Mark Twain, Henry Clay, and the others — were famous contemporaries, and are shown partaking of the product, famous then as now.

The scene in the engraver's copperplate etching is entirely imaginary, yet quite plausible. The numbered, outline picture key, at lower right, helps the reader identify the guests and, of course, James Crow.

The body copy explains that "Only an artist's imagination could bring these famous men together...And of course Old Crow would have been at the meeting too...Enjoy it yourself tonight..." The slogan: "Old Crow/'The Greatest name in Bourbon.'"

131

HOW MANY OF THESE FAMOUS AMERICANS CAN YOU IDENTIFY?*

... all were friends of Old Crow

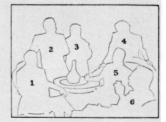

Scrooge himself would love styling like this...

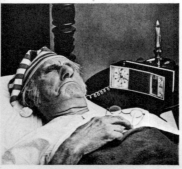

Weighs less than a fat goose. General Electric's new Escort—a scant 22 pounds of portable picture. Enjoyable in any room in your manse which boasts a baseplug. Generous 16-inch diagonal, 125-sq.-in. screen. Reliable as a sunrise. Front speaker *and* earphone for bedchamber use.

Deck the halls with hi-fi stereo. New G-E Custom Decorator fits a table or bookcase—even hangs on a wall. Flip-down Garrard° changer. That extra speaker beneath the changer plugs into any 110-volt outlet, gives you a flexible Home Music Distribution System (Optional).

Hark! Stereo from a radio. General Electric unites FM/AM/FM-Stereo with fine furniture in the T-1000. A 9-inch oval hi-fi speaker resides in each detachable wing. Resonant hardwood cabinet in Walnut or Antique Cherry veneer. Plug in a turntable, hear stereo records, too.

Miserly with space. G.E.'s new plug-in clock radio is transistorized for power without bulk. Features abound: lighted clock and radio dial. Pillow speaker for solo listening. Slumber switch shuts radio off if you doze. Snooz-Alarm° for morning catnaps. Model C-501, about $50.

Hail the hues of General Electric's high-fidelity color television. Colors are vivid, true, *real*. And so they stay—locked in as you switch from channel to channel. Like money in the bank, thanks to 1,486 General Electric quality-control checks.

Even the Cratchit budget can afford high-fidelity stereo; praised be the new General Electric Adventurer portable. Styled like a console with swing-out speakers, flip-down Garrard changer. Three color schemes in scuff-proof vinyl. FM/AM/FM-Stereo radio optional.

Bah! Trickery! How can a radio so compact yield sound so strong? No tricks—eight transistors and a heavy-magnet speaker give the new G-E Sportmate its husky voice. And it's as sturdy as a strongbox, due to its die-cast steel case. Model P-860, with carry harness, about $40.

Prithee, what be you? The Custom Decorator be *everything* in one compact package: 19" diagonal, 175-sq.-in. TV. FM/AM/FM-Stereo radio. Garrard changer. Detachable hi-fi speakers. General Electric designed it to fit on a table, in a bookcase—even hang on a wall.

Be you haunted by the spectre of Christmas presents? These delightful gift ideas will put your mind to rest. Withdraw to your General Electric dealer's. See, hear, examine them all. Consider their modest prices. And be comforted by this: each is styled by General Electric to bring pleasure through many, many Christmases yet to come.

Progress Is Our Most Important Product

GENERAL ⒼⒺ ELECTRIC

133 Chesterfield

A familiar indoor sport — card playing — is used to set the scene. The picture of the girl is done in reverse, for very good reason: she is pointedly holding the white package of the product in sharp relief against the red heart shape. She is, of course, the Queen of Hearts.

©Liggett & Myers Tobacco Co.

136 Stetson Hats

This ad appeared during World War II, when a lot of advertising was patriotic in nature. "Keep it under your hat," the familiar, colloquial admonition to not give away secret information, supplies a valuable mnemonic aid, as paraphrased here.

137 Cream of Wheat

Al Capp, in his comic strip, *Li'l Abner*, portrays a melodramatic sequence with Cream of Wheat, the product, as hero.
   Daisy Mae is threatened with extinction by the ugly brute McGoon. The report goes out to Li'l Abner. As he skis vertically downhill to the rescue, he swallows a bowl of Cream of Wheat — the job, of course, calls for quick energy. As he saves Daisy Mae, she hollers the product's praise.

134 Bekins

This ad tells of the problems faced by movers and the believe-it-or-not success they have in meeting them. For example, one problem is transporting the replica of the Lincoln log cabin, made of 16,360 pennies, from New York to Ripley's "Believe it or not Museum" in San Francisco. "One slip," the copy says, "and exhibit would have arrived in a sack!"
   Or consider the life-size Japanese man. "Move did not shake up statue in any way. (Which is more than we can say for our movers)."

135 General Electric

Old Scrooge, lifted out of Dickens' *Christmas Carol,* has come alive in this holiday spread. The few props — wreath, rocking chair, candle — help us to relate the old curmudgeon with the season of giving. He changes in scale as he moves from background, to middle, to foreground.
   The caption beneath each photo relates to the ad theme and gives the reader the product's specifications. Each begins with an attention-getting lead: "Weighs less than a fat goose," etc.

138 Camels

The Phil Silvers TV show is successfully adapted here to the print medium, featuring Silvers as Sergeant Bilko. A short story uses photographs in comic-strip sequence.
   The resilient Sergeant asks the Colonel for permission to enroll at night school (on account of the pretty teacher). The Colonel is not fooled. He immediately replaces the pretty teacher with the elderly Miss Crabshaw. The class, after an interminable hour, rushes out gratefully for a smoke — Camels, of course.

R. J. Reynolds Co.

139 Hertz (see following pages)

After years of being browbeaten, plus a change of agency, Hertz made this astonishingly successful comeback, using the attacks by the underdog as a basis for the ad. Sympathy was the first reaction to the initial Avis campaign, "We're only No. 2." But after a few years, readers became indifferent to the fate of Avis.
   Hertz surprises the reader by not countering Avis' argument. Explaining what rent-a-cars are all about, the copy tells the reader why Hertz is No. 1.

©Hertz System

136   **137**

For years, Avis has Hertz is No. 1. Now we're going to

We're No. 1 because we're better at helping you get to where you're going.

A car where you need it.

The first step in renting a car is getting to the car. Hertz makes that easier for you to do than anybody else.

We're at every major airport in the United States. And at some airports that are not so major. Ever fly to Whitefish, Montana? Some people do. And have a Hertz car waiting.

No matter how small the airport you fly to, if it's served by a commercial airline, 97 chances out of 100 it's also served by Hertz or by a Hertz office within 20 minutes of it.

We also have locations throughout the downtown and suburban areas of every major city.

And because you don't restrict your travel to city areas, we don't restrict our locations to city areas. We're also out in the country. And out of the country, too. Windy Hill Beach, South Carolina has a population of 100. It has a Hertz office. Chichiri, Malawi in Africa has a population of 2,059. It has a Hertz office.

In all, Hertz has over 2,900 places throughout the world where you can pick up or leave a car. Nearly twice as many as No. 2.

Can't come to us? We'll come to you.

We have a direct-line telephone in most major hotels and motels in the U.S. It's marked HERTZ and it's in the lobby. Pick it up, ask for a car, and we'll deliver one to the door. You often can't get a cab as easily.

What kind of car would you like?

When you rent from Hertz, you're less likely to get stuck with a beige sedan when you want a red convertible. We have over twice as many cars as No. 2.

Not only is our fleet big, it's varied. We do our best to give you what you want. From Fords, to Mustangs, to Thunderbirds, to Lincolns and everything in between.

And because we know that travel can be a bore if you travel a lot, we've even got something to ease your lot. The Shelby G.T. 350-H. If you know what cars are all about, you'll know what this car is all about.

What kind of service will you get?

When you rent a new car from us or anybody else, you expect it to be sitting there waiting, ready to go, looking like new.

On that score we claim no superiority over our competition. They goof once in awhile. We goof once in awhile.

Except when we goof it bothers us more because people don't expect the big one to goof. And to make up for it, if our service is not up to Hertz standards we give you $50 in free rentals.* Plus an apology.

No. 2 gives a quarter plus an apology. And advertises that he "can't afford" to do more.

We feel the other way about it. We can't afford to do less. Besides, the $50 comes out of the station manager's local operating funds. This tends to keep him very alert …and our service very good.

Hot line.

When you're in one city and you're flying to another city and you want to have a car waiting when you arrive

*There's one thing you have to do for us though: fill out our Certified Service form and mail it to our main office in its self-addressed envelope. Upon verification we'll send you $50 in rental certificates by return mail.

been telling you

tell you why.

and you want it confirmed before you leave, we can do it for you. Instantly. In any one of 1,038 U.S. cities. No other rent a car company can make that statement.

The major reason we can do it is because we recently installed one of the world's largest private electronic reservations systems.

After all, with the supersonic jets in sight and one hour coast to coast flights in prospect, you'll need some quick answers.

We can give them to you today.

About rates.

We probably offer more kinds of rates than you care to know about.

You can rent a car from Hertz by the day and the mile, by the weekend, by the week, by the month, by gift certificate, by revolving credit, by sundry other ways in between.

We offer all these rates for two reasons. To stay ahead of competition. To get more people to rent cars.

When you go to rent a Hertz car just tell the Hertz girl how long you want the car and roughly how much driving you'll be doing.

She'll figure out the rate that's cheapest for you. She'll figure it from our rate book that states loud and clear, "Hertz people must use the lowest applicable rate on all calculations."

About credit.

If you've got a national credit card with most any major company, you've got credit with us.

A businesslike way of doing business.

If you own your own firm or are instrumental in running a firm, you know what a nightmare billing can be.

Have your company rent from us and we'll help ease that nightmare. We can even tailor our billing cycle to fit your paying cycle.

We'll bill by the rental, by the month, by division, by department, by individual, and by blood type if it'll help you.

And now about trying hard.

No. 2 says he tries harder. Than who?

Hertz

Facts are facts

Dial does more than just get you clean. Lots more. Dial removes the skin bacteria that cause perspiration odor. Removes them so effectively it's America's leading deodorant soap. And that's a fact.

Aren't you glad *you* use Dial Soap!

dial

(don't you wish *everybody* did?)

140

**Abu Ben Ali,
test pilot for the Persian Airforce,
reports on the performance of this exciting new rug.**

"What most impressed me about this **Aldon** rug is its durability and strength. As you know, I must fly low over some very pointy buildings. So I need a very strong rug. And this rug outperforms all others of its type in actual durability tests.

Also very important to me is soil resistance and washability. Here, in the Middle East, we have many oil wells: lots of smoke and soot in the air. I used to ruin rugs right and left. But with this **Aldon** rug all it takes to look new again is a quick machine washing.

And boy! Does this gold rug look good! Now all the girls wave to me. There are other colors the girls wave at too: sapphire blue, moss green, white, petal pink, red and amethyst.

As for comfort, it's unbeatable. The dense velvety pile by Borg is 100% Kodel® polyester. It stays unbelievably soft and luxurious even after repeated washings.

One final thing: It has a nice name, Antoinette. Available in many sizes. Prices from $6.96 to $39.98." a **B**org fabric

Borg

Borg Fabrics, a division of Amphenol Corp., Delavan, Wisc.

141

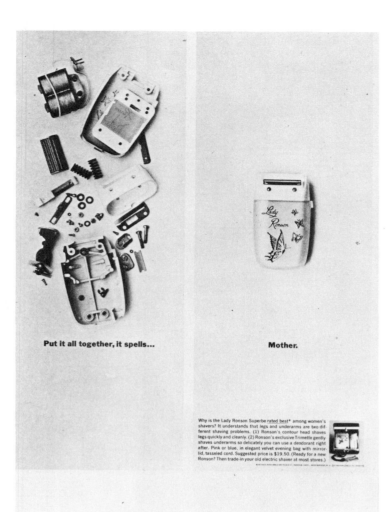

Put it all together, it spells...   **Mother.**

Why is the Lady Ronson Superbe rated best* among women's shavers? It understands that legs and underarms are two different shaving problems. (1) Ronson's contour head shaves legs quickly and cleanly. (2) Ronson's exclusive Trimmette gently shaves underarms so delicately you can use a deodorant right after. Pink or blue, in elegant velvet evening bag with mirror lid, tasseled cord. Suggested price is $19.50. (Ready for a new Ronson? Then trade-in your old electric shaver at most stores.)

Now he can't have anything up his sleeve.

And why should he? He already rules half the world of fashion in his short-sleeved cardigan by Drummond. It's as new and popular as the mickey-fest ban and it comes in red naturally, black, white, butterscotch, sage green and electric blue. Of 60% fine looped mohair, 35% virgin wool and 5% nylon; $15.95. Also in pullover and long-sleeved versions or in 100% virgin wool styles. At the finest stores, or write Drummond Knitwear Co., Ltd., 350 Fifth Avenue, New York 1, N.Y.

DRUMMOND

Can a girl who marries a promising young sculptor find happiness with a carpet of Polycrest in the studio?

If Gregor had to be an artist, Natasha wondered, why couldn't he do something neat? Like writing poetry or composing symphonies.

But no. Gregor wasn't happy unless he was making a mess. She was glad they'd chosen a carpet of Polycrest olefin.

"You can't buy a more stain-and-wear resistant carpet fiber than Polycrest," she reflected aloud.

"Ahh, yes," pondered Gregor. "I get inspired every time I look at it. Those artistic patterns. That warm color. That deep, lush, lofty pile. Look how Harry digs his toes into it.

"Shhh, I'm thinking," said Harry.

"And Polycrest," she said, "costs only about half what you'd expect to pay for such luxury."

"An important consideration for struggling young sculptors like myself," he agreed.

"Yeow!" cried Gregor, dropping his mallet into the deep Polycrest pile.

"Another inspiration?" she asked.

"No," he said, "I think I just broke my thumb."

Carpet is Bigelow's "Bountiful."

  POLYCREST **UNIROYAL**

We finally found a guy who looks good in a metal zipper.

We just looked over a rainbow and there he was. The only man in the world who prefers a hard, gleaming metal zipper on his trousers over the soft invisible Talon Zephyr nylon zipper. Score one for the metal zipper. Now the score is only 60,000,000 to 1 in favor of Talon Zephyr zippers. Not bad when you figure that the only dissenting vote comes from a guy who hasn't even got a heart.

Talon ZEPHYR

THE INCONGRUOUS

146 Charles of the Ritz

Since the product is one that helps keep skin young, the "skin" of the model's cheek is rolled back to reveal the casual copy that talks about the aging that may take place "between your twenty-fifth and twenty-sixth birthday, those intriguing and attracting little laugh lines around your eyes suddenly seem a mite deeper. And is it possible that your neck and jaw sag just one iota?" Even the instructions are pleasant: "Fingerprint it on, don't rub." And it ends, "Eye Oil Concentrate, 6.00. Throat Cream 5.00. Are you worth it?"

The shadow under the curled up "skin" intensifies the contrast with the flatly lit profile.

©Charles of the Ritz

146

147 5th Avenue

It is inevitable that popular movements or fads be reflected in advertising. A form of Pop art is used effectively in this ad to bring home the point in the headline. The surprise is in the photograph in which the photographic chin is replaced by a painted smile which the headline is talking about.

The copy relates to the headline and makes an offer: "If there's a song in you, 5th Avenue candy bars will draw that out too. Because for just one 5th Avenue wrapper and 50¢ we'll send you an LP-record."

"There goes my husband with the car keys!"

A lady who had just seen her husband off at the Jacksonville airport discovered he'd taken off with the car keys. A United passenger agent helped her get home. And he saw to it that the keys came back—on the next inbound flight from her husband's destination—and were delivered to her.

Stories like this about United passenger agents could go on and on. These fellows in Mainliner® blue are usually seen behind the counter or at the gate . . . figuring fares and routings, selling tickets, checking baggage, answering your questions. But their main job is people. And the way they handle this job is often an inspiration.

Our passenger agents are not perfect, of course. But on the whole, in their efficiency and understanding they demonstrate an attitude that all of us at United must have.

Extra care—for *people*—is the briefest way to say it. You'll find it at the heart of everything we do at United.

<u>P.S. to husbands:</u> Take your car keys *and* your wife on your next trip using United's Family Plan. Your wife gets 25% off (the car keys go free)!

UNITED

THE NATION'S LARGEST AIRLINE
KNOWN FOR EXTRA CARE

12H

The more rooms you have to paint the more reasons you have to use Lucite® Wall Paint. (Clean!) Lucite never needs stirring or mixing. It's ready to use when you lift the lid. Lucite does not drip, run or spatter like ordinary wall paints. Lucite loads roller or brush, takes more paint to the wall each time you dip. (Quick!) Flows smoothly over wallboard, wallpaper, old paint. Brush marks don't show. You can start or stop at any point. Lucite dries flat and lovely in half an hour. It's extremely durable and completely washable. Painting tools (and hands) wash up (Easy!) with soap and water. There is no other wall paint just like Lucite. Made only by Du Pont for beauty without bother. **DU PONT**

Better Things for Better Living . . . through Chemistry

For outside, there's LUCITE House Paint. It's the nearest thing to permanent house paint. LUCITE needs no primer on most jobs. Resists blistering, cracking, peeling, chalking and discoloring. Protects your house like a plastic shield. Specify LUCITE House Paint. It's as easy to use as it is durable.

This is an ad for a razor blade.

That's right. A razor blade.

A new razor blade from Gillette that brings shaving one step closer to the effortless.

(But what about that frying pan over there? What in the world does that have to do with a razor blade?)

Ah. We were just coming to that.

Baked onto the cutting edge of this blade is a miracle plastic which is closely related to the coating that's used on the non-stick frying pans.

It's known as a solid fluorocarbon polymer, and it's fantastic stuff.

On a frying pan, the scientists know why it does what it does. But when we put this coating onto the cutting edge of a razor blade, something mysterious takes place: You can slice through your beard with a fraction of

the pull you would feel if the same blade didn't have the coating.

You have to experience it to believe it.

But even Gillette, which invented this type of blade, and has a patent on it—even Gillette can't explain why it works.

This solid fluorocarbon polymer has many secrets, and it gives them up grudgingly.

After working with this substance for years, Gillette has found a way to make it behave on the edge of a razor blade. It is a microscopically thin film, extremely hard and smooth, and it stays on the blade edge to do whatever it does for shave after shave.

Try this new razor blade yourself and see if you don't notice the difference immediately.

Ask for the Gillette <u>Super</u> Stainless. One of the sweet mysteries of life.

148 United Airlines

This ad could almost have been copied from a famous *New Yorker* magazine cartoon by Charles Addams which shows the shadow, on a beach, of a large eagle with a man in its beak. A running woman is looking up and shouting: "George! George! Drop the car keys!"

The picture of the woman pointing upwards is too incongruous a sight to pass up; the reader simply has to know more about what is going on. The copy explains that United got back those keys on its very next return flight. "Extra care — for people — is the briefest way to say it."

149 Lucite

The woman is shown trapped behind a "wall" that separates the reader from the ad; with her handy roller, and some ingenuity, she is painting herself in.

In the usual photograph, the page of white space is the "wall," and so, logically, the model is shown standing in front of it with her back to the reader. But suppose the wall were transparent and the photographer made his shot *through* the wall? This is what was done here, at minimal expense, by photographing the girl with the roller, doing a simple retouch job (the white roller marks across her body), and using the white space at right to represent the painted wall.

Three words were spotted in the copy in a second color to make them extra clear in summing up: "Lucite Wall Paint: (Clean!) (Quick!) (Easy!)" Wherever the word "Lucite" fell in the copy, it was in gray instead of black to make it stand out better.

DuPont

150 Gillette

That's right. This is an ad for a razor blade. The ad is a stopper, all right. "A new razor blade from Gillette that brings shaving one step closer to the effortless," the copy says. Still, you go on asking yourself, what has that to do with eggs in a frying pan? At the end of the fifth paragraph is the answer, a simple scientific one.

"Baked onto the cutting edge of this blade is a miracle plastic which is closely related to the coating that's used on the non-stick frying pans. It's known as a solid fluorocarbon polymer..." And still the copy leads you on, explaining that the scientists know how it does what it does on a frying pan, "But even Gillette, which invented this type of blade, and has a patent on it — *even Gillette can't explain why it works.*"

© Gillette Co.

151 Johnson & Johnson

The copy must be read. But it explains the headline's incongurity in the very first sentence, "Touch, more than talk, is what a baby best understands. Every inch of him responds to your touch."

The idea is well thought out. The cliché would have been a mother's big hand holding a baby's tiny hand.

If you consider that the sense of touch is a baby's way of communicating, and realize that the sense of touch exists all over the body, you will see how well the idea has been dramatized in the close-up photograph. The headline leads visually right into the point of information.

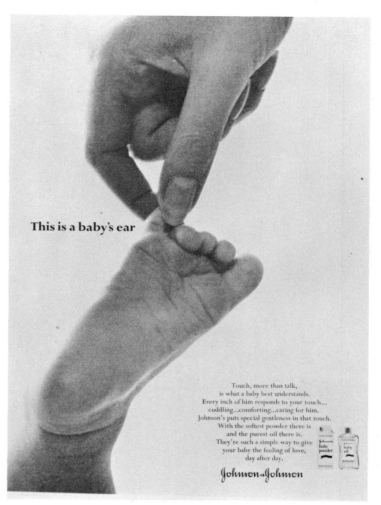

This is a baby's ear

Touch, more than talk, is what a baby best understands. Every inch of him responds to your touch... cuddling...comforting...caring for him, Johnson's puts special gentleness in that touch. With the softest powder there is and the purest oil there is. They're such a simple way to give your baby the feeling of love, day after day.

Johnson & Johnson

151

152 Australian National Travel Association

The visual matches the headline: a most uncommon place. If the girl is standing on a beach, where is it? Only a faintly bumpy horizon indicates that she is standing against the sky. Is she standing on water? If not, where did she get that live starfish? Didn't she just pick it out of the water down under? Most uncommon photograph.

The copy describes uncommon attractions in Australia: the 600 paradise islands of the Great Barrier Reef; ivy-covered ruins; "Kangaroos, wallabies, bandicoots — and other animals Noah forgot..."

See the wonders down under Down Under. See Australia: the uncommon place.

Do you speak Réplique?

(The perfume with a language all its own.)

153

Jet National to the moon

over Miami.

154

153 Réplique.

In France they speak *francais*; in love they speak Réplique — at least, she does.

This nice product shot in no way helps to confirm the idea expressed in the headline. But the effectiveness of product recognition and the simplicity of layout can be appreciated because they do not distract the reader from the important headline copy.

155 Mennen Baby Magic

The wide expanse of background on this re-touched photograph, with the curled up baby at the center, simulates the protected world of the fetus. The cast shadow against the flat background gives the impression that a tiny baby is lying right on the page. If the light tone of the photograph were bled off the entire page, the illusion might be heightened. The copy explains that the vernix, the protective covering of the newborn, wears off after a few days. "Baby Magic...inspired by nature's own protection" can be an artificial substitute for the natural protection just lost.

Bold copy at the end exploits the general market, "Specially for new borns...better for all babies...by Mennen."

156 Endust

The headline is a lie — the reader knows he is looking at a dust cloth. The contradiction is resolved only by reading the ad. The copy makes the point neatly, comparing the pull of a magnet with the attraction of Endust for particles of dust and dirt.

"It catches even the tiniest, sneeziest bits... You can make a magnet out of any cloth or mop. Just spray it with *endust*. It's just for dusting — it's just wonderful!"

©The Drackett Co.

154 National Airlines

The visual clinches the headline in two ways. First, it leads the reader off-base by showing him the moon; second, it serves as a space-pause for the eye as it travels downwards to the bottom of the ad to find out if the headline is really true.

The ad was printed in two colors, black and orange; the orange gave the photograph the full-color look of a warm, moonlit beach scene.

A logo might have tipped off the reader too soon and lessened the impact of the ad.

157 Knorr Soup

The three-dimensional photo of soup has been turned into a flat slice of Swiss cheese. A slight shadow near the holes serves to thicken the slab.

Instead of branding a product with "Made in," a different gambit can actually exploit the romance inherent in many imported goods. One might say, and still keep within the import law, "Precision-crafted in France" or "From the hand looms of Turkey." A few moments of thought can save a product from the brush-off by the consumer that a "Made in" label evokes.

158 Corvette

Turning the tables on the foreign sports car image, Chevrolet has shown that it, too, is a foreign sports car — in Europe. This shiny blue Corvette stands out well against the brown-beige beam-and-plaster background of a European village. The owner looks like a well-to-do European; with a car that carries a price tag upwards of $10,000 (in Europe), he would probably have to be.

The high-priced, imported sports car, symbol of the exotic as conjured by Americans, applies equally to the Corvette over there. The copy says: "We think the Corvette would be quite a buy at 10 thousand. At around five thousand it's a steal. And that, duty-free, is about what it costs over here...Aren't you glad you live near the factory?"

General Motors

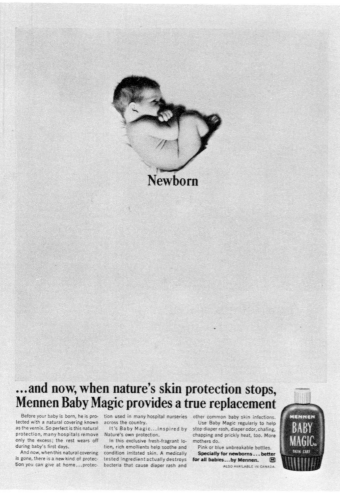

Newborn

...and now, when nature's skin protection stops, Mennen Baby Magic provides a true replacement

Before your baby is born, he is protected with a natural covering known as the vernix. So perfect is this natural protection, many hospitals remove only the excess; the rest wears off during baby's first days.

And now, when this natural covering is gone, there is a new kind of protection you can give at home...protec-

tion used in many hospital nurseries across the country.

It's Baby Magic...inspired by Nature's own protection.

In this exclusive fresh-fragrant lotion, rich emollients help soothe and condition irritated skin. A medically tested ingredient actually destroys bacteria that cause diaper rash and

other common baby skin infections.

Use Baby Magic regularly to help stop diaper rash, diaper odor, chafing, chapping and prickly heat, too. More mothers do.

Pink or blue unbreakable bottles.

Specially for newborns...better for all babies...by Mennen.

ALSO AVAILABLE IN CANADA.

155

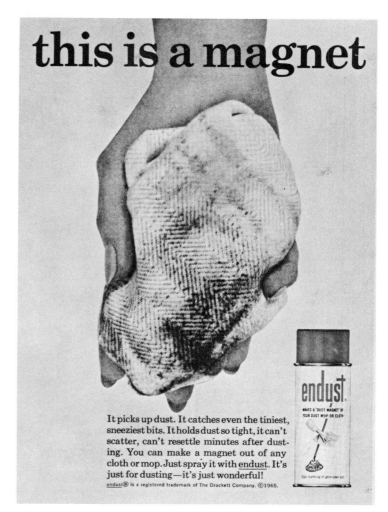

this is a magnet

It picks up dust. It catches even the tiniest, sneeziest bits. It holds dust so tight, it can't scatter, can't resettle minutes after dusting. You can make a magnet out of any cloth or mop. Just spray it with endust. It's just for dusting—it's just wonderful!

endust® is a registered trademark of The Drackett Company. ©1965.

156

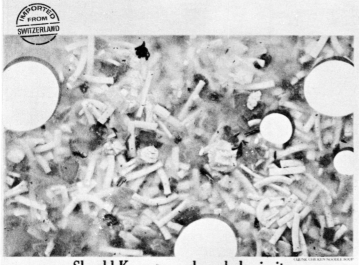

QUICK CHICKEN NOODLE SOUP

Should Knorr soup have holes in it just because it's Swiss?

No. The only Swiss delicacy that needs holes is Swiss cheese. But Swiss cheese isn't the only delicacy the Swiss are famous for. Now there's Knorr Swiss soup. Rich, hearty, robust soup that doesn't have any-

thing in common at all with the kind you get out of a can.

Your first tantalizing whiff of Knorr simmering on the stove tells you you're in for something special. Your first steaming spoonful tells you what that "something special" is. FLAVOR! European flavor. Subtle, delicate, distinctive flavor. The

product of centuries of European soup making "know-how."

Ready for a wonderful new soup experience? Then call for Knorr...the Swiss soup that doesn't have any holes in it. Just FLAVOR. Lots and lots of it.

25¢ SAYS YOU'LL LOVE IMPORTED KNORR SOUP.

Fill in your name and address. Send it to us, along with the boxtop from any package of Knorr

Mail to Knorr Refund Offer, Box 1478A, Brooklyn, N.Y. 11202. We'll send you 25¢ cash. We're out to make friends. Offer expires December 31, 1966.

NAME

ADDRESS

STATE

THERE ARE 7 DELICIOUS KNORR SWISS SOUPS. AND THERE AREN'T ANY HOLES IN ANY OF THEM. JUST FLAVOR. LOTS OF IT!

157

Corvette Sting Ray Coupe with eight safety features now standard, including two-speed electric wipers for better vision in the worst weather.

In Europe Corvette is a high-priced imported sports car.

Ah, the high-priced imported sports car! Mere mention of the phrase conjures visions of the exotic, the forbidden: of wild forays into the night; of secret agents and clandestine gatherings; of howling engines and winding roads. It must indeed rank as one of man's greatest desires, suppressed or otherwise.

Few, however, realize that Corvette

is just such an animal. Some Europeans do, and gladly pay upwards of ten thousand dollars for one.

And frankly we don't blame them. These people have a deucedly sharp eye for Grand Touring machines, and they know Corvette compares feature for feature, spec for spec with Europe's finest.

In fact, with four wheel disc brakes,

fully independent suspension and up to 425 horsepower available under the bonnet, we think the Corvette would be quite a buy at 10 thousand. At around five thousand, it's a steal. And that, duty-free, is about what it costs over here where it's built, depending on equipment.

Aren't you glad you live near the factory?

GM

'66 CORVETTE BY CHEVROLET

158

©1962 VOLKSWAGEN OF AMERICA, INC.

Think small.

Our little car isn't much of a novelty any more.

A couple of dozen college kids don't try to squeeze inside it.

The guy at the gas station doesn't ask where the gas goes.

Nobody even stares at our shape.

In fact, some people who drive our little flivver don't even think 32 miles to the gallon is going any great guns.

Or using five pints of oil instead of five quarts.

Or never needing anti-freeze.

Or racking up 40,000 miles on a set of tires.

That's because once you get used to some of our economies, you don't even think about them any more.

Except when you squeeze into a small parking spot. Or renew your small insurance. Or pay a small repair bill. Or trade in your old Volkswagen for a new one.

Think it over.

159

"WHY DIDN'T WE CALL HIM DADDY SAM?"

IN some nations he might have been called "Daddy" Sam or "Papa" Sam, or something of the sort. But not in America.

The people who wrote our Constitution decided that our Federal Government should not be a Great Father. They limited its role rather strictly, to assure freedom and opportunity for individuals.

One result has been America's unparalleled record of industrial achievement. The investor-owned electric power industry is just one example. Financed in the traditional way of American business, it provides the best electric service in the world.

Yet billions have been spent for Federally owned electric power plants and lines. And billions more are proposed. This would not only burden the taxpayers unnecessarily, but it would also do something worse. It would endanger the spirit of American enterprise and the faith we all ought to feel in our relationship with Uncle Sam.

Investor-Owned Electric Light and Power Companies
more than 300 companies serving 140,000,000 people

Sponsors' names on request through this magazine

160

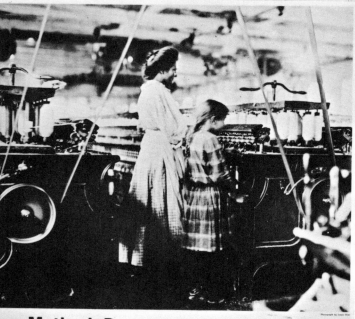

Mother's Day.

Those were the days when many working mothers always knew where their children were.

In the factory. Working ten or twelve hours a day, seven days a week.

Little time was "wasted" on play or school. Even when Mother's Day was established—back in 1914—many women and children couldn't celebrate it. They had to work.

Gradually organized labor whittled away at the long work week: 55, 50, 45 hours. Today, throughout most of the ladies' garment industry, the 35-hour work week prevails.

Through our union, 450,000 members of the International Ladies' Garment Workers (80% of us women) have won many benefits: fair wages, decent working conditions, security on the job.

The ILGWU label, sewn into ladies' and children's garments, is our signature. It is a symbol of progress made; and more progress to come.

Look for it when you shop.

A handsome 64-page publication with historic photographs of labor's progress—is available. Send $1.00 to: ILGWU, Union Label Dept., 275 Seventh Ave., New York 10001, Dept. T-2.

SYMBOL OF DECENCY, FAIR LABOR STANDARDS AND THE AMERICAN WAY OF LIFE

Photograph by Lewis Hine

161

Six Dunbar chairs out for the night will stay just as the campfire catches them. Dunbar knows no phases. The youngest chair here is pushing half a decade. Which one? Who can tell but Edward Wormley and his staff. And they design without calendars to give Dunbar all the time in the world. See Dunbar at showrooms in New York.

Boston, Chicago, Dallas, Denver, Kansas City, Los Angeles, San Francisco, Seattle, St. Louis and Athens. Order through your interior designer at stores fine enough for Dunbar. Suggested retail prices on customer-covered material (starting with the seventh chair and left-ready): $875, $875, $325, $685, $525.

$290. Dunbar Furniture Corporation, Berne, Ind.

TOMORROW IS A FRIEND OF

DUNBAR

162

159 Volkswagen

The volume of light tone contrasts so effectively with the car that it actually *is* small in relation to the whole area. The copy says that, in America, Volkswagen has grown from being a novelty to an accepted mode of transportation. The gags about the Volkswagen are gone, but not the big value provided by its durability and economical maintenance.

© Volkswagen of America, Inc.

163 Zenith

This ad makes sense. And it happens to be true. "When you want to hear, is it a strain on your face?"

"You know. You squint. Lean forward. Or swivel your head. It's not very attractive...And a Zenith can do a lot for your looks. In case you haven't heard."

The follow-up copy tries to help the reader overcome the embarrassment of admission of deafness, by offering a booklet "for folks a little bit deaf."

Zenith Radio Corp.

160 Electric Light and Power Companies

Since the familiar is instantly recognizable, when our concept of Uncle Sam is used in a way unfamiliar to us, it becomes a stopper. In some other countries he might have been called Daddy Sam but not in America. Those who framed our Constitution would never have consented to the federal government's sticking its two cents in where American free enterprise could so ably handle the job.

The message from investor-owned Electric Light and Power Companies is that the government should keep out of power projects. "Financed in the traditional way...it provides the best electric service in the world."

161 ILGWU

The incongruity in this ad lies between the headline and the harsh implications of the photograph. The reader expects a simple, sentimental image evoked by the words "Mother's Day."

The copy says that the advertiser, the International Ladies Garment Workers Union, worked to improve the conditions, hours, wages and security of garment workers. Mothers working in the factories of those days always knew where their children were: "In the factory. Working ten or twelve hours a day, seven days a week."

ILGWU, the union label, is the logo. But the slogan is the message. "Symbol of decency, fair labor standards and the American way of life."

164 Ritter Brothers

The girl in the Saga Blue Fox is a real swinger. As the copy says, she "might suddenly take it into her head to swat a few with the little league team she passes in the park."

Blue Fox is for the young, the fun-loving "So watch yourself when you wear fox. But then, you probably won't have to. Everybody else will be watching you."

162 Dunbar Furniture Corp.

Chairs, elegant upholstered chairs, grouped around a campfire are an unusual sight. The whole idea of camping is to rough it in the great outdoors.

The boys' attention is directed to the scoutmaster; the furniture has not interfered with the telling of the tale. If the children seemed aware of any incongruity, they might give the ad a stilted, posed look. But nobody loves a braggart, whether it sticks out in his advertising copy or the models. Since the children ignore the furniture, the readers are all the more aware of it.

A Zenith Hearing Aid can do a lot for your looks.

When you want to hear, is it a strain on your face?

You know. You squint. Lean forward. Or swivel your head. It's not very attractive.

But there's hope. Visit your Zenith Hearing Aid Dealer.

We make 16 different kinds of hearing aids. If you have an electronically correctible hearing loss, your Zenith Dealer can match the right aid to your special hearing difficulty. Your Zenith Dealer is listed in the Yellow Pages.

See him soon. For many good reasons. But one in particular. He sells Zenith "Living Sound" Hearing Aids. And a Zenith can do a lot for your looks.

In case you haven't heard.

Yours free! Vital information for folks a little bit deaf.

> Important, new book. Frank. Informative. It could change your life. Send for a copy.
>
> Name
>
> Address
>
> City   State   Code
>
> Zenith Radio Corporation, Dept. 72-P
> 6501 W. Grand Ave., Chicago, Ill. 60635
>
> Zenith

163

The things that can happen when you wear fox!

Saga Norwegian Blue Fox is the gay fur, the young fur, the fun fur. A light heart just naturally goes with it. And a girl might suddenly take it into her head to swat a few with the little league team she passes in the park. Anything can happen. So watch yourself when you wear fox. But then, you probably won't have to. Everybody else will be watching you.
SAGA BLUE FOX BY RITTER
RITTER BROTHERS, NEW YORK/GARTENHAUS, WASHINGTON/RICH'S, ATLANTA/HOLT, RENFREW, CANADA

Old Volkswagen Station Wagons never die.

The things some people can do with an old box.

But then, he didn't start with any old box. He started with a Volkswagen Station Wagon. Which has about twice the amount of space as an ordinary wagon.

There was room for everything. A refrigerator, a stove, a table, an in-

stant chili dispenser, and of course, the proverbial kitchen sink.

And a way for it all to get in. The two side doors open into a huge 4' by 4' hole.

Also, its roof may be high compared to other wagons, but its overhead is low. Our Standard VW wagon costs only $2,337.*

However, if you're planning to go into

the restaurant business, better not buy one new. (The body's been welded into one solid piece of steel, the tires alone will last for 35,000 miles, and on top of everything else, there are four coats of protective paint.)

It'll take too long to get a new one into bad enough shape.

©Volkswagen of America, Inc. *Suggested Retail Price, East Coast P.O.E., 152454 West Coast P.O.E., Local Taxes and Other Dealer Delivery Charges, If Any, Additional.

Youth is a wonderful thing. What a crime to waste it on children.

— George Bernard Shaw

MUSTANG
YOU'RE AHEAD IN A FORD

In this year 5727 we're not about to stop.

This is hardly the people of Israel's first crisis. When a people's history dates back well over five thousand years you can be sure they have learned to prevail and endure.

Granted this is not the moment to plan an idyll in Eilat. But we want you to know we're still flying our regular schedules to Europe and Tel Aviv. This is not the time for us to stop flying. Our history demands this.

If you are wary about going to Israel at this time, we understand. But don't worry. We'll be flying there in 5728, 5729. In fact, we plan on flying there for a long, long time.

EL AL

The airline of the people of Israel.

165 Volkswagen

The use of an old Volkswagen for a snack bar is not just for the sake of novelty; it helps prove a few selling points.

The copy describes what was fitted inside to create this eatery: "A refrigerator, a stove, a table, an instant chili dispenser, and of course, the proverbial kitchen sink... And a way for it all to get in."

Then it warns not to buy a new Volkswagen bus if you are planning to go into the restaurant business because (with a welded solid steel body and four coats of protective paints) it will take too long to get a new one in bad enough shape.

©Volkswagen of America, Inc.

168 Bengal Gin

Here is a product placed in its natural surroundings — the jungle! If a product has a built-in graphic theme, it is a good idea to illustrate that theme in advertising it.

The copy is well married to the full-color photograph. Here it is in full: "Bengal Gin. Imported (and undomesticated)/ Keep it behind bars. Yours. Grrrr! 94 Proof."

166 Mustang

In this ad, the incongruity is the elderly couple sitting in a car that boasts the most successful mod look and followers. The quote from George Bernard Shaw is well chosen. The idea was to release the car from the stereotype of any particular age group.

The slogan: "Mustang/You're ahead in a Ford."

Ford Motor Co.

169 Lord West

The little girl in the photo is the lady who approves. Besides the discrepancy in age between her and Lord West, the incongruity is heightened by having his head at the very top of the ad and hers close to the very bottom.

167 El Al Israel Airlines

At the time of the 1967 Middle East war, El Al ran this newspaper spread: "In this year 5727 we're not about to stop...We'll be flying there in 5728, 5729. In fact, we plan on flying there for a long, long time." This statement helped to reassure travelers and investors who might be skeptical about the future of the airline.

168

170

170 Ambassador

No headline. No copy. Only a well executed idea. It can't be repeated too often that an idea well conceived on the part of the copywriter or a hint dropped by an art director can bring a quiet smile to the reader's lips, and make a simple ad memorable.

Two straws alone would have served to tell the story of the "World's Lightest Scotch," but the touch of lipstick on one of them creates deep-dyed intrigue. If the couple were shown, the reader would have everything handed to him on a silver platter. Done this way, the ad might even inspire a short short about the camera-shy couple.

172 Perma-Lift

Surrealism still has its place. It's used here strictly as an attention-getter. The whimsical approach is supported by a sound composition: the ceiling and floor lines lead into the corner where the girl stands with the telephone at her ear; the bare white walls offset the full color of her skin. The "under-whimsy" includes the "Bra-la-la Bra" and the "Kikini Brief."

Kayser-Roth

173 Oil Industry Information Committee

Rather like a "What's wrong with this picture?" test, this ad depicts a great modern city ac-. cessorized with the heavy machinery, especially transportation equipment, of the nineteenth century: the horse and carriage, balloon, sailing vessel, ferryboat, and steam engine using soft coal for fuel.

The incongruities in this scene demonstrate the great impact on technological progress that has sprung from American petroleum research in the uses of oil: better gasoline for autos, better aviation fuel, special lubricants for thousands of machines and engines, "diesel fuels for modern trains and tractors, fuel oil for giant ships and home heating, synthetic rubber, plastics...the complete list would fill pages."

171 Wallace Sterling

Four different patterns of sterling silverware dig into a common package of Kellogg's Corn Flakes.

Silverware is sometimes locked up only to be taken out on special occasions. Wear and tear is taboo and, it is reasoned, the simplest thing is not to use the silverware.

Not so with Wallace Sterling. The copy declares that everyday use is good for it. "So is peanut butter. And chocolate ice cream...Life... Plain old everyday family life...The tiny, tiny scratches that are battle scars of bouts with corn flakes and dishwater are actually what make the famous Wallace patina glow."

Hamilton Watch Co.

174 Ritter Brothers

The bare skin of the baby against the Saga mink shows the coat to advantage. We usually think of mother and child in a warm setting, with baby wrapped in a blanket. The plain background in this ad, however, lets the reader's attention focus on the baby and the coat.

The copy has a hidden headline in the third sentence, "Two purely feminine joys..." These are, of course, "The clinging tenderness of a baby's finger. The lingering rapture of a rare Mink coat by Ritter...caught here in a moment of perfect rapport... The baby is heaven's latest model, purely one-of-a-kind."

175 Dorothy Gray

The whole setting for these Dorothy Gray colors implies that they are waterproof, and certainly the girl in the fish tank helps to put over the illusion. The only indication that the tank is not empty is the goldfish swimming past the model's face.

The copy is fast and the names appealing: "Up with the rousing, rosy glow of 'Pink Plunge'... with the kiss-me dash of 'Coral Splash'..."

PLAZA 8, A WILD YOUNG UNDER-WHIMSY, IS HAPPENING. (IT SHOULD HAPPEN TO YOU.)

BRA-LA-LA BRA, NYLON LEVERS LACE, VELVET STRAPS, WHITE, BLACK. $5.00. KIKINI BRIEF. SHEER LYCRA® SPANDEX, LACE INSERTS. BLACK, WHITE. $4.50. FROM THE NEW PLAZA 8 COLLECTION BY PERMA-LIFT.

ANOTHER FINE PRODUCT OF HOLLYWOOD-MAXWELL

172

What's missing here?

FORTUNATELY, only the artist has turned back the wheels of progress. He did it by drawing a modern city with one thing missing. He left out the thing that makes modern transportation possible—the energy of oil.

Fortunately, the wheels of progress are not turning back—they are turning forward and will keep on turning forward. The benefits we get from oil will be even greater tomorrow than to-day. The thousands of men and women working in the great field of petroleum research are your guarantee of that. Their past record confirms their promise of further progress.

Out of American petroleum research has come better gaso-line for your automobiles, better asphalt for your roads, better aviation fuel for America's planes, special lubricants for thousands of different types of machines and engines, diesel fuels for

modern trains and tractors, fuel oil for giant ships and home heating, synthetic rubber, plastics, insecticides, paint, cosmetics, modern medicines—the complete list would fill pages.

With research—and with the rivalry of many companies each trying to make better products and invent better ways to serve you, the oil industry sets the pace for progress. It is break-ing new records almost every day: in production—in refining—in marketing—in service. The 34,000 individual oil companies in America are progress minded. And their progress makes for "better living"—means more comfort and convenience for you.

Oil Industry Information Committee
650 Fifth Avenue • New York 19, N. Y.

THERE'S A PLUS FOR YOU IN PETROLEUM'S PROGRESS

173

The clinging tenderness of a baby's finger. The lingering rapture of a rare Mink coat by Ritter. Two purely feminine joys...caught here in a moment of perfect rapport. The Mink is that rare magnificence known as Saga...imported elegance from Denmark, Finland, Norway and Sweden...The baby is heaven's latest model, purely one-of-a-kind.

ritter
originals

174

COMING UP-UP-UP! ***NEW UNDERWATER COLORS* BY Dorothy Gray**

Down with timid tints! Up with the rousing, rosy glow of "Pink Plunge"...with the kiss-me dash of "Coral Splash," the new Underwater Colors by Dorothy Gray. Light in hue...yet radiant with the sea's own haunting shimmer. Sheer Velvet formula. Reg-ular case $1.00. Fashion Slim $1.50. Matching shades in Fashion Finish Nail Enamel.

175

The Parker touch

New pen writes with no pressure at all!

The Parker 51's remarkable new Electro-Polished point is so smooth that there is absolutely no scratch—or catch! It writes with perfect ease even on the most sensitive mousetrap!

You get the same feeling of silken smoothness on paper. The Parker touch. Flawless writing that no other pen can match because only Parker Pens have the Electro-Polished point—smoothed to a mirror finish by a new, electro-chemical process. Add to this

Parker's two-finger filling. Its wonderfully sleek design. Its tremendous ink capacity. And you wonder. Isn't it time to put the Parker touch to every word you write? You *can* for as little as $5.00!

If you're gift buying: See the new *Parker Smart Set* . . . Parker EP Pen and matching Jotter ball point, from $8.95.

The Parker Pen Company

176

177

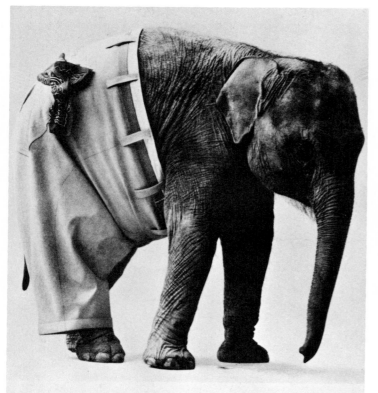

178

179

176 Parker

It is hard to imagine anyone writing on a set mousetrap; the reader knows any light touch will set it off.

The selling idea for this new Parker pen is that it will write with no pressure at all because of "Parker 51's remarkable new Electro-Polished point."

©Parker Pen Co.

180 Löwenbräu

The headline is a simple suggestion implying that this is a beer without peer. "From Munich where Löwenbräu has been brewed since 1383."

The rich golden beer in the heavy, sweating beer goblet contrasts with the clear, sparkling champagne in its fine crystal stemware. The copy offers the decorative beer goblet in sets of two as a premium (at a price).

177 Coats & Clark

Types who insist upon wearing stretch fabrics are shown doing a modern dance (rear view, of course, to emphasize the stretch). Unhappily, one of them is coming out at the seams slightly.

The urgent need of using thread especially made for sewing stretch fabrics is pressed home to the textile industry, the needle trades in particular.

178 Sanforized

One look at this baby elephant and the Clothing-for-Animals Society may be inspired to renew its campaign. Credit certainly can be given to those solemn souls who carried this great idea to its logical end, with a special award to the one who put that handkerchief in the back pants pocket.

"This is an elephant," the copy begins, "wearing a pair of pants. The elephant is loxodonta africana. The pants are 'Sanforized-Plus.' The elephant is wrinkled. It's not his fault. He was made that way. The pants are never wrinkled. They were made that way, too."

After explaining the difference between "Sanforized" (won't shrink out of fit) and "Sanforized-Plus" (tested wash-and-wear), the copy winds up: "So always be sure to look for our label. Our model never forgets. Don't you!"

Cluett, Peabody & Co.

181 Grandoe

You may be surprised to know that some people don't notice that the female model has three hands. Did you miss it?

The chessboard and the girl's bright yellow dress distract the eye (possibly to delay the double take?). The fact that each hand is correctly posed may help the deception, and enables her to show three styles of gloves.

The chess player is apparently unaware of the physical idiosyncrasies of his girlfriend. Well, each to his own taste.

179 Four Roses

The result of "cultivation" is shown by depicting glasses of whiskey rising gradually out of the earth, and at the same time increasing the size of the glass. For the product label, an identification seed packet is set in a garden row. The extraneous bottle is set in the background.

The rake and trowel in the foreground are props to better relate the idea to the headline.

Frankfort Distilleries

If they run out of Löwenbräu.....order champagne.

IMPORTED BY HANS HOLTERBOSCH, INC. OF NEW YORK IN BOTTLES AND BARRELS FROM MUNICH, WHERE LÖWENBRÄU HAS BEEN BREWED SINCE 1383. THE HAND-BLOWN LÖWENBRÄU CRYSTAL GOBLET PICTURED HERE IS AVAILABLE IN SETS OF 2 IMPORTED FROM GERMANY. FOR EACH SET MAIL $2.00 IN MONEY ORDER OR CHECK MADE PAYABLE TO "LÖWENBRÄU GOBLETS", P.O. BOX 37, WESTBURY, N.Y. 11590. PLEASE ALLOW 6 TO 8 WEEKS FOR DELIVERY.

180

WHISPERWEIGHTS HAVE A GAMBIT ALL THEIR OWN. They're soft as suede, smooth as suede, supple as suede...yet washable as cotton. Because they *are* cotton. The very finest in the world. Doesn't that make your next move practically inevitable? Left to right: EUGENIE, about $4; ISLE, about $4; SLEEK, about $5. At fine stores everywhere, or write Grandoe Glove Corporation, Gloversville, New York.

grandoe WHISPERWEIGHTS

181

182 House of Bianchi

If the copy feeds the art director a line, he can play it back. By being specific and using the word "surgeon" instead of "doctor," the concept suggested a wedding in the groom's operating room rather than in a church. The wedding dress stands out well, feminine and glamourous, against a cold, clinical setting.

184 Worthington Air Conditioning Co.

A luxury such as an air conditioner is to be shared by the entire family. The photograph has concentrated in one scene the several activities that may be going on all at once. This situation might exist anywhere; the boy is watching TV, the girl is studying, and the father is typing. It would be difficult for any of the three to concentrate if the others were close by. So the need for air conditioning the whole house is strongly brought home.

185 Rolls-Royce

The headline in this ad for one of the finest cars in the world contrasts the noise of its electric clock with the silence of the car. It is said that one of the car's engineers remarked, after seeing this ad, "We really must do something about that clock."

There is no magic about the excellence of this car, the copy explains. The secret is "merely patient attention to detail." And the details are given: "Every Rolls-Royce engine is run for seven hours at full throttle...easy to drive and to park. No chauffeur required...the engineers use a *stethoscope* to listen for axle whine...five coats of primer paint...before *nine* coats of finishing paint go on...picnic table, veneered in French walnut , slides out from under the dash...three separate systems of power brakes." The price: $13,995.

The photo shows a woman driver — remember, "No chauffeur required."

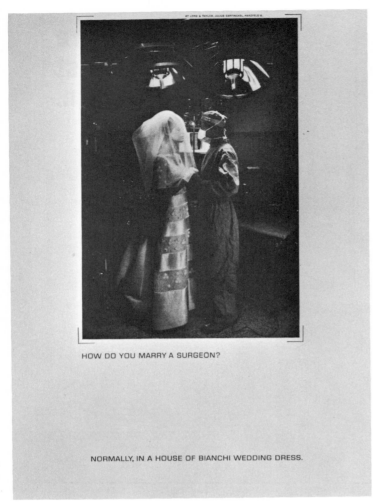

HOW DO YOU MARRY A SURGEON?

NORMALLY, IN A HOUSE OF BIANCHI WEDDING DRESS.

182

183 London Fog

This ad is a visual paraphrase of the Morton's Salt shaker which shows a little girl standing under an umbrella in the rain, a symbol of oxidized salt that doesn't cake up in wet weather. Morton's slogan is: "When it rains, it pours" — which has also been played upon here.

The copy advises that "London Fog's Manchester keeps you tastefully well dressed in all weather...available with either a dash of plaid or a touch of checks." This ad came off better when it was re-run: the background was changed to white so that the shape of the shaker was better defined.

Available with either a dash of plaid or a touch of checks, London Fog's Manchester keeps you tastefully well dressed in all weather. Third Barrier® Construction. Exclusive Clipper Mill Plaid of 65% Dacron® 35% cotton—about $40.
LONDON FOG, BALTIMORE 11, MD.

186 Macy's

A few enterprising art directors have copied good ideas right out of their layouts. For example, there's this Macy's ad.

Usually, when a layout is done for a retail store ad, the price of the merchandise is left out until publication date. Prices are either "greeked in" or indicated by a few zeros. In this case, the zeros were kept in the finished ad to indicate the uncharged-for benefits of shopping at Macy's.

Some of these are listed: low prices; the vast assortment in the world's largest store; Macy's watchdog, the Bureau of Standards; experts to consult with on buying; Macy's one-year warranty, trade-in allowance, shopping account, etc.

The slogan is: "Macy's/It's smart to be thrifty."

Why air condition just the bedroom?

Worthington can air condition your whole house for less than the cost of carpeting.

If you've put off air conditioning your house because you think it's too expensive, get rid of that idea. Know how much carpeting costs? About $10.00 a square yard? Air conditioning costs less . . . much less. If you have a warm air duct system, it will only cost you about $1.00 per square foot to install a complete Worthington Climatrol System in your house.

And since air conditioning is a home improvement, you can finance the work over three years.

For free folders on whole-house air conditioning mail the reply card (or call your Worthington Dealer; he's listed in the Yellow Pages). You'll find that a Worthington Climatrol System costs far less than you think. Much less than the cost of carpeting your home.

WORTHINGTON AIR CONDITIONING COMPANY

HEATING & COOLING FOR HOME, BUSINESS AND INDUSTRY

The Rolls-Royce Silver Cloud—$13,995

"At 60 miles an hour the loudest noise in this new Rolls-Royce comes from the electric clock"

What makes Rolls-Royce the best car in the world? "There is really no magic about it— it is merely patient attention to detail," says an eminent Rolls-Royce engineer.

1. "At 60 miles an hour the loudest noise comes from the electric clock," reports the Technical Editor of THE MOTOR. Three mufflers tune out sound frequencies—acoustically.

2. Every Rolls-Royce engine is run for seven hours at full throttle before installation, and each car is test-driven for hundreds of miles over varying road surfaces.

3. The Rolls-Royce is designed as an *owner-driven* car. It is eighteen inches shorter than the largest domestic cars.

4. The car has power steering, power brakes and automatic gear-shift. It is very easy to drive and to park. No chauffeur required.

5. The finished car spends a week in the final test-shop, being fine tuned. Here it is subjected to '98 separate ordeals. For example, the engineers use a stethoscope to listen for axle whine.

6. The Rolls-Royce is guaranteed for three years. With a new network of dealers and parts-depots from Coast to Coast, service is no problem.

7. The Rolls-Royce radiator has never changed, except that when Sir Henry Royce died in 1933 the monogram RR was changed from red to black.

8. The coachwork is given five coats of primer paint, and hand rubbed between each coat, before nine coats of finishing paint go on.

9. By moving a switch on the steering column, you can adjust the shock-absorbers to suit road conditions.

10. A picnic table, veneered in French walnut, slides out from under the dash. Two more swing out behind the front seats.

11. You can get such optional extras as an Espresso coffee-making machine, a dictating machine, a bed, hot and cold water for washing, an electric razor or a telephone.

12. There are three separate systems of power brakes, two hydraulic and one mechanical. Damage to one will not affect the others. The Rolls-Royce is a very safe car—and also a very lively car. It cruises serenely at eighty-five. Top speed is in excess of 100 m.p.h.

13. The Bentley is made by Rolls-Royce. Except for the radiators, they are identical motor cars, manufactured by the same engineers in the same works. People who feel diffident about driving a Rolls-Royce can buy a Bentley.

PRICE. The Rolls-Royce illustrated in this advertisement—f.o.b. principal ports of entry—costs $13,995.

If you would like the rewarding experience of driving a Rolls-Royce or Bentley, write or telephone to one of the dealers listed on opposite page. Rolls-Royce Inc., 10 Rockefeller Plaza, New York 20, N. Y. Circle 5-1144.

$00.00

You get a vast assortment of cameras from which to choose, both still and movie . . . all the models of all the famous makers, all clearly priced . . . . this costs you **$00.00**

You get experts to instruct you in the use of your camera when you buy it . . . and to consult at any time on everything from back lighting to action shots . . . . this costs you **$00.00**

You get the maker's one-year warranty and Macy's as well: if parts and workmanship are not perfect, we'll pick up your camera for repair and send it back to you . . . . this costs you **$00.00**

You get the extra of being able to trade in your used equipment here . . . at fair market value . . . . this costs you **$00.00**

You get the convenience of ordering by mail or phone if you can't come in. And you get speedy delivery . . . this 8mm Home Movie Outfit is right in Macy's stock . . . . this costs you **$00.00**

You get the fun of browsing around our complete Camera Centre on Macy's 5th Floor, seeing all the news in everything from filters to film . . . . this costs you **$00.00**

You get our watchdog, Macy's Bureau of Standards, checking and approving every word in our ads about the performance of cameras . . . . this costs you **$00.00**

You get the pleasure of being able to say: "Charge this movie outfit to my Macy's Shopping Account and I'll pay for it when I get my bill" . . . . this costs you **$00.00**

You get the solid confidence that comes from buying at Macy's . . . with our 104 years of pleasing customers and our 104 years of thrift . . . . this costs you **$00.00**

AND you get the low Macy price for this four-piece, 8mm home movie outfit of Kodak #143 camera, Bell & Howell #253RV projector, roll of Kodak 8mm Kodachrome film and Kodak processing. Macy's Comparison Shoppers, the world's biggest, most knowledgeable staff of shoppers, have just rechecked prices around town on these items and they say:
NO LOWER PRICE THAN MACY'S FOR THIS 8MM MOVIE OUTFIT **$94.89**

ALL THIS COSTS YOU **$94.89**

Yes, you get more than the low price at Macy's . . . but it's the things that cost you $00.00 that make the world's largest store such an exciting, such a satisfying place to shop.

MACY*S
IT'S SMART TO BE THRIFTY

$00.00

You get 48 different portable TV sets alone from which to choose . . . a huge magnificent collection, all clearly priced, all where you can see and buy them . . . . this costs you **$000.00**

You get expert salespeople to explain the differences between sets to you. They're specialists, sell only TV . . . . this costs you **$000.00**

You get the assurance that if your set doesn't arrive in perfect condition, we'll come to your house or pick it up for repair or replacement . . . . this costs you **$000.00**

You get our watchdog, Macy's Bureau of Standards, checking any unusual claims in our ads for any set . . . . this costs you **$000.00**

You get the convenience of ordering by mail or phone if you can't come in. And you get speedy delivery . . . this RCA Victor portable TV is right in Macy's stock . . . . this costs you **$000.00**

You get the fun of browsing around one of the world's biggest TV and Music Centers on Macy's 5th floor, seeing all the news in everything from radio to stereo . . . . this costs you **$000.00**

You get the pleasure of being able to say: "Charge this RCA Victor portable TV set to my Macy Shopping Account and I'll pay for it when I get my bill" . . . . this costs you **$000.00**

You get the solid confidence that comes from buying at Macy's . . . with our 104 years of pleasing customers and our 104 years of thrift . . . . this costs you **$000.00**

AND you get the low Macy price for this Model #193A52 RCA Victor Sportsman 19" deluxe new vista portable TV set with telescoping antenna. Macy's Comparison Shoppers, the world's biggest, most knowledgeable staff of shoppers, have just rechecked portable TV set prices and they say:
NO LOWER PRICE THAN MACY'S FOR THIS RCA VICTOR SET **$151.89**

ALL THIS COSTS YOU **$151.89**

Yes, you get no lower price than Macy's on this RCA Victor portable TV . . . but it's the things that cost you $000.00 that make the world's largest store such an exciting and satisfying place to shop.

MACY*S
IT'S SMART TO BE THRIFTY

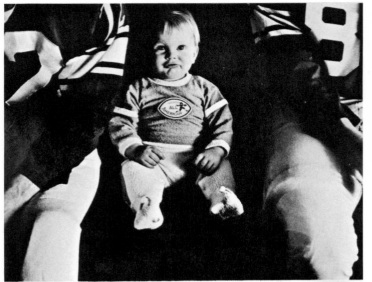

Wait 'til you see the rest of our All-American line
before you load up your bench with a bunch of substitutes.

In the little leagues this fall, ours is the team to beat. From end to end, we're loaded with the big league soft-stretch fashions, the exclusive comfort and freedom features that can jam your stadium to capacity. And in the backfield we've got an all-star squad of styles for infants and toddlers in active soft-stretch terrys, nylons and cords - even a new thermal knit that's going to be the rookie of the year. If you're looking to go undefeated this season, don't start calling signals until you get the game plan from us. We'll be seeing you in plenty of time for the opening kick-off. Kapart, Inc., 950 North 4th St., Allentown, Pennsylvania.

Babygro.

187 BabyGro

The expression on this baby's face forecasts the football player he will probably grow up to be. The two players beside him are but partially seen so as not to divert interest from the baby and the outfit he is wearing. Other styles are shown below — the ski baby, the safari baby, and the cowgirl baby.

The copy uses football idiom throughout: "In the little leagues this fall, ours is the team to beat...we're loaded with big league soft stretch fashions, the exclusive comfort and freedom features that can jam your stadium to capacity. And in the backfield we've got an all-star squad of styles for infants...a new thermal knit that's going to be the rookie of the year...don't start calling signals until you get the game plan from us."

Kapart, Inc.

What Max Bogen fur should a woman own at age three?

Sunshine colored Palominos perhaps. Angora kittens absolutely, but she's not quite ready for a Max Bogen fur. When she begins liking tea roses and matadors, bring her to us. We have flair. 350 Seventh Ave., N.Y.C. PE 6-9305

188 Max Bogen

This tiny girl wrapped up in fur is developing an early taste for things that are hard to get. A woman model, sitting at ease in a fur coat, might also prove an attention-getting break from the conventional standing model.

A lot of fashion shots are standardized by photographers too busy tending to the many exacting details of their complex art to worry about the art director's concern with the finished ad. Often photographs are made by the photographer on his own; the art director then designs or tries to contrive a layout to fit the pictures. This was not the case here.

The copy answers the headline question: "When she begins liking tea roses and matadors, bring her to us. We have flair." And they have.

NOSTALGIA

IF BABIES RAN THE WORLD...

LAW: BABIES GET SWAN BATHS EVERY DAY

They'd pass a great big law to say
All babies get a bath a day
With gentle Swan. So pure! So mild!
(It's simply *perfect* for your child!)

They'd tell the world what doctors know—
Swan's mild as fine castiles! And so
Its suds are safe for tender skin.
Just right to dunk a baby in!

They'd splash in tubs so happily
With snowy Swan that folks will see
That Swan's the bestest soap by far
For baths—no matter *who* you are!

Then watch the babies' mamas beam
'Cause Swan complexions are a dream.
So soft! So smooth! So very fair!
(Why don't you try Swan's pure, mild care?)

Then see the babies' daddies grin
'Cause Swan agrees so well with skin.
They like that lather . . . creamy! Thick!
Swan's one pure soap that lathers quick!

In kitchens and in laundries, too,
There's lots for baby's Swan to do.
Dishwashing with this grand, mild bar
Leaves soft hands lovelier by far!

While pretty duds stay fresh and bright
With Swan's pure suds to treat 'em right.
Yep, babies know what grownups should—
For *every* job, Swan's mighty good!

So doesn't it seem pretty smart
To use pure Swan right from the start?
For baby! Bath! For dishes! Duds!
Buy Swan! Get *baby-gentle* suds!

P.S. To all new babies that arrive
Sometime in 1945
We'll send a pure, *free* cake of Swan!
Just ask your dealer for coupon.

FREE A CAKE OF SWAN TO EVERY BABY BORN IN 1945! ASK YOUR DEALER FOR FREE BABY COUPON

SWAN PURE WHITE FLOATING SOAP

BABY-MILD FOR EVERYTHING SWAN IS PURE AS FINE CASTILES

TUNE IN: George Burns & Gracie Allen, CBS, Monday Nights

Ad No. 577
Life—March 28, 1945
Look—March 26, 1945
Ladies Home Journal—May, 1945

THIS IS SPAT.

Spat is a Gamin.
Gamin Gamin Spat.

See Spat go.
Go go Spat.

Spat is part suede and part calfskin in a variety of colors for about $24 at all Andrew Geller stores. GAMINS*

Sing a song of sixpence, sing a little ballad.
Serve the King some Jell-O, fixed in a salad
The salad's so refreshing, the King is overjoyed—
And four and twenty blackbirds are now unemployed.

JELL-O BRAND TEN DELICIOUS FLAVORS

COPR. 1957, GENERAL FOODS CORP.

JELL-O IS A REGISTERED TRADE-MARK OF GENERAL FOODS CORPORATION

Now...a witch-proof policy for both home and life

A Very Adult Fable in which Insurance Company of North America plays Fairy Godmother

Hansel and Gretel were imprisoned by a witch just because they chewed on her gingerbread house. "Vandalism like that worries me half to death!" she cackled, throwing wide the oven door.

"Obviously, you haven't heard about INA Homeowners-Instant Life protection," chorused the children. "Package Homeowners coverage, plus optional Term Life insurance both at very low cost."

"No medical exam required, I suppose?" sneered the witch. "None," averred Hansel. "That's why it's called 'Instant' Life; additional low-cost coverage with no bother or red tape."

"You mean INA offers Life coverage AND Homeowners protection that insures my house against windstorm, fire, burglary and people chewing on it?" "All that and more!" chorused the kids.

Charmed, the witch turned into a beautiful princess and they all lived happily ever after in the little gingerbread house with a passing INA agent, who was really a prince after all.

INA
INSURANCE COMPANY OF NORTH AMERICA
Life Insurance Company of North America
World Headquarters: Philadelphia

Moral: Be sure, insure with INA. Just ask your INA agent or broker about new INA Homeowners-Instant Life. Then, have him pass the gingerbread and feel free to eat all your heart desires.

189 Swan

In this lyrical, hard-sell baby commercial, each panel of rhyme mentions the brand name at least once without seeming intrusive. The rhymes are easy to read; they make medical facts easy to digest. The first panel: "Law: Babies get Swan baths *every* day." Then, "They'd tell the world what doctors know —/ *Swan's mild as fine castiles!* And so / Its suds are safe for tender skin./ Just right to dunk a baby in."

Other purposes for the soap: "In kitchens and in laundries, too, / There's lots for baby's Swan to do. / Dishwashing with this grand, mild bar / Leaves soft hands lovelier by far!"

An offer of a free cake of soap is made in the last panel for any baby born that year (1945).

193 Armstrong Cork

A scrap of copy, coupled with the gold flooring and dim white arches, set this picture in a fairy-tale palace, where the King has enjoined the miller's daughter to spin straw into gold. The deformed and angry dwarf. Rumpelstiltskin, has promised to do it for her, but under one heart-breaking condition...However, as with most fairy stories, all turns out well in the end — except for the dwarf.

190 Gamins

Using the child's primer as inspiration, this ad follows the style and language meant for five-year-olds. It was not geared to the masses but to the sophisticated taste of *New Yorker* magazine readers. (However, this approach might work even if it were used in a mass-circulation medium for an inexpensive product.)

The copy has a nice rhythm to it — even though it spoofs the *"First Reader."*

191 Jell-O

A Mother Goose rhyme sparked this and other ads in a memorable campaign. Taken from "Sing a song of sixpence," this ad substitutes Jell-O for the "four and twenty blackbirds baked in a pie" as the king's dessert: "Sing a song of sixpence, sing a little ballad. / Serve the King some Jell-O, fixed in a salad / The salad's so refreshing, the King is overjoyed —/ And four and twenty blackbirds are now unemployed."

The illustrations in this series were gay, neat, and colorful.

©General Foods

194 Insurance Company of North America

Another bit of nostalgia from Mother Goose launches a message, this one about the old lady who lived in a shoe — a football shoe. The cleated football shoe is converted into a shingled, three-story house. At the small windows are members of the team, variously occupied. The color of the house was blue with a red band running along the white lacing.

The copy tells us that the Insurance Company of North America protects the New York Giants' football team "with a business insurance program that's great both on offense and defense... sets up a solid line of protection while it blocks overlapping coverage."

192 Insurance Company of North America

Fairy tales can come true. INA has based a whole series of ads on a child's world.

"A Very Adult Fable," taken from the story of Hansel and Gretel, "in which Insurance Company of North America plays Fairy Godmother." The witch imprisons the children for eating away at the gingerbread house. " 'Vandalism like that worries me half to death'." The children answer in chorus, " 'Obviously, you haven't heard about INA Homeowners—*Instant* Life protection'." " 'No medical exam required, I suppose'?" " 'None'," Hansel replies. And so on. The moral is, of course, "Be sure, insure with INA."

There's a rumor going around that it takes a bit of magic to make Montina Vinyl Corlon floors. Please help us spread this rumor. But first, see the magic for yourself. For a free sample of Montina Corlon, write: Armstrong Cork Company, 6511 Maple Ave., Lancaster, Pa. In Canada: Dept. 115-K, Box 919, Montreal, P. Q.   vinyl floors by ⒶArmstrong

193

Ⓘ**NA** INSURES FOOTBALL

Insurance Company of North America protects the New York Giants with a business insurance program that's great both on offense and defense.

Custom-made for the Giants, the INA program sets up a solid line of protection while it blocks overlapping coverage. Efficiency wins, premiums plummet.

INA can do the same for your business, large or small. We've been at it since 1792, and today we have more than $1½ billion in assets.

Phone your broker or INA agent about INA business insurance programs. He also knows about thrifty INA Package policies for home, car, health, life. Be sure, insure with INA. **Insurance Company of North America. World Headquarters: Philadelphia.**

194

The day New York almost vanished

It didn't happen all at once.
They did it very gradually.
"We can't alarm the people!" they said.
So they removed a little house here. And a great
hotel there. And then a few limestone banks
and all the cast-iron store fronts they could find.
And very quietly one night they stole a railroad
station and buried it in New Jersey.

A few people grumbled.
Some found temporary shelter at The Dakota
when Park Avenue disappeared. Others moved
to Westchester. And some completely
disillusioned out-of-towners went to Philadelphia
instead. But most people were complacent. Until
the day they discovered that their city had
been entirely replaced with glass.

Then they complained. But it was too late.
So the faces of the city grew grimmer
than they had ever been before. Clocks stopped.
And the glass began to crack.

Soon after this on one ghastly glittering
morning, an observant executive walking to work
paused on Fifth Avenue at Fifty-Ninth Street
to clean his heavy dark goggles. Squinting,
he looked around. And gasped!

There was The Plaza where he had always
remembered it. "It can't be!" he said and rubbed
his eyes. He looked again. "It *is* there!" he said.
And ran to work.

He called his wife.
"We'll go there tonight, before it's too late.
Don't tell anyone!" he hissed. So she only told
her very best friend. Soon everyone knew.

Crowds gathered. They wandered in the
lobbies. They caressed the marble, admired the
gilded cherubs. And the caryatids in the Palm
Court where palms still swayed. They feasted in
the baronial splendor of the Edwardian Room.
And discussed mergers over martinis and lunch
in the Oak Bar.

That night, they danced to *real* music
again in the Persian Room. And laughed with
Julius Monk in his red velvet world at PLaza 9-.
The lucky ones who had made reservations
retired upstairs, to spacious rooms where they
were waited on hand and foot by manicurists and
podiatrists and chambermaids and valets and
waiters with trays and florists with roses.
They loved it.

After all, people of taste are like everybody
else. They're very grateful when great demands
are met. And incurably sentimental.

Eventually word spread out of town. And
out-of-towners came again to see a part of the
city they thought had vanished. Some never
left The Plaza. They didn't have to. They had
the world on a golden chain.

The Plaza had thought of everything. It
always does.

It always will.

THE PLAZA
HOTEL CORPORATION OF AMERICA

This advertisement is fantasy, of course.
But then so is life at The Plaza. Come live it.

"It didn't happen all at once. They did it very gradually. 'We can't alarm the people!' they said. So they removed a little house here. And a great hotel there." Well, they can have the Ritz, perhaps, and the Savoy Plaza. Very regretfully, they can have the Lafayette. But not The Plaza.

Waves of nostalgia engulfed bred-in-the-bone New Yorkers at the mere thought of losing The Plaza. Read the copy to find out why. But first read the footnote below. That strip of skyline slowly fading out is a visual telegram flashing the ad theme.

Hotel Corporation of America

196 Chevrolet

This old sampler has the words "Higher Resale" and a Chevy logo as its motif. The headline below the sampler is elaborated in the copy which says: "Chevrolets have commanded higher resale value than the other two leading makes of fleet cars. The reasons that make this true are the same reasons that make Chevy desirable in the first place."

General Motors

197 Utica Club

This imitation "period" photograph conveys the atmosphere of an old-time bar, an achievement which was enhanced by printing the photograph in sepia tones. The idea of being 50 years behind the times implies that this beer is brewed with the traditional craftsmanship and time consuming ways of the past, with the character and body of pilsener.

"It's brewed by the West End Brewing Company of Utica, N. Y. With stubbornness and pride." What is the authentic touch that really dates this saloon set-up? No ladies allowed.

©West End Brewing Co.

It's an old family tradition

And we're proud of it. Since 1953, Chevrolets have commanded higher resale value than the other two leading makes of fleet cars.* The reasons that make this true are the same reasons that make Chevy desirable in the first place. A Jet-smooth ride, for instance. All Chevrolet models have that. And Body by Fisher. It's rugged and solid. Not to mention a whole list of 1964 easy-care features that save time and money. Like self-adjusting brakes, battery-saving Delcotron generator, long-life exhaust system and rust-resisting wash-and-dry rocker panels. When you consider Chevrolet's overall popularity, that should make it unanimous. . . . Chevrolet Division of General Motors, Detroit, Michigan.

*Source: 10 years of NADA Reports

CHEVROLET—A credit to your business . . . on the road . . . on the ledger

196

Our beer is 50 years behind the times
(and we're proud of it)

198 Old Crow

If your product has had famous acquaintances and there is proof in old correspondence that they praised your product, make the most of it.

Old Crow has run contests paying $250 to anyone who could dig up written reference to Old Crow by famous people.

The caption under the picture says that Mark Twain once ordered 25 barrels of Old Crow to assure his supply at Klaproth's, his favorite tavern. The copy informs us that it is rare indeed for any product to be singled out for public praise over a period of 125 years. "In every generation great Americans have praised it by name."

The painting is realistic, re-creating a convivial scene that could not have been recorded photographically.

199 Warner's

The name of Warner's pajamas, Silent Flicks, takes the reader back to the twenties, including nostalgia for the quaint days when bathing suits like these were considered daring. The Keystone cops arresting the girls on the beach prove how times have changed.

But "Warner's snatched oldtime swimsuits for you to sleep in...more darling than daring... Soft, stretchy, deliciously silky, crushproof... Anyone for a historical pair of pajamas?"

PERSONALIZING

You'll soar like an eagle or plummet like a stone when you ski-sail in the Austrian Tyrol

1 "Even the pros can't predict what will happen after the takeoff," writes Toni Walkner, American friend of Canadian Club. "The warm updraft from sun-drenched slopes gives you the 'lift'—and the gusty cold winds coming down from the shadowed regions above give you the necessary 'carry' for a long, breathtaking, birdlike ride through the air.

2 "All you need is the lucky combination of strong legs, good balance and air currents to catch your balloonlike sails and float you off into space for a long, easy glide.

3 "My Tyrolean pro friend had that combination—but I didn't! The gusty downdraft slammed me down into drifted snow seconds after I jumped, and I wound up head over skis for a very undignified finale.

4 "A bit wobbly but all in one piece, I gladly called it a day and went off with my friend for a drink of his favorite whisky and mine—Canadian Club." Why this whisky's universal popularity? It has the lightness of Scotch and the smooth satisfaction of Bourbon. No other whisky tastes quite like it. You can stay with it all evening long—in short ones before dinner, in tall ones after. Enjoy Canadian Club—the world's lightest whisky—tonight.

Canadian Club

"The Best In The House"® in 87 lands

To the best of our knowledge, no airline has seats like this. In fact, seats on all the major airlines are pretty much the same (except that our jet Coach has only 5 seats across instead of 6 like most other airlines). Indeed, today there are few important visible differences between airlines. Yet—one airline is different. You can't see the difference—you feel it! The name of this airline is Continental and the difference you feel is pride—the pride of Continental's people . . . in their jobs, in themselves, in their airline. The reason they have this extra measure of pride is that Continental, as major airlines go, is not a great big, impersonal one. So—Continental's people can and do maintain their individuality, their interest and involvement in how their airline is run. It's not so much what they do as how they do it. That's what you feel and you feel good—comfortable—confident. All airlines don't feel the same. Come travel with us and feel the difference pride makes. It's almost like being at home. Your travel agent or Continental Airlines will arrange it. Please call.

CONTINENTAL The Proud Bird with the Golden Tail

Don't let the sun burn out your weekend fun!

Sunburn doesn't *have* to spoil your weekend or vacation. Today there's a product that does more than just soothe sunburned skin—*it actually stops the sensation of skin pain!*

SOLARCAINE stops sunburn pain!

Stops it faster, more completely than ordinary "first aids"

Takes the pain out of pain nerves with benzocaine, used by doctors! Solarcaine cools your sunburned skin instantly. Then it actually *blocks pain-sensations* with a surface anesthetic. That's why it's much more effective than first aid products that have no real pain killing ingredient!

Helps prevent infection, promote healing with multiple antiseptics. And Solarcaine's emollients soothe and *moisturize* dry, sunparched skin . . . keep skin soft and pliable, help prevent peeling. Solarcaine is greaseless. Won't stain. Get this unique formula—praised by skin specialists—today.

Blocks pain of scrapes, scratches, dozens of skin irritations that hurt, burn or itch . . . cookout burns, mosquito bites, hot, sore feet. You will use Solarcaine for skin pain all year round.

Solarcaine comes in popular Lotion, first aid Cream and convenient "no touch" Spray form. Lotion and Cream both come in cartons now. You get big saving on 6 oz. Lotion. Also buy Solarcaine Lip Balm. All are quality products of Plough, Inc.

Even the next morning a little Taji still lingers

Taji is a hauntingly beautiful new fragrance in a totally new perfume form. All pure perfume oil, instead of the traditional blend of oil and volatile alcohol, a few drops of Taji touched to your skin will last throughout the day or night. Why, the Taji you wear when you go out in the evening will even still linger a little by morning. Taji in Perfume Oil 7.50, also in a Spray for bath and shower and a Soap.

TAJi

200 Canadian Club

This campaign has been running for years. Personal experiences in various sports have typed the Canadian Club man as one who tries but doesn't always make it.

Ski-sailing in Austria inspires this dramatic story. "Even the pros can't predict what will happen after the takeoff." The reason-why copy leads the reader step by step through the event in which our hero doesn't have that necessary combination of expertise and luck. Did he "plummet like a stone?"

The conclusion is not in a hospital; friends of Canadian Club come out alive. In the last picture, the two ski-sailors are shown, "a bit wobbly but all in one piece," having their favorite drink — Canadian Club.

204 Goodyear

With the headline as the slogan and theme, this idea was easily adapted to TV. In the commercial the situation was even more frightening — a re-creation of Ichabod Crane's flight through the forest — with a woman getting a flat in the midday dusk of the woods.

The copy says, "She'll never have to change tires with Life Guard Safety Spare." It describes how "You would help her if you were there. But you're not," and the concept of "a tire-within-a-tire" lets her keep on driving until she is out of the woods.

The photograph's cut-away tire shows the Safety Spare.

201 Continental Airlines

To bring home the personal care given you, at low cost, on Continental Airlines ("It's almost like being at home"), a plane seat is converted into an armchair much like the one you have at home. There are slippers, a pipe, and even the evening newspaper awaiting you.

The copy tells you that "all the major airlines are pretty much the same (except that our jet Coach has only 5 seats across instead of 6 like most other airlines)." The real difference is the employees' pride. "Continental, as major airlines go, is not a great big, impersonal one."

202 Solarcaine

This ad used red as the second color for the beet-bright shade of the girl's skin. The model is well posed and makes an appealing center of attraction because of the diagonal line of the body and the triangular shape formed by the bent leg and extended arm. The intruding hand holding out the product gives the model prospect of relief from sunburn.

The small insert at top right shows the model on a beach blanket. The headline over it advises, "Don't let the sun burn out your weekend fun!" The copy says, again and again, that the product — *"actually stops the sensation of skin pain!"*

Plough, Inc.

205 Hamilton Watch Co.

This ad alternated black-and-white action shots with full-color photos of the watches.

The color and size of the watches attract the reader, but the black-and-white photos have human-interest appeal, creating a minor visual conflict between the two. The copy upholds the headline: "Where important events occur, you're likely to see the 505 Electric."

203 Taji

Here is a mood shot married to the headline, visually depicting why you should use Taji: just because it does linger.

The conductor near the train is an essential character in this soap opera because he establishes the early morning hour and is a symbol of human activity at the station. Without the conductor as a necessary intruder, the station might have seemed abandoned. The anxiety of the departing one might have been lost (and the effectiveness of the perfume in holding a man a little longer).

©Shulton

When there's no man around...Goodyear should be.

She'll never have to change tires with LifeGuard Safety Spare. You would help her if you were there. But you're not. That is why every woman should drive on Goodyear Double Eagle tires with LifeGuard Safety Spares (optional, to give her *extra* safety).

It's a "tire-within-a-tire," so if the outside tire is ever damaged, the LifeGuard Safety Spare takes over, lets her keep driving until she is safe. Good tires are especially important when there's no man around. And that is when Goodyear should be.

Double Eagle, LifeGuard—T.M.'s
The Goodyear Tire & Rubber Company, Akron, Ohio

GO GO GOODYEAR
MORE PEOPLE RIDE ON GOODYEAR TIRES THAN ON ANY OTHER KIND

204

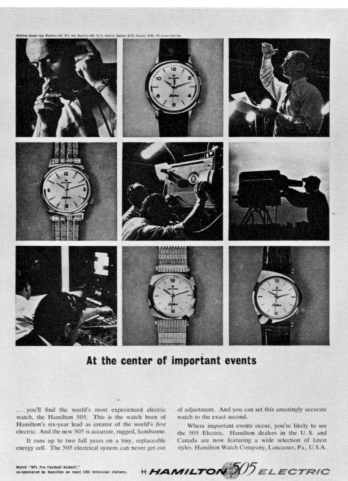

At the center of important events

...you'll find the world's most experienced electric watch, the Hamilton 505. This is the watch born of Hamilton's six-year lead as creator of the world's *first* electric. And the new 505 is accurate, rugged, handsome.

It runs up to two full years on a tiny, replaceable energy cell. The 505 electrical system can never get out

of adjustment. And you can set this amazingly accurate watch to the exact second.

Where important events occur, you're likely to see the 505 Electric. Hamilton dealers in the U. S. and Canada are now featuring a wide selection of latest styles. Hamilton Watch Company, Lancaster, Pa., U.S.A.

Watch "NFL Pro Football Kickoff," co-sponsored by Hamilton on most CBS television stations.

HAMILTON 505 ELECTRIC

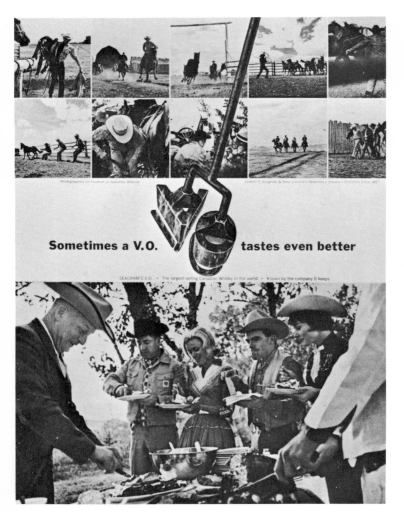

206

206 Seagram's V. O.

Without any words, a simple montage of the day's routine in a cowboy's life ends with his having a drink of the product.

The bottled product is not even shown. The headline, which is the only real copy in the ad, says, "Sometimes a V. O. tastes even better," with "after a hard day's work" implied. "The largest selling Canadian Whiskey in the world. Known by the company it keeps."

Joseph E. Seagram & Sons

207

207 Shalimar

We can read only a part of this very personal note, but it is enough to send our imagination soaring. The reader gathers, from key words, that "Lilly" either has been or is keeping company with books until whoever-he-is heeds her "Hurry, hurry back," sign-off. The drops of Shalimar near the words "Love, Lilly" are well placed. They serve as a fine mnemonic for the loved one Lilly is writing to.

The colors in this photograph were well planned too: the wide expanse of green blotter, the handwriting in the letter and the watery-blue color of the perfume stopper. The gold-colored bottle was shown against gradations of green.

Guerlain

208 Shalimar

In Paris, in 1926, the brothers Guerlain heard the story of the great romance between the Indian Maharajah, Shah Jahan, and the loveliest of his wives. They decided to pay homage to the legend, creating the perfume Shalimar, meaning "abode of love."

During her lifetime, the Shah had built for them the Gardens of Shalimar; he commemorated her death by building the Taj Mahal. Guerlain decided to call the perfume Shalimar rather than Taj Mahal..."You see, Taj Mahal marks the end of a story. And this perfume has nothing to do with endings." But read the copy. It flows smoothly in this dreamy world of fantasy.

Note that however poetic the copy, the bottle of Shalimar is shown (telling the *sales* story).

Guerlain

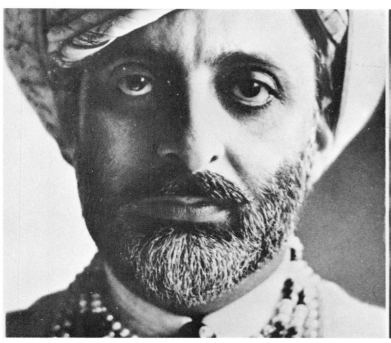

Before Shalimar was a perfume, it was a garden of love.

Our story begins in India, some 300 years ago. It belongs, however, to no place and no time.

His name was Shah Jahan, ruler of India.

Her name was Mumtaz Mahal, the loveliest of his wives.

And although he had many wives, it was only for her that his soul thirsted.

Some say that he loved her unto madness. That she was not his wife, but his fever. But in his eyes she was the balm that made the world bearable.

Victories, new empires and riches were as dust compared to her.

So great was his love for her that when she died, he would not let her die. He had built in her memory a place you may still see and wonder at.

The Taj Mahal.

But long before there could be a Taj Mahal, there had to be yet another place which the Shah also built.

The Gardens of Shalimar in Lahore.

All that the Taj Mahal keeps alive for the ages flowered in Shalimar. Here it was that their love grew and became a legend.

Its very name, "Shalimar," means "abode of love" in Sanskrit.

And truly it was.

The Shah allowed into this garden only those things which would nourish their love. Joyful fountains. Deep, limpid pools. Marble terraces. Rare song birds. Fragrant blossoms from every corner of the earth. Lanterns to rival the stars.

Only in Shalimar were the lovers truly alone.

Thus, even though many miles apart, if you wish to see the foundations of the Taj Mahal, you must look for them in Shalimar.

All this, dear reader, was also told to Pierre and Jacques Guerlain by a Maharajah. It was in Paris, in 1926.

Naturally, being human and being French, and being, above all, Guerlains, they were deeply moved.

They decided to pay homage to this man and woman by creating a perfume of intoxicating, yet subtle sensuousness.

A perfume not for children.

They decided, also, that this perfume should not be called "Taj Mahal," but "Shalimar."

You see, Taj Mahal marks the end of a story.

And this perfume has nothing to do with endings.

SHALIMAR BY GUERLAIN

THE STORY OF L'HEURE BLEUE

Or how a certain time of day led to Guerlain's creation of, perhaps, the most tenderly beautiful perfume in the world.

Twilight on the Seine: 1911.

The art of the perfumer, like the art of the musician, is elusive and mysterious.

But even the musician has certain laws of harmony and the eight notes of the scale to rely upon, while the perfumer is faced with an infinite range of fragrances, and only his intuition to guide him.

Common to all great art, however, is that moment, or event, which compels the artist to attempt to preserve it forever. (Who amongst us has led such a shallow existence that he was never moved to say "I wish I could paint that," or at least, "I wish I had a camera with me"?)

A moment such as this is the story of L'Heure Bleue.

A man pauses to reflect on his walk home from work. The year is 1911. It is summer. There is nothing spectacular about the scene. No vivid sunset. No heavenly rays penetrating dark clouds.

To the contrary. The air is dark blue. The sky has lost the sun but not yet found the stars. And yet it is as if all the elements were conspiring to say something.

Something infinite. Something . . . tender. Something that simply cannot be translated into words.

The following morning M. Guerlain returned to his laboratory and began work. For almost a year he struggled to capture that vibrant hush, the beguiling sweetness of closing flowers, the tender, infinite something that had overwhelmed him.

The result was L'Heure Bleue, a finely balanced perfume composed with the passion of Musk and Rose de Bulgarie, and the naive loveliness of Iris and Heliotrope, subtly blended with fragrances from the far corners of the earth.

What happens when you apply L'Heure Bleue to your pulse points, and its delicate scent starts to permeate the air around you? Ah . . .
That's another story.

Twilight on the Seine: 1966.

209 L'Heure Bleue

The validity of the idea is, of course, essential but the rendering of the idea can add to or detract from the effectiveness of the ad.

The full warmth of color tone that carries over from the background with the rich golden perfume bottle is suddenly interrupted by an unusual, blue-shaded rectangle of twilight on the Seine.

All I can say about the copy is read it.

Guerlain

210 Eveready

An actual experience can be put into readable comic strip form; it's one of the best ways to tell a complete story in a short time.

The amusement park to which a woman took her little twin cousins turned into a nightmare when the lights blacked out. Thinking quickly, to avoid panic, she reached into her purse for a pocket flashlight...Would the battery work?

You know it would — it's the advertiser's product.

The slogan: "The battery with 'Nine Lives'."

Union Carbide and Carbon Corp.

211 Breck

The Breck girl is as famous as Miss Rheingold although she has never been promoted in the same way or given an identity. The point is that this is not a photo of a ravishing model ohing and ahing the praises of the product. It is the portrait, slightly idealized, of an ordinary gal, pleasant and feminine, easy for a housewife to identify with.

The ad simply promises beautiful hair and shows that the product keeps that promise. Straightforward copy repeats (remember that old standby of good advertising) the words "Breck Shampoo" as it describes the three types recommended for different kinds of hair, what it does when you use it, and how it leaves you afterwards.

The spacing between the letters in the word "Breck" spreads it across the full width of the ad, serving to establish the identity of the company as well as any of the latest logo designs. It presents the name, large and clear, while retaining the light touch desirable for a woman's product.

©John H. Breck, Inc. Reproduced by permission.

210

211

...and Pillsbury says it best. **Pillsbury**

212

"Now?"

How long can a fellow hold out against that aroma, the tender white chicken meat, the firm, delicious rice? This is Lipton Chicken Rice soup, the one that tastes like Mother just cooked it. All Lipton soups taste that way.

ALPHABET VEGETABLE · BEEF NOODLE · MUSHROOM · TOMATO · TOMATO VEGETABLE · GREEN PEA · CHICKEN NOODLE · CHICKEN NOODLE WITH MEAT · ONION · CREAM STYLE CHICKEN · COUNTRY STYLE POTATO

212 Pillsbury

Is this your little girl reaching for the fresh cup-cakes on the counter? It might well be, after your wife has seen this ad.

The full-color photograph is brought up so close to the reader that he can almost smell the cakes. When the reader happens to be some-one's wife, she might rush off to find her cook-book and start baking — preferably with Pills-bury flour.

214 Aphrodisia

Fabergé made an "extra-dry Aphrodisia for him" to complement a "sparkling, full-bodied Aphrodisia for her. Both terribly mutual, not at all neutral."

His-and-Hers sets are common in pillow cases (whence the idea sprang), certain apparel and various appliances. The problem of making the idea work is that there are many products to which it can't apply: for instance, stockings, makeup, cigars.

Another difficulty is in creating look-alike packaging appropriate to both sexes. The appear-ance of the product must convince the consumer — man or woman — that it "belongs" to the op-posite sex, too. (This was a problem that Marl-boro, originally a cigarette for women, overcame with its sophisticated tattooed-man campaign.)

Fabergé

215 Ivory

The photograph of mother and child gives about 85% of the picture's area to skin — two beauti-fully toned complexions; the rest of the space for their hair and the cake of Ivory Soap.

The copy bears out the slogan (not the old "99 44/100% pure," but the new one): "For that young Ivory look." It explains that your skin hasn't changed as much as you think since you were a baby. The suggestion is that "Maybe the way you wash your face is leaving it a little rough and dry. Why not try a change to regular Ivory care?"

Procter & Gamble

213 Lipton

How long can they keep a guy sitting like that in front of an appetizing bowl of soup? Either that kid's mouth is watering or he has already started in on the soup. (Let's hope for his sake he has.)

216 Vistaril

Personalize your ad by giving case histories. The detailed close-up of the aged woman is excellent. The little dog is pathetic, but com-forting to her. And we can't help paying attention to the content of the advertisement: "Her only comfort in life is her dog...Crowds distress her... She grows agitated when her pension check is late." And the headline and subhead: "No other tranquilizer is as precise, as uncomplicated as Vistaril (hydroxyzine). Its site of action *is* the seat of anxiety."

Pfizer

If you can't lick 'em, join 'em.

Her Aphrodisia. His Aphrodisia.

It's the newest way to show who's whose — fragrance in two genders! Extra-dry **Aphrodisia** for him; sparkling, full-bodied **Aphrodisia** for her. Both terribly mutual, not at all neutral. Both, tellingly two-faced, by the one with The Knack— *Fabergé*

cheek-to-cheek softness

for skin more like a baby's, try using Ivory...
the purest, mildest complexion soap possible

Of course your skin has changed since you were a baby... but maybe not so much as you think. Maybe the way you wash your face is leaving it a little rough and dry. Why not try a change to regular Ivory care? It helps keep your skin looking so fresh, and

soft, and glowingly alive... so young. Pure, mild Ivory doesn't irritate... even with the extra washings you give your face in hot summer weather. Did you know that more doctors recommend Ivory than any other soap for babies' skin—and yours!

99⁴⁴/₁₀₀% pure*

FOR THAT YOUNG IVORY LOOK

in senile agitation...

Her only comfort in life is her dog...
Crowds distress her...She grows agitated when her pension check is late.
This anxious patient and others can feel more comfortable on Vistaril... because Vistaril calms smoothly, makes them feel better without the euphoria or psychic overgratification that fosters habituation.

What is Vistaril? Vistaril is hydroxyzine, a tranquilizer entity, totally different from the diazepines, meprobamates and the phenothiazines. While equal to the diazepines and meprobamates in effectiveness, Vistaril has been remarkably free of the unwanted psychic and somatic reactions associated with other tranquilizing agents because its primary effect is exerted at the seat of anxiety.

Vistaril tranquilizes with less complication than do the phenothiazines. Unwanted effects, such as hepatotoxicity, blood dyscrasias, skin pigmentation, and opacities of lens and cornea, are not characteristic of Vistaril activity.

Vistaril tranquilizes with less complication than do the minor tranquilizers. Withdrawal symptoms, possible psychotropic drug incompatibilities, blood dyscrasias and hepatotoxicity, seen with some minor tranquilizers, are not characteristic of Vistaril.

No other tranquilizer is as precise, as uncomplicated, as Vistaril®
(HYDROXYZINE)

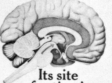

Its site of action is the seat of anxiety

Pfizer Since 1849.
Science for the world's well being®

Turn page for brief summary...

OUR CURIOUS WARS WITH THE ANIMAL WORLD

(In defense of your telephone service)

Ever since the telephone business began, birds, beasts and insects have been doing their best to disrupt it. The struggle never ends. Here are a few of the many amusing skirmishes.

A belligerent Minnesota moose butted down a telephone pole. Another tore-out a mile and a half of line serving a forest fire station. We put in tougher and taller replacements!

An Illinois cat kept chewing the spring cord on her owner's phone. We pleased everybody by providing a piece of *old* spring cord the cat could safely chew on.

A hungry goose in North Dakota pecked the long worm that ran up the side of the house until he cut it through. We just hope he doesn't bust his beak on the *new* telephone wire!

Prairie gophers have tough teeth and an insatiable appetite for the lead sheathing on buried cable. We *think* our new steel-jacketed cable is gopher-proof.

We try hard to win each little war. In these and many more important ways, we do our human best to bring you good service—service so free from trouble that most people take it for granted and can't remember the last time they had to have a phone fixed!

217

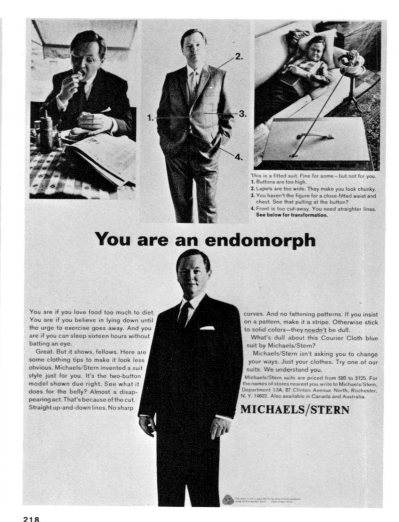

This is a fitted suit. Fine for some—but not for you.
1. Buttons are too high.
2. Lapels are too wide. They make you look chunky.
3. You haven't the figure for a close-fitted waist and chest. See that pulling at the button?
4. Front is too cut-away. You need straighter lines. **See below for transformation.**

You are an endomorph

You are if you love food too much to diet. You are if you believe in lying down until the urge to exercise goes away. And you are if you can sleep sixteen hours without batting an eye.

Great. But it shows, fellows. Here are some clothing tips to make it look less obvious. Michaels/Stern invented a suit style just for you. It's the two-button model shown due right. See what it does for the belly? Almost a disappearing act. That's because of the cut. Straight up-and-down lines. No sharp curves. And no fattening patterns. If you insist on a pattern, make it a stripe. Otherwise stick to solid colors—they needn't be dull.

What's dull about this Courier Cloth blue suit by Michaels/Stern?

Michaels/Stern isn't asking you to change your ways. Just your clothes. Try one of our suits. We understand you.

Michaels/Stern suits are priced from $80 to $125. For the names of stores nearest you, write to Michaels/Stern, Department 13A, 87 Clinton Avenue North, Rochester, N. Y. 14602. Also available in Canada and Australia.

MICHAELS/STERN

218

Marriage is not all beer and tarantellas.

But that's not a bad way to start. At an Italian *sposalizio*, after the bride and groom have danced together, they dance some more—with fathers and mothers, aunts and uncles, cousins, nephews and nieces, and well-wishers in general.

Which makes everybody thirsty. And of course they have to keep their strength up by nibbling at the mortadella, soppressate, scampi, calamari, sardines and anchovies. Which makes them thirstier. And what then?

Ecco! Rheingold Extra Dry, the beer that refreshes all kinds of happy occasions. In fact, in New York City, where there are more different kinds of celebrations than anywhere else in the world, more people buy Rheingold than any other beer.

How come?

We don't know. But we must be doing something right.

Buona fortuna e molti figli! Rheingold

219

Don't make the mistake that George did!

1. George Sewall bought (one July one)
A brand-new sport shirt just for fun.
It was somewhat red and debonair,
And the label said 'twas Wash-and-Wear.

2. George thought what a fine thing this is,
No more ironing for the Missis.
Alas, the rosy vision sank—
The shirt, when washed, *wrinkled* and *shrank*.

3. Said George, "Oh, No! This cannot be
The Wash-and-Wear they promised me."
But he would be victorious
If he had looked for "Sanforized-Plus."
These words assure the best degree
Of wash-and-wear-ability.

4. Just keep in mind this simple rule,
Avoid the fate of poor George Sewall.

5. Remember you can always trust,
All fabrics labeled "Sanforized-Plus."

·SANFORIZED·

SANFORIZED for shrinkage protection in all cottons

SANFORIZED plus

New SANFORIZED-PLUS for excellence in wash-and-wear performance

220

217 Bell System

Few big companies are smart enough to take the consumer into their confidence about seemingly small jabs, pin-pricks in the great body corporate, which nonetheless threaten the perfection of service to the customer. Here the advertiser recounts some bizarre encounters with a moose, a cat, a goose and a gopher. Multiplied many times, these add up to a continuing war with animals, birds, and insects.

In presenting this picture to the individual consumer, the company puts the problem on a level with the individual's problems. The company becomes suddenly human, not a vast impersonal communications machine. The consumer's response is one of tolerance. It is easier to excuse man's failure than that of a machine.

American Telephone & Telegraph

218 Michaels/Stern

This is a break-away from those stereotyped ads for men's brand-name suits which reduce the choice to one of style or material.

The reason for you to buy this suit is made clear: "you are an endomorph." The problem of fitting you properly is a special one. The black-and-white photos above show who the endomorph is and how poor a fit the standard suit is for him. The copy, numbering its faults, is very specific. The full-color photo shows how a suit properly designed for an endomorph should fit. It's by Michaels/Stern, of course. This ad was one of a series that identified body types.

219 Rheingold

To emphasize Rheingold beer's place as a necessary adjunct to hospitality and happy times, this ad — one of a series featuring celebrations by New Yorkers of various national descent — makes its appeal to Italian-Americans, literally talking their language and conveying to everyone the timeless, robust delight of the wedding reception. *Buona fortuna* ring out the toasts—drunk, of course, in frosty Rheingold. A good example of ethnic advertising with a universal appeal.

Liebmann Breweries

220 Sanforized

This is the personal saga of George Sewall, who bought a wash-and-wear shirt that didn't have the Sanforized label. Our hero is not identifiable in those black silhouettes. The simple shapes of his figure are in sharp contrast with the highly ornate borders of each picture.

The second picture, showing the Missis hanging up the wash-and-wear shirt, sums up: "George thought what a fine thing/this is,/ No more ironing for the Missis./ Alas, the rosy vision sank—The shirt, when washed,/ *wrinkled* and *shrank*."

Cluett, Peabody & Co.

221 Trifari

A few black-and-white snapshots interspersed with expensive-looking jewelry in full color, against a rich blue background, make this ad first, human; second, provocative (until the headline is explained).

The copy says that the women in this man's life are his niece, his daughter, his cousin and his sister. How can a married man afford so much jewelry? Simple, when it's made of expensive-looking rhinestone and gold or platinum-toned trifanium.

Trifari, Krussman and Fishel, Inc.

222 Jacqueline Cochran

Personalize familiar scenes for mnemonic value. The everyday experience occurring in your ad becomes even more personal when the model looks the reader in the eye.

The black border frames the picture so that the reader is looking into a neighborhood scene. The perspective of the sidewalk and houses heightens the effect of proximity.

221

222

223 Roosevelt Raceway

It seems that every advertiser knows a guy named Charlie. Charlie's activities within a typical American interior pretty well sum up everyone's. It simply isn't in the cards to have an exciting time at home *every* evening.

In this ad, one of a series, vignettes of "characteristic" scenes of a dull or frustrating evening at home are contrasted, finally, with the excitement at Roosevelt Raceway and the oversize lettering of the word "Roosevelt." "C'mon, hop over to Roosevelt Raceway instead. Tonight may be your lucky night."

223

224 Florists' Telegraph Delivery

Automation has really set in when you can "say it with flowers" by number. The idea of making up thirty-nine flower arrangements and numbering them to facilitate ordering is an excellent one; the concept is well presented, showing individuals with different tastes ordering their favorite arrangements.

The arrangements are shown first, the special purpose next, and the individuals last—each one on the phone reading from the Flower Selection Guide. "Making people happy. Spreading holiday cheer. Bucking no crowds..." A final footnote advises that the FTD member guarantees quality and delivery or your money back.

225 Bell Telephone System

Again that vast network of affiliated companies, Bell Telephone System, presents a warm and human image. Read the copy.

The Telephone Pole

That Became

a Memorial

The cottage on Lincoln Street in Portland, Oregon, is shaded by graceful trees and covered with ivy.

Many years ago the owners, A. H. Feldman and his wife, remodeled the house to fit their dreams . . . and set out slips of ivy around it. And when their son, Danny, came along, he, too, liked to plant things and watch them grow. One day, when he was only nine, he took a handful of ivy slips and planted them at the base of the telephone pole that stood in front of the house.

Time passed . . . and the ivy grew, climbing slowly to the top of the pole. Like the ivy, Danny grew too. He finished high school, went to college. The war came along before he finished—and Danny joined the Army and went overseas. And there he gave his life for his country.

Not very long ago the overhead telephone lines were being removed from the poles on Lincoln Street. The ivy-covered telephone pole in front of the Feldman home was about to be taken down. Its work was done.

But, when the telephone crew arrived, Mrs. Feldman came out to meet them. "Couldn't it be left standing?" she asked. And then she told them about her son.

So the pole, although no longer needed, wasn't touched at all. At the request of the telephone company, the Portland City Council passed a special ordinance permitting the company to leave it standing. And there it is today, mantled in ivy, a living memorial to Sergeant Danny Feldman.

BELL TELEPHONE SYSTEM

TOWLE INTRODUCES CONTESSINA

Contessina.® A romantic new pattern in sterling silver. Inspired by the beautiful young countess who captured Michelangelo's heart when they met in the Medici gardens. (The Contessina shown here is played by Diane Cilento in a scene from "The Agony and the Ecstasy.")

Contessina: timeless as a renaissance garden.

"The Agony and the Ecstasy" is produced by 20th Century-Fox

32-piece service for eight, $264. ©TOWLE, 1965 Newburyport, Mass.

226 Towle

Contessina, the name of a pattern in flatware, was "Inspired by the beautiful young countess who captured Michelangelo's heart when they met in the Medici gardens." Rather than a silver pattern alone, the contessina, a human element, is introduced, by reflection in the bowl of a spoon. After flipping through pages of patterns, the reader is stopped by the face; then, perhaps, on to the pattern and, finally, to the copy to see the connection.

The countess (actress Diane Cilento) is in "The Agony and the Ecstasy," a movie about Michelangelo. The promotional tie-in is apropos; the sign-off: "Contessina: timeless as a renaissance garden."

© Towle

Cut this out and put it in bed next to your child.

Go ahead. Try it, if you have the stomach for it. Lay it next to your baby and let him play with it.

You can't?

Then you have a lot more imagination than some of the members of our House of Representatives.

They don't even think real rats are anything to worry about.

That's why they laughed when they killed a bill that would have given $40 million to our cities and states to help them pay for rat-control programs in our slums.

But the real shame is that they didn't even vote on the bill itself. They only voted on a rule that asked them to consider it.

And they voted 207 to 176 against it.

They had their reasons, of course. Economy was the most quoted one. They felt this country couldn't afford $40 million.

Yet they were told that rats cause us an estimated $900 million worth of damage each year.

Does that make economic sense?

They were also told that rats have killed more humans than all the generals in history put together. And that thousands of our children are bitten by rats each year—some killed or disfigured.

Does that make social sense? Especially when we're already spending Federal money to protect livestock and grains from rats?

Maybe those men have never lived in broken-down tenements where you could hear the rats scurrying inside the walls at night.

Maybe they've never seen a rat dash across their kitchen floor and into some hole under the sink when a light was snapped on.

Maybe. But then a lot of us have been that lucky. Does that excuse our ignoring those who haven't?

There are 90 million rats in this country. Where do you think they go when their slum homes are torn down?

They go into our finest hotels and restaurants; into modern apartment buildings, cellars, garages. They go everywhere and anywhere.

And they breed more rats.

That's why when our congressmen vote against all of us. Not just the poor people. But all of us.

Fortunately, there's still hope.

The vote was 207 to 176. That means if we can get just 16 men to change their votes when the bill comes up again, the tally will be 192 to 191—enough to pass it.

Below is a list of congressmen and how they voted.

If yours voted for the bill, write him and let him know you support him and anything he can do to change the minds of those who voted against it.

If yours voted against the bill, write and let him know you want him to change his vote.

Write to: Honorable_____

House of Representatives, Washington, D.C.

It's time we stopped giving rats equal rights with people.

227 Rat Control

This full-page newspaper ad showed a life-size rat menacing the reader. Repulsive as it is, it carried an emotion-packed visual/verbal impact, one that might move the reader to write his congressman urging reconsideration of the vetoed rat-control bill.

Following the headline, "Cut this out...," the copy reads: "Lay it next to your baby and let him play with it. You can't? Then you have a lot more imagination than some of the members of our House of Representatives."

PARTICIPATION

In just five minutes Wellington will move his cavalry into position on Charleroi Road.

And across the Channel while England waits, this Bracket Clock will watch the hour. Has measured the minutes since 1775. Is ticking now. On the shelf in our collection of beautiful and rare clocks. That tell the times. French Carriage Clocks that traveled with Victorians. Japanese Pillar Clocks that kept daylight savings time before Commodore Perry steamed into port. But hurry, see them all. The clock collection at Fields, Chicago. On First. There's nothing like it back home.

Marshall Field & Company

228

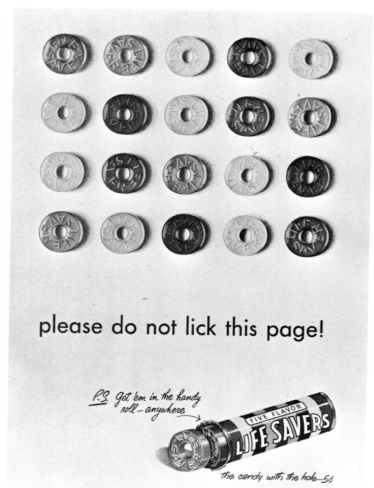

please do not lick this page!

P.S. Get 'em in the handy roll - anywhere

FIVE FLAVOR LIFE SAVERS

the candy with the hole...5¢

230

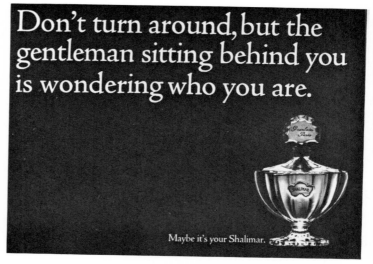

Don't turn around, but the gentleman sitting behind you is wondering who you are.

Maybe it's your Shalimar.

231

228 Marshall Field

Copy can transform a deserted road into a corridor of time. We are whisked back to the Duke of Wellington's era and, through the clock, we witness the impending Battle of Waterloo.

According to the copy, "across the Channel while England waits, this Bracket Clock will watch the hour. Has measured the minutes since 1775. Is ticking now." One indirectly related event has been singled out to dramatize the clock, an inanimate object, and make it human. As a witness, in existence for nearly two centuries, it links us with that time. The copy tells about the rest of the collection of rare old clocks to be seen on the shelves at Field's.

232 Goodall Fabrics

Pity the poor chair and the pains it goes through adjusting itself every time someone sits down. "Up, down, turn, twist, scrunch. Forty times a day and sometimes more, active office furniture takes a beating. But woven Goodall Fabrics love it."

This ad is selling fabrics that last. "Goodall fabrics are tailored expressly for the contract field. They're built to last without showing wear under the hardest use...in offices and theaters, buses and airplanes! ... engineered to the exacting standards of Burlington Industries."

229 Reader's Digest

When the reader sees the headline of this ad, he will say to himself: "I didn't do a thing. How am I contributing?" The subhead answers his question: "you have just registered an *exposure* for our advertisement" Again the reader asks himself: "How is this important?" In the second paragraph, he receives a fair answer: "No matter how many people buy this publication, they are worthless to us unless they open to *our ad* and read *our news.*"

Converse with the reader. Anticipate the questions the headline will bring to his mind, and give him time to absorb the words. Then surprise him by giving him a precise answer.

The slogan: "People have faith in Reader's Digest."

230 Life Savers

This advertiser received irate letters from mothers who caught their children actually licking the page!

The full-color ad showed the flavors of the candy sitting on the page. A soft shadow to the right of each piece helped to achieve the three-dimensional effect.

The germ for this idea was a billboard for ice cream saying, "Please do not lick this billboard." The copy was simply boiled down and used for the candy ad. The slogan is "the candy with the hole...5¢."

231 Shalimar

This ad appeared in a theater program. The sense of participation is very strong. The impulse to turn around and see who is sitting "behind you" is overpowering.

No matter what sort of person is actually sitting there, the ad will sooner or later induce a woman to turn around and satisfy her curiosity. The reason: "Maybe it's your Shalimar."

Guerlain

232 a

232 b

If you liked what you read before this page,

and if you like what comes after this page,

why not enjoy LIFE every week?

Send in the attached card and you'll receive LIFE for 20 weeks for just $1.99—about 10¢ copy. You'll enjoy LIFE's fresh, lively reporting each week plus the many special features coming up in the next 20 issues.

If the card is missing, just print your name and address on a postcard and send it to LIFE, Time-Life Building, Chicago, Illinois 60611. Send no money. We will bill you for $1.99 after your subscription begins.

Give your ad a sense of immediacy by talking directly to the reader. What better way of getting him to participate than being at his side as he reads your ad? In this way, the use of the space becomes an essential part of the ad.

The parts of the headline are divided and positioned with careful forethought, deliberately; the hands serve to create natural pauses. The momentary visual break lets the first part of the message sink in as the eye travels down to the beginning of the next phrase. The reader is almost bound to give an answer to the question, "why not enjoy LIFE every week?"

234 Trend Mills

The center of the little "start" button on the first page of this ad was red, and too tempting not to push (see following pages).

It is really a marvelous ad experience to see a piece of plain tufted carpet transformed before your eyes. You can almost hear the thud of the four-color presses. Those little "Ka-chunk, Ka-.chunks" lead and hold the eye momentarily, picture by picture, through the printing process. More words would be superfluous.

A very simple pattern was chosen, and just enough of it to show the four-color process. More of the pattern might have distracted the reader to the pattern rather than the process.

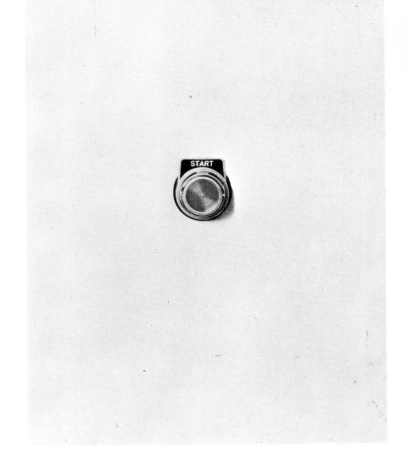

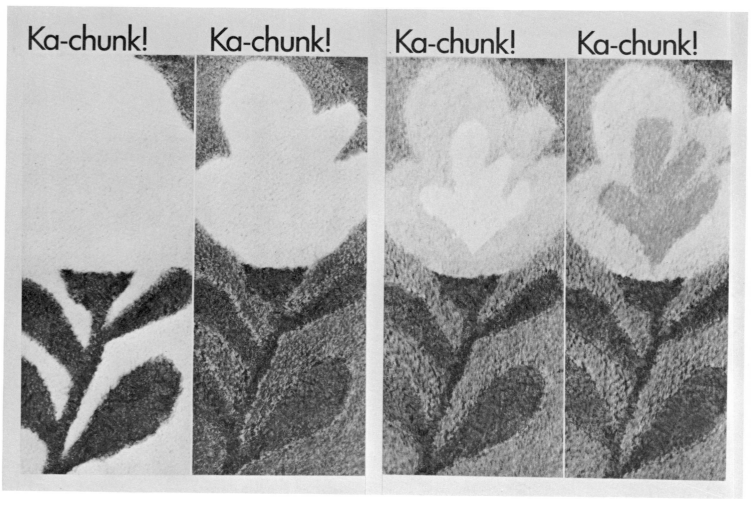

235 Ancient Age and Tupperware

Here is an example of two ads combining to make use of the same medium. Holding the page up to the light or turning to the next page is an essential procedure. Tupperware shows the "inside" first, while the Bourbon package. or the "outside," is shown. Both ads tell the reader what to do. They don't just sit there waiting for the reader to figure it out.

The Bourbon ad expresses the idea well by advising the reader to take an "x-ray peek," but forgot to put in a headline — or else saved it for the other side.

©Ancient Age Dist. Co.

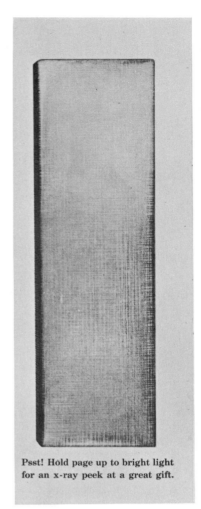

Psst! Hold page up to bright light for an x-ray peek at a great gift.

235 a

You have just watched a demonstration of Trend's new Auto-Dyeing* process in the world's first fully automated carpet mill.

The carpet industry has been strapped for too long with those same old designs in mass-produced tufted carpets.

But not Trend any more. We've turned on our new Auto-Dyeing machine, and now we can make tufted carpets in patterns and styles that always had to be woven. Geometrics, leaves, medallions, even Orientals. In as many as eight colors.

You name it, and Trend can make it in tufted. And you can sell it at a tufted price.

It works like this. Broadloom moves along the machine and one by one— ka-chunk, ka-chunk—colors are applied to the surface and pulled through the pile by a powerful vacuum. It all happens very fast with perfect register and detail.

A whirlwind tour

The Auto-Dyeing process is just one step in a completely new carpet-making operation that's full of news. This new mill at Rome, Georgia, has a production line that stretches 672 feet from the tufting machines to the wrapping machines. These operations and everything in between—cleaning, brushing, Auto-Dyeing, steaming, washing, drying, backing, shearing, rolling, cutting, weighing, inspecting—march along in one continuous high-speed line. Without blowing a fuse, we can make a roll of carpet every three minutes (in 12 or 15 foot widths).

The different machines on the line come from all parts of the world, including Rome, Georgia (because we built some of them ourselves). We put the parts together and pressed the button. And it works!

For the carpet retailer

They say you're not supposed to show pictures of your factory in advertising. But we've broken the rule this one time, because this particular factory happens to be big news for the carpet retailer.

Our new mill means we can do even more of what you like best—producing and delivering great carpets at great prices. With Auto-Dyeing, we can bring you the widest selection of patterns and styles you've ever seen in tufteds.

It goes to show what you can do with a few well-placed ka-chunks.

*Registration pending

TREND MILLS

Trend Mills, Inc., P.O. Box 162, Rome, Georgia • New York, Chicago, Plainville, Los Angeles, San Francisco, Dallas, Atlanta

14   *June 1965* • Modern Floor Coverings

What's the secret that keeps them fresh for days? Just hold this page up to the light!

Great holiday gift idea! This magnificent decanter plus the gold gift wrap shown on the back of this page — both yours at no extra cost.

If you can give a better bourbon . . . give it!

KENTUCKY STRAIGHT BOURBON WHISKEY • 86 PROOF • ©ANCIENT AGE DIST. CO., FRANKFORT, KY.

235 b

It's Tupperware that does the trick — and a very wonderful trick it is! Just imagine: For days and days, moist foods stay moist, crisp foods crisp, dry foods dry. Everything stays delicious (and nutritious) in these famous plastic containers. And famous, too, are the delightful home parties where Tupperware is demonstrated and sold. Have a party. And make it soon!

Call local Tupperware distributor, listed in Yellow Pages under Housewares or Plastics, for dealer's name. Or write Tupperware, Dept. J-1, Orlando, Florida. **TUPPERWARE**

72

235 d

236 Glissando

To convey the idea that a new lipstick, Glissando, by DuBarry, has become fashionable in a fabric and in a dress line as well, what could have been simpler than to superimpose the lipstick on a fold-down, and then convert that into a dress? (See following right-hand page.)

The copy ends: "Glissando...the lipstick that inspired a fashion...the lipstick that is fashion!"

©DuBarry

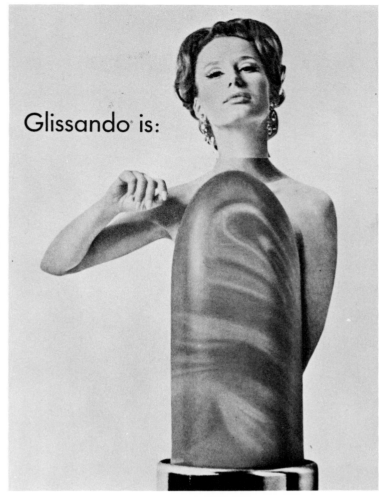

Glissando is:

236 a

The disadvantages of advertising Benson & Hedges 100's.

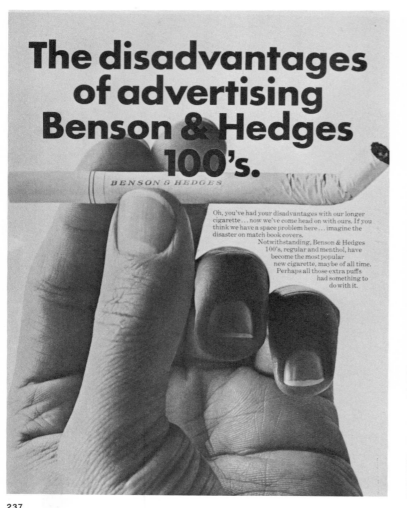

Oh, you've had your disadvantages with our longer cigarette...now we've come head on with ours. If you think we have a space problem here...imagine the disaster on match book covers.

Notwithstanding, Benson & Hedges 100's, regular and menthol, have become the most popular new cigarette, maybe of all time. Perhaps all those extra puffs had something to do with it.

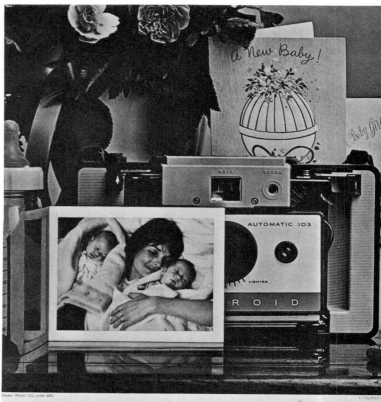

Shown: Model 103, under $85.

You can get color prints like this in 60 seconds with a Polaroid Color Pack Camera. Is there any other way to take pictures?

Prices start at under $60.

Growth.

In architecture, you grow when you're successful. In advertising, you grow when you're successful, too. And the more a magazine grows, the more its advertisers do.

The growth of ad pages in Progressive Architecture for January-through-April this year is the largest in architecture by far: up 169 pages, or 33.7%.

In growth, as in circulation, the big one is **P/A**

Progressive Architecture, a Reinhold publication, 430 Park Avenue, New York, N.Y. 10022, MUrray Hill 8-8600 (area code 212)

237 Benson & Hedges

In this ad, the cigarette is bent at the tip because the new Benson & Hedges 100 is too long to fit even a full page of a newspaper. This campaign played up with humor the "disadvantages" of the longer cigarette. TV commercials backed it up, devising various ludicrous situations.

Since the headline mentions the name of the product and the brand name is on the cigarette itself, there is no logo. Nor was it necessary to show the cigarette pack.

238 Polaroid

This bedside setting with significant props — flowers, birthday cards, and especially the snapshot of the young mother with her newborn twins — will come as a revelation to some readers. Many people still are unaware of the miracle of getting finished color prints in one minute, black-and-white in ten seconds.

The headline asks, "Is there any other way to take pictures?"

239 Progressive Architecture

Here a page of the medium itself is used to contain the cramped figure. The posture is well designed; however, if the dark areas of the suit had been filled in with solid black, it would have made an even more interesting abstraction.

Glissando is:

a lipstick
a fabric
a fashion.

The whole beautiful concept originated when DuBarry created Glissando...the never-before, never-dreamed-of lipstick. Not just one color but a wonderful whirl of separate colors... separate hues that fuse as one on your lips. Then (it had to happen!) Glissando caught on like wildfire...ignited a whole new fashion. The lipstick became a misty-soft fabric (ours alone)...colors and pattern inspired by the Glissando whirl and swirl. Then a gown...all motion...all grace... designed to move in the marvelous world you move in. Glissando...the lipstick that inspired a fashion... the lipstick that is fashion!

Glissando by DuBarry
the most elegant name in cosmetics

There's no stopping Glissando! So unique...so exciting... it inspired the Glissando original by Malcolm Starr.

©DuBarry, 1966

236 b

The End
after Six
22ND & MARKET STS., PHILA. 1290 AVENUE OF THE AMERICAS, NYC

240

HELLO, NEW YORK!
HELLO, BROADWAY!
HELLO, GREAT NECK!
HELLO, STATEN ISLAND!
HELLO, SCARSDALE!
HELLO, BROOKLYN!
HELLO, THE BRONX!
"Come on down" to Florida on the new Northeast Airlines!
Jim Dooley says "come on down!"
Chilly up there? Come on down! Think what a little Miami sunshine would do for you right now!
Have a ball getting here, too. On the new Northeast Airlines. This year, Northeast is doing even more to make you feel like a guest, not just a passenger.
The superb gourmet food and refreshing beverages on Northeast are just like you get in Miami's top restaurants. You'll be pampered by the prettiest gals in the sky—those Northeast stewardesses in their chic new Florida Blue uniforms.
You'll get to the beach faster, thanks to speeded up baggage delivery.
We've increased our service with the brand-newest jets to Florida. And now you can charge your Northeast trip on American Express, Carte Blanche, Diners Club or Air Travel card. So come on down. Call a Travel Agent or Northeast Airlines at TW 7-1000.
55 non-stop flights per week to Miami/Ft. Lauderdale.
NORTHEAST AIRLINES

241

"It's for you, dear..."

THE JOYOUS SEASON

continued from page 45

any sense at all until Daddy said, "He means you talk too much, kid." I also suffer from something known as "total recall." Daddy had what seemed to me a very good suggestion when he said, "Couldn't Kerry just shut up?" But the school psychiatrist said that would cause a lot of repressions and like that and that my "garrulity should be harnessed and channeled into verbal productivity." Anyway, I'm supposed to talk until I run out of things to say. Now back to last Christmas.

I was so doggone bushed that I almost told her there wasn't any Santa Claus and to go back to bed until morning. But like Gran, who is Mom's mother, says, we all try to "keep her simple faith alive." Besides, Maxl, our dog, was licking my ear, and by the time I got them both off me I was wide awake.

So I got up and we went into the living room, which was also dark except for the Christmas tree, flickering away in front of the middle window. Our Christmas trees are different each year—usually to match whatever color the room happens to be. This year it had nothing but green ornaments and millions of little white lights going off and on at different times like a sign in Times Square. I mean it would drive you crazy to look at it for more than a couple of minutes, but like Ga-ga, who is Daddy's mother, said, it was very chic.

There were about a million packages under the tree that hadn't been there the night before, but they were all wrapped up, and in our house a wrapped-up package or a sealed envelope always meant "Hands off!"

Our stockings were hanging over the fireplace where Daddy had taped them (it's very difficult to drive a nail into a marble mantel) before he and Mom went off to their Christmas Eve bash, only now the stockings were full instead of empty. So, to keep Missy's simple faith alive, I put on a big act about how wonderful it was that Jolly Old Saint Nick had parked his sleigh up on top of the Cushings' penthouse, carefully avoiding the television aerials, and made his jolly old way through all the vents and the elevator works with a sack full of junk and right down the chimney to dear old Sixteen East, going "Ho ho ho" every inch of the way. Some kids will swallow *anything*.

Well, the stockings weren't filled with much except some candy and little things from the five-and-ten. Besides, Missy has a very small foot, so it didn't take her long to go through all that stuff and break most of it. It wasn't even six A.M., and Missy was itching to get at the real swag under the tree.

"Well, what time is it *now?*" Missy said.

"Five minutes till six."

"Shouldn't they be getting *up?*"

"No, they shouldn't, for cripes sake."

Missy was getting so het up that I finally took pity on her. "You can open this one and that will have to hold you till everybody else gets up."

"From Santy Claus?"

"It's from me! I bought it with my own money. I wrapped it myself too."

"It looks it," Missy said.

Well, maybe it wasn't the prettiest package under the tree, but when Missy opened it, she sang a different tune. It was a genuine Martian Outer Space Squirt Gun. It holds a pint of water and, depending on which knob you turn, shoots either a hundred Instant Locomotor-Paralysis Rays or one full-pint Gamma Death Ray, which means curtains for Earth Mortals.

"Gee, Kerry, it's *beautiful!*" I could tell that even Missy was impressed. "Can I work it now?"

"Not in the apartment. Remember that time with the glass clock and the Johnny Reb Cannon?"

That shook her, but not enough.

"Well, at least show me how to fill it."

The Martian Outer Space Squirt Gun comes with a full set of instructions, but they're kind of complicated and Missy can only read beer signs and cigarette packages and "Run, Jack! Jump, Jane!" and the kind of stuff they teach in the first grade at Miss Farthingale's.

"OK," I said, "we'll fill it, but don't shoot it at anything except Daddy's shower and *don't* make any noise."

We went to Daddy's bathroom, which is all tile and positively leakproof (except the time Daddy let his tub run over) and has a great big shower stall with lots of water spouts that get you in terrible places if you don't watch out. I filled the squirt gun in the washbasin, aimed and fired half a dozen Instant Locomotor-Paralysis Rays into the shower stall right at heart level. Pow, pow, pow, pow, pow, *pow!* Let me tell you, that Martian Outer Space gun was everything they claimed it was on TV. It sent out a fine spray that hit the wall so hard it splashed halfway back into the bathroom.

"Now let me try, Kerry," Missy said.

"Be my guest, kid, it's your gun."

Well Missy's aim wasn't all it should have been, like with the Johnny Reb Cannon two Christmases ago, but it made five or six beautiful splashes right into the shower stall.

"Now let's fill it all the way up again and try the full-pint Gamma Death Ray," I said. Hell, I was just trying to keep Missy quiet until Mom and Daddy woke up.

Missy ran the cold water full tilt and reloaded. But when she tried to turn the faucet off she knocked over Daddy's shaving bowl. It's some kind of plastic and unbreakable, but it made a terrible racket when it hit the tile floor. There was a groan from the bedroom.

"Wh-who's there?" Daddy moaned.

"Shhhhhhh," I said to Missy and switched off the lights. The sun was beginning to come up over the East River and a little bit of gray dawn filtered in through the bathroom window—just about enough so that you could see your hand in front of your face.

There've been a lot of robberies in our neighborhood over the past year. (Only last week some fool dame left half a million bucks' worth of diamonds on top of her dressing table, like a cook's-night-out supper, and a burglar came in, helped himself and walked right out.) Anyhow, Daddy keeps this great big revolver left over from the Army in the drawer by his side of the bed, and the next thing we knew, the door opened and there he was standing stark naked pointing the gun right over our heads at his reflection in the bathroom mirror.

"Daddy . . ." I started to say. A shot rang out and the mirror busted into a million pieces. Then Missy did *something* with her squirt gun, and Daddy got it up and down his whole front with a full pint of ice-cold Gamma Death Ray. There was a bellow like he'd grabbed a live wire and then a stream of language

like even *I* had never heard. Then he made a lunge for us, and *then* there was even a worse yell and worse language because he'd cut both bare feet on all that broken mirror.

By that time Mom was up struggling into her robe and saying, "Darling, what's the matter?" Missy went into hysterics, and I was so confused I didn't know whether to laugh or to cry. I laughed. It was the wrong choice.

Well, what happened right after all that is still too painful even to think about. The lights went on. Daddy took one look to see that we were OK. We were. I got a good one across the side of the head, and Missy got such a crack on the rear end that she forgot to have hysterics and *just* plain cried. Then Daddy turned all gray and went staggering back toward the bed, leaving a trail of bloody footprints on the white rug and clutching his head like he was dying. By then Mom was awake enough to start putting the whole picture together.

From what the other guys at school tell me about *their* parents, Mom and Dad got along like two peas in a pod most of the time. But this wasn't one of the times.

"My God, there's blood all over the place. What are you doing with that *gun?*"

"Only trying to protect my family."

"*Protect* them? You nearly killed the children! Kerry, Melissa! Tell Mother! Are you all right?"

"If those two don't get out of here I'm just as likely to kill them as not."

"You great, drunken oaf! Look what you've done. The whole room a shambles and company coming. Just *look* at the place!"

In addition to the blood and the water and the broken glass, the bedroom looked the way it does when Daddy has a Difficult Night and is about to have a worse day. Usually he's very neat and tidy, like an architect ought to be, with his clothes all hung up and trees in his shoes and his dirty linen put in the laundry hamper.

But today was One of Those Mornings. His evening clothes were partly on the chaise longue, partly on the floor. His shirt was draped over a chair with the studs still in it. One shoe had been kicked off near the door and the other one was almost under the bed with the socks scattered in between. His tie was over a lampshade and his underwear crumpled up on the desk. And, what with Mom's new evening dress rolled up like a sleeping bag on her dressing table instead of out of sight in her dressing room, it didn't take me long to get the general idea.

Then Mom said in that kindly cold tone of voice, "De-ar, don't you think you might try to get a little help with your drinking problem? There was a Doctor Gumbiner who helped Liz's first husband before he killed himself. . . ."

"Liz's *first* husband? Well, if that poor guy drank, it was because Liz drove him to it. And if your great chum Liz would serve something decent instead of her hot Swedish *Glögg* that nobody ——"

"*I* thought it was delicious."

"So I noticed."

"And it didn't seem to me that *you* were being force-fed. I mean social drinking is one thing, but when it gets to the point of having hallucinations and shooting at the children ——"

"I *didn't* fire at the children. I thought it was a prowler. What were they doing in my bathroom anyway?"

"What anyone would be doing in a bathroom."

"They've got their own bathroom to use. Why don't they?"

"And look at you! You're soaking wet. Liz told me what Doctor Gumbiner said about those terrible sweats ——"

"Sweat, hell. I'm freezing to death."

"*And* chills. One of the first signs of acute alcoholism ——"

"Alcoholism! One of those brats sprayed me with a damned hose."

"A *hose?* Now where would they get a hose? I really think you're on the verge of delirium tremens, darling, honestly I do. And would you look at what you've done to my brand-new rug!"

"*Your* rug? Who paid for it?"

"Nobody, as yet. And that reminds me, a man from the credit department at ——"

"Oh, shut up about it!"

Since she hadn't attracted much of an audience, Missy had stopped crying and wiped her tears on the sleeve of her robe. Now she took advantage of the silence to do things up brown. "Merry Christmas, Mommy! Merry Christmas, Daddy!" Missy yelled. "Look what Kerry gave me. It's a genuine Martian Outer Space Gun." I had thought that the squirt gun had fired its full charge at Daddy in the bathroom doorway, but I was wrong. There was just enough water left in it to do a little more damage. Missy raised the gun proudly and Mom got it full in the face.

An hour or so later, with the Martian Outer Space Gun under lock and key, we were all in the living room to see what Santa Claus had brought. In other years Mom and Daddy used to sit on the floor beside the tree in their robes and slippers drinking coffee while Daddy read out the names and passed the presents around. This year Daddy couldn't get his slippers on for all the Band-Aids on the soles of his feet, and he was drinking a brandy-and-soda. "Do you think that's entirely wise?" Mom asked.

"You're damned right I do, and if you had any sense you'd join me. You must feel fierce."

"Perhaps. But *someone* has to think about the children's Christmas. Besides, your mother is coming to lunch."

"Isn't yours? *And* your idiot brother?"

Mom suddenly got very interested in a stuffed giraffe her friend Liz had sent to Missy. It was big, I'll say that for it, but not all that fascinating.

The Christmas presents were much fancier than usual—especially the ones Daddy gave Mom and vice versa. I guess it must have had something to do with the big new building he designed. Daddy gave Mom a green ring and a brown fur jacket and a gallon of some kind of French perfume and quite a lot of other stuff. She gave him a whole new set of drafting instruments in a cool leather case and a kind of machine to make copies of plans right at home and some spiffy books on architecture and a couple of special golf clubs and a new squash racket. They said thank you very politely, but they didn't seem to like the stuff very much, fancy as it all was.

My haul was the usual run of stuff—a few things I'd asked for and a lot of things I hadn't. Gran gave me a big old book on the blood lines in her family and she'd written, "Kerrington—This is so you'll know who your ancestors were—at least on your mother's side," on the flyleaf so I couldn't take it back and turn it in on

(continued)

"Thanks -- I'll take it here, honey..."
Talk About A Bargain!
A second phone costs only a fraction more a month than the first . . . but gives you twice as much telephone convenience . . . and saves you many steps and minutes every day.
To order an extension phone for bedroom, kitchen or any location—in your choice of color and style—just call the Business Office or ask your telephone man.
Bell System
American Telephone and Telegraph Co. and Associated Companies

242

240 After Six

This ad appeared on the inside back cover of a men's magazine. This is excellent positioning and, in this case, a vital one for the ad's success. One line of copy amplifies the headline and adds its own fun: "Blind dates, summer festivals, wedding receptions, cruises or coronations. Everything turns out better in The End with after-six formal wear by Rudofker." The logo is part of the sentence.

Rudofker

243 Breck

In this case the medium creates a pause as the copywriter talks to the reader. The reader has said "no" if she has turned the page, and the ad (see following page) reminds her to think twice before passing up this offer. The ad has communicated twice (maybe three times, if the reader turns back). That is good exposure for any ad at one reading.

243 a

241 Northeast Airlines

The excitement, the warm sunshine, the beach — all this was well presented on TV for the airline by announcer Jim Dooley. The "come on down" theme stressed all the enjoyment missing from the lives of those in the north-eastern sector of the United States. The implication is that if your neighbor can go to Florida for a vacation, so can you. "Neighbors" from various boroughs and suburbs of New York sent their regards back home, localizing the ad appeal.

242 Bell System

Maybe it isn't good manners to reach across a table, but calling across a spread greatly increases the visual size, or space, of the ad. The wife manages to bring her husband to the phone without shouting At the same time, all that unpaid-for space — the reading matter in the center of the magazine layout — is acquired.

The wife is shown close-up, in part one of the ad; her husband would have had to make a mad dash for the kitchen if he hadn't had the extension phone in the bedroom.

The subhead is: "Talk about a bargain!...A *second* phone...saves you many steps and minutes every day "

American Telephone & Telegraph

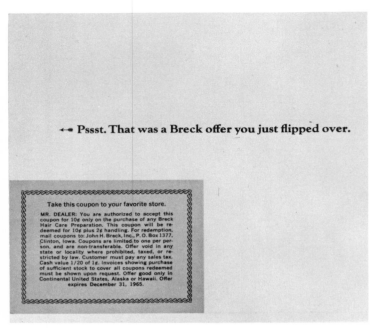

← Pssst. That was a Breck offer you just flipped over.

Take this coupon to your favorite store.
MR. DEALER: You are authorized to accept this coupon for 10¢ only on the purchase of any Breck Hair Care Preparation. This coupon will be redeemed for 10¢ plus 2¢ handling. For redemption, mail coupons to: John H. Breck, Inc., P. O. Box 1377, Clinton, Iowa. Coupons are limited to one per person, and are non-transferable. Offer void in any state or locality where prohibited, taxed, or restricted by law. Customer must pay any sales tax. Cash value 1/20 of 1¢. Invoices showing purchase of sufficient stock to cover all coupons redeemed must be shown upon request. Offer good only in Continental United States, Alaska or Hawaii. Offer expires December 31, 1965.

243 b

244 Glissando

Three different shades of lipstick were shown on models on three separate, consecutive right-hand pages.

The note near the dotted line says, "Tear here, dear." The page could be held up over the reader's chin and she could, by looking in a mirror, see herself with either plunging neckline or one of the other styles. The model is holding up the shade of lipstick she has on, and the matching nail polish. A woman could tell at once which shade of lipstick she likes by following the instructions hidden in the copy: "What do your eyes tell you when you hold this page over your lips?" But because the headline doesn't mention anything about tearing out the page or holding it up to a mirror, many readers who didn't read the copy missed the point altogether.

© DuBarry

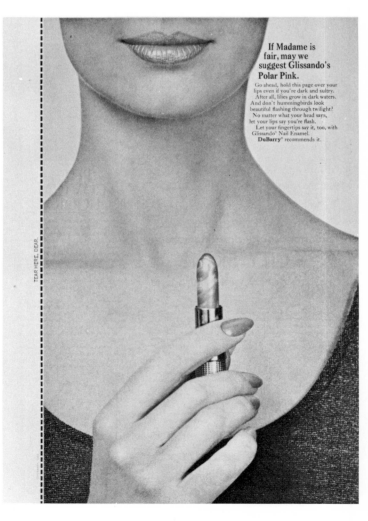

244 a

244 b

Madame is wearing black this evening? She must try on Glissando's Iced Poppy.

What do your eyes tell you when you hold this page over your lips? Too marvelous? The way these new Glissando® lipsticks and nail enamels pick up light, even the moon will give you away. And DuBarry can't help you then.

DuBarry®

the most elegant name in cosmetics

244 c

Don't read this before going to bed

(You may not sleep)

This is the sad, sad story of the man who left no stone unturned—except one.

He went to bed just as you will do tonight. He awoke hale and hearty—and on the brink of ruin.

He had every kind of insurance known to man. Fire insurance, use and occupancy insurance, liability insurance, and casualty. **Protected against every loss—except one!**

His office was in a *"fireproof"* building. It conformed with every fire law. It was as well protected night and day as the Pentagon. And like the Pentagon, where fire destroyed 14 truckloads of valuable papers, *he had a fire!*

Here's what his business lost through his neglect:

Their customer list and prospect file.

All current personnel records.

The company's current legal correspondence and tax records.

All current orders, quotations and correspondence.

The accounts receivable records.

His own income tax records, data and checks; and those of his associates.

This tragedy is typical of scores. In one, a million dollar "fireproof" building fire, the walls and floors of the building remained standing, but thousands of irreplaceable records in steel files were burned to ashes.

In another "fireproof" building, housing a dozen firms in the title, real estate and insurance business, fire destroyed all of the essential records of these businesses that were filed in non-insulated steel files.

records will be vault-safe, and always ready for instant use, even after a fire. Your records will be fire-protected not just at night but also during the daytime hours when most fires (actually 58% of them) occur. Shaw-Walker Fire-Files have a **34-year successful record of performance!**

Fire-Files also *pay their cost* by saving time and space. Hours are saved and so is floor space because you eliminate entirely the need for housing records in separate safes or vaults.

If these words fail to convince you, perhaps this one statistic will: 93% of the businesses that are victims of a fire are so seriously handicapped that 43% of them fail. And only the 7% with Fire-File protection carry on without costly delay. To ignore these facts is business neglect of the first order.

All the information on this subject that any business needs is available for the asking . . . in the famous 248-page Shaw-Walker "Office Guide," now in its 12th edition. Write for it. A program of fire protection for your essential records can be started for less than $200.

N.B. Many businessmen have Shaw-Walker Fire-Files at home, *not only for their own private papers but also to protect stamp or coin collections, keepsakes, rare books, document collections and other valuables.*

SHAW-WALKER

Muskegon 66, Michigan
Largest Exclusive Makers of Office Equipment
Representatives Everywhere

Moral: In Shaw-Walker Fire-Files your

245

The Parker touch

Try it! Touch it to any writing surface. New ball point writes a clear, dark line!

This is good news—especially if you've had trouble with ball points that balk at writing on this or that kind of paper. With finer craftsmanship and improved ink, Parker has developed the Jotter—a ball point that lets *you* decide where it will write. And that's anywhere!

A sure touch is only one of the Jotter's virtues. With *a choice of four point sizes* from broad to extra fine, it's the only ball point that writes *your* way. A

single cartridge will write nearly 100,000 words! And the new Parker "51" Jotter has no telltale ball point button. Its handsome *sliding cap* extends and retracts the point.

Stop at the nearest pen counter and ask to see and try this remarkable new Parker "51" Jotter ball point. With Lustraloy cap, $5.00; gold-filled cap (illustrated) $8.75. Other Jotter ball points, $2.95 up.

Parker Jotter
ball point pens
from $2.95

246

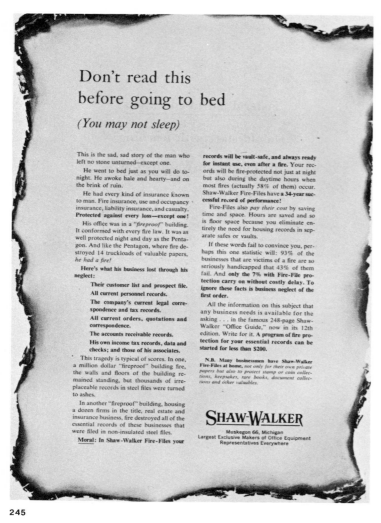

This is Braille. It says:

"You've got only one pair of eyes. Have them examined once a year."

Better Vision Institute.

247

248

245 Shaw-Walker

This ad, addressed to businessmen, must have
produced an increase of inquiries about Shaw-
Walker office Fire-Files. Its charred edges tell
you that this ad has to do with fire; the effect
is to instill the fear of fire.

The copy tells about one businessman who
"went to bed just as you will do tonight: He
awoke hale and hearty — and on the brink of
ruin." The copy tells you further that his office
building was "fireproof," but "like the Pentagon,
where fire destroyed 14 truckloads of valuable
papers, he had a fire!"

More fears are instilled by the climax in the
story: 43% of the businesses that have had fires
fail. After all this, an owner of a company might
really not get any sleep.

246 Parker Jotter

When many ball point pens were still shoddy and
inferior to fountain pens, the biggest problem
was that they blotted. Furthermore, they didn't
take to all surfaces because the ball wouldn't
start easily on some.

Different kinds of paper are shown in the ad —
a postcard, a paper bag, a check, cleansing
tissue, a scrap of tablecloth, a snapshot. These
are tough surfaces to write on with any pen.
An ordinary ball point might not work at all. The
reader's eye can skim across the different
surfaces as he reads the headline, which claims
the Parker Jotter will write on all of them.

The pen is shown upside down — unusual
placement for a product — and seems to be
lying on a desk in front of the reader. The cast
shadow establishes this as another trompe l'oeil.

©Parker Pen Co.

247 Better Vision Institute

In this ad, the reader is made vividly aware of
how a blind person has to read. The cross-
lighting used in photographing the page gives
those raised braille dots long shadows to
emphasize the poignant reality of their purpose.
The copy quite simply says: "You've got only
one pair of eyes. Have them examined once a
year."

249 Loving Care

Women with graying hair who do not wish to
change their natural hair color are tempted to
use this Loving Care hair color lotion which
promises a ten-years-younger you. "Has your
hair aged faster than you have?" the copy asks
(see following right-hand page), then explains
that the lotion "seeks out the gray and colors it
young again without changing your natural hair
color."

The question in the headline "Why not try a
little Loving Care and see!" is answered when
the left-hand page flap is opened and discloses
the gray-haired husband embracing his young
wife. Surprise, on opening the flap, is total; the
reader is actually startled by the newcomer in
the picture.

The caption under the package: "Hairdressers
agree it's a fountain of youth for graying hair."
The slogan: "Hate that gray? Wash it away!"

©Clairol

248 Sealtest

Setting the ice cream and spoon and the package on the paper gives the reader a sense of
participation. This feeling was intensified by the
contrast between the black-and-white newspaper
and the full-color ice cream.

This, of course, is a mock-up of a newspaper
with headlines, subheads and type set in
columns. But the news is all about ice cream —
Sealtest. The copy extols Sealtest ice cream
from every angle. It hints, too, that the checkerboard is not merely a surface pattern, but goes
right through the bricks. Subtle shadows
increase the impression of the three-dimensional
objects.

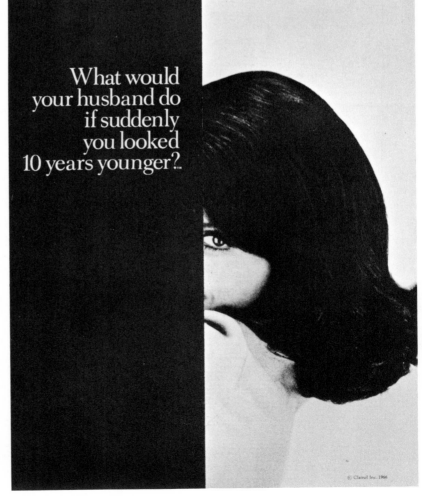

249 a

250 a

250 b

250 c

250 d

In this section, actually a 16-page brochure, the ad itself is a top-notch idea for selling many Aurora models, not only those pictured in the section, but also Aurora hobby kits. Stories presented on the cover are followed up well on the inside. The illusion of a color comic section held, although about half of it was in black-and-white.

However, it was the medium chosen for the insertion of this ad — the Sunday *New York Times* — that made it a stopper and got it the exceptional acclaim it deserves.

The New York Times is a conservative newspaper. It never runs comic strips. To find there a colorful section with Superman and other familiar characters comes as a delicious shock. The comic strip stories themselves lead nicely into the selling copy for Aurora models.

SUPER-STICK

PATENTS PENDING

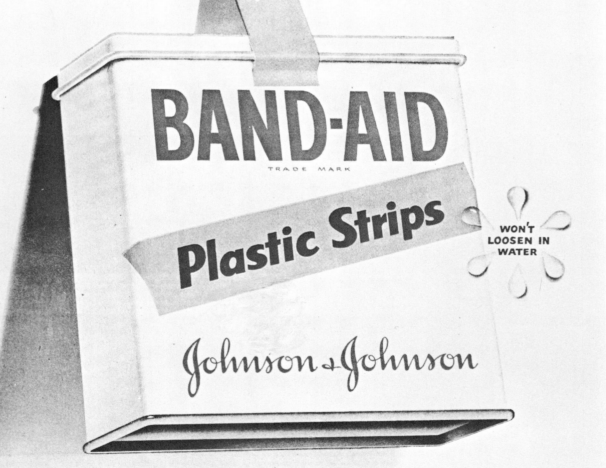

BAND-AID
TRADE MARK

Plastic Strips

WON'T LOOSEN IN WATER

Johnson & Johnson

Now with **SUPER-STICK**. They stick better, protect better. Won't loosen in water.

This *trompe-l'oeil* package almost hangs off
the page because of the severe shadow on the
"wall" of the page. The Band-Aid, stuck to the
lettering, plays up the effect that the tin stuck
to the page.

At the right-hand side of the page are droplets
of water, surrounding a bit of copy: "won't loosen
in water." The difficulty with this is that, if the
tin is three-dimensional and resting on the page,
how could the droplets rest on the tin and on
the page as well? This confuses the visual
planes.

The reason why Super-Stick makes Band-Aids
better is hidden in the one line of copy at the
bottom: "They stick better, protect better."

Johnson & Johnson

252 Mead Papers

Using the principle of participation (to invite the
reader to use what he usually has with him), this
trompe-l'oeil color print of a hand stands out as
close to real when printed on Mead paper. The
shadow of the hand achieves the three-dimensional effect.

On the reverse side (see following page) the
fingerprints are shown, with the subhead: "Hands
down. Mead Printflex Enamel's a winner."

Since the Mead paper this insert was printed
on is the product to be sold, the copy invites the
reader to feel how smooth it is and to look at
its brilliant whiteness.

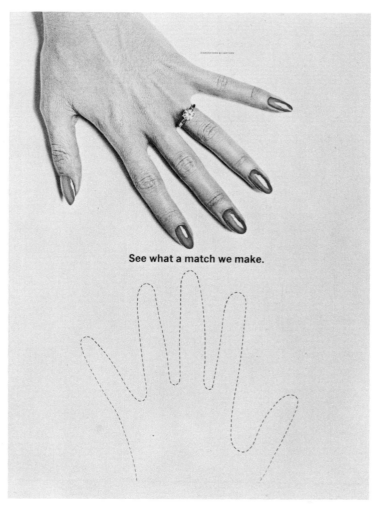

See what a match we make.

MEAD *papers*

Run your fingers across its surface. Feel how smooth and even it is. Take a good look at the white of it. Pretty brilliant. All this, along with excellent ink receptivity and rapid ink drying. That's why, with Mead Printflex Offset and Letterpress Enamels and their matching Coated Covers, you always get the depth and contrast, the full rich color essential for finest quality reproduction. Take it in hand for your next folder, manual or booklet. It's readily available through your local Mead Merchant.

Mead Papers, a division of The Mead Corporation, Dayton, Ohio 45402   Lithographed on Mead Printflex Offset Enamel, Dull Finish, 100 lb.

Hands down, Mead Printflex Enamel's a winner.

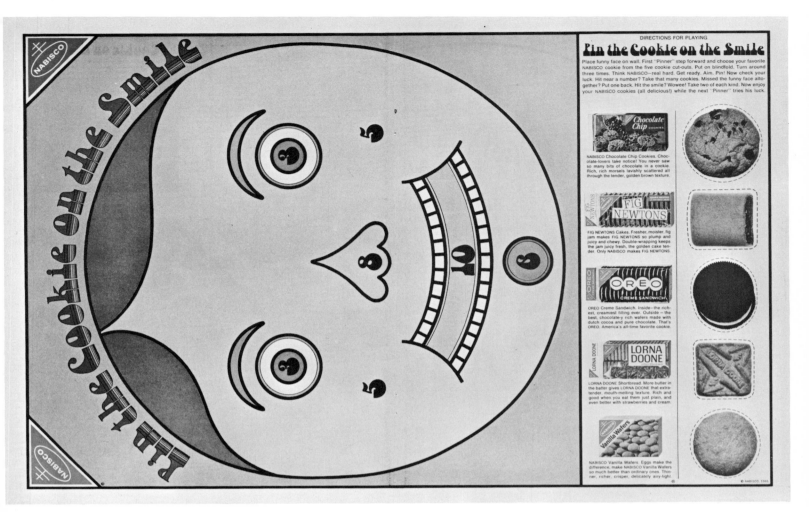

255 Itkin Bros.

Rather than make up new ads to eliminate the listed items that were sold the previous day, these newspaper ads, running on consecutive days, simply showed the items crossed out and let the reader see for himself the progress of the "Sorry Sale." The idea was successful and has since been used a number of times by the advertiser.

It is human to procrastinate. People also tend to believe that they can buy what they want when they want it, at the price they want to pay. This ad convinced them otherwise on the second day it ran. Notice that, proportionately, most sales were made on the last day, after the stampede had begun.

The last ad is an "I-told-you-so," and a warning to buy at the beginning of the next "Sorry Sale."

256 California Fashion Creators

On insert ads you can use a tip-on bag, cellophane it in front to show the contents (see following right-hand page) and thereby induce the reader actually to do the puzzle. It's not complicated, so it shouldn't take more than a minute.

As the reader tries to match the pieces, he also reads the clues for matching them, that is, the copy on the puzzle pieces. A number of impressions are thus conveyed for both the ad and the puzzle parts. Should the information on the puzzle be repeated in case the reader doesn't want to do the puzzle?

The trade reader would know what's going on at Palm Springs Holiday Inn, but it would be wise to include, for a newcomer, as much information as possible about the fashion show.

IF YOU ARE

PUZZLED ABOUT SPRING?

PUT THE SUN TOGETHER · DISCOVER THE ANSWER

OCTOBER 23·24·25
AT PALM SPRINGS
HOLIDAY INN

SPONSORED BY CALIFORNIA FASHION CREATORS. 110 E. 9TH ST., LOS ANGELES 15, CALIF.

McCALL'S SPORTSWEAR MERCHANDISER, OCTOBER 1965   23

2 1965 VONDA KAY VAN DYKE ☐ 1964 DONNA AXUM ☐ 1963 JACQUELYN MAYER ☐ 1962 MARIA FLETCHER ☐ 1961 NANCY FLEMING

1   2 BONUS GIVEAWAY: THIS BABY IS VONDA KAY VAN DYKE.   3   4   5

Enter the Pepsi-Cola
Miss America
"Matching Picture"
Contest!

Match Miss Americas with their baby pictures! Win thousands of prizes!

How good are you at spotting resemblances? Use your skill and judgment and match each Miss America with her baby picture. It's interesting—and fun! To help make you a winner, here's one of the answers to the "Matching Picture" Contest.

BONUS GIVEAWAY
Vonda Kay Van Dyke is Baby #2
Now match the others! Send in your completed Entry Blank today. Free Entry Blanks are available wherever Pepsi-Cola Company products are sold. Hurry—enter now! Contest open for limited time only.

1st PRIZE—$10,000 Scholarship!
A golden opportunity! Pick your favorite career and study at the school or schools of your choice! Or $10,000 in cash, if preferred.

2nd PRIZE
New Oldsmobile Cutlass Convertible with powerful 315-HP, V-8 engine and extras! Plus a free year's supply of auto equipment and services (worth $500).

3rd PRIZES
20 Frigidaire Refrigerator-Freezers. Frost-free 12 cu. ft.—each filled with $300 worth of food that you select!

2,035 4th PRIZES
2,035 Gift Certificates worth a total of $80,000, redeemable where you buy Pepsi-Cola Company products. Values range from $25 to $500 each!

OFFICIAL ENTRY BLANK

Fill in the blanks below, placing the numbers of the baby pictures next to the name of the Miss Americas to which they correspond. (To get you started, we have correctly placed the number 2 next to Vonda Kay Van Dyke.) Then enclose six corks from under the caps of any Pepsi-Cola Company product (DO NOT MAIL BOTTLE CAPS) or enclose six plain pieces of paper on which you have hand-printed "Pepsi-Cola" in plain block letters and mail to: "MATCHING PICTURE" CONTEST, Box 474, New York, N.Y. 10046.

BONUS GIVEAWAY:
☐ 1965 Vonda Kay Van Dyke ☐ 1962 Maria Fletcher
☐ 1963 Jacquelyn Mayer ☐ 1961 Nancy Fleming

NAME
ADDRESS
CITY   STATE   ZIP CODE
DEALER'S NAME
DEALER'S ADDRESS

photo quiz
How many of our "salesmen" do you recognize?

Davis Holbrook and Harper

MEMPHIS

30/30

M$M

1. **Major Mudd** . . . typical of the exciting local personalities developed by WNAC-TV Boston, for greater audience acceptance and advertising impact.

2. **The Yankee Network** . . . with radio stations in all major New England markets, for efficient advertiser saturation of the entire 6-state area.

3. **Beethoven** . . . representative of WGMS radio Washington, D.C., programming classical music and news to the best educated, most influential audience in America.

4. **Davis, Holbrook and Harper** . . . the exciting radio personalities who have switched morning listening habits with their new radio show on KFRC San Francisco.

5. **WHBQ radio Memphis** . . . programming and coverage designed to dominate three important trading areas.

6. **"The Information Station"** . . . KHJ radio Los Angeles, newly programmed to meet the needs of America's No. 1 market.

7. **30/30 Plan** . . . exclusive new sales plan developed by RKO General Broadcasting, now available on CKLW Detroit, and other RKO General radio stations.

8. **Dobie Gillis** . . . first run off the network and already the top-rated show in its time period on WHBQ-TV Memphis.

9. **"Talk Radio"** . . . WNAC Boston and WOR New York reach large, attentive, adult audiences with this compelling format.

10. **MSM . . . Million Dollar Movie** on stations WOR-TV New York, CKLW-TV Detroit, and KHJ-TV Los Angeles. TV's most famous prime time movie program affording full minute movie program availabilities.

11. **The New Breed** . . . experienced, national sales executives of RKO General Broadcasting will tell you **how**, the RKO General "station salesmen" (shown above) can move more of your merchandise in seven major U.S. markets. For full information call, wire or write.

RKO General Broadcasting • National Sales:
NEW YORK, 1290 Ave. of the Americas, LO 4-8000
CHICAGO, Tribune Tower Building, 644-2470
LOS ANGELES, 5515 Melrose Avenue, HO 2-2133
SAN FRANCISCO, 415 Bush Street, YU 2-9200

new need . . . new breed

257   258

NABISCO

TAKE AN OREO COOKIE TO SCHOOL
Enjoy that creamy filling, chocolate-y goodness all the way.

GO TO PENALTY BOX

SCHOOL BUS

BACK 3 BOXES

NABISCO
CHEWZACOOKIE
GAME

THINK OF A GLASS OF MILK

HAVE A PARTY! You're host so everybody gets a NABISCO cookie but you.

PENALTY BOX Give back next cookie you win.

WATER FLOWERS Take a FIG NEWTONS cake, flow ahead 3 spaces.

PEEL OFF Back off 2 spaces, but you may have a crisp NABISCO VANILLA WAFER.

BACK 3 BOXES

FEED THE KITTY And take one NABISCO cookie for you.

BOO! (HOO!) All get a chocolate-y NABISCO CHOCOLATE CHIP cookie but you.

PENALTY BOX Give back next cookie you win.

COCOA BREAK

FEED THE BABY And take one egg-rich NABISCO VANILLA WAFER for yourself.

GO TO PENALTY BOX

NABISCO VANILLA WAFERS

LORNA DOONE Shortbread

NABISCO CHOCOLATE CHIP Cookies

OREO Creme Sandwich

FIG NEWTONS Cakes

Extra butter in the batter gives LORNA DOONE Shortbread lightness, dairy-rich deliciousness. Serve with strawberries or other fresh fruit and watch the smiles.

Luscious, creamy filling and rich chocolate-y crisp wafers make it hard to stop eating OREO Creme Sandwich, America's favorite chocolate sandwich cookie.

Eggs, eggs and more eggs make the delicious difference in airy-light NABISCO VANILLA WAFERS. Luscious plain, with pudding or ice cream.

Moist-fresh fig jam tucked into tender, golden cookie cake. These nuggets of luscious flavor are called FIG NEWTONS Cakes. Easiest lunch dessert you ever packed.

Golden, tender-textured NABISCO CHOCOLATE CHIP Cookies are plumped with sweet chocolate morsels. Look for them in the bright blue package.

LORNA DOONE

OREO CREME SANDWICH

Vanilla Wafers

FIG NEWTONS

Chocolate Chip COOKIES

HOME

259

257 Pepsi-Cola

A contest is an effective form of participation. The most effective is one that ties in well with the product and is interesting in itself.

Here the interest is in matching a popular personality, a Miss America of a previous year, to a snapshot made of her when she was a baby. As a bonus give-away, the current year's winner, Miss Vonda Kay Van Dyke, is matched up for you.

The only connection between the contest idea and the product is that you have to send in six corks from under the caps of any Pepsi-Cola product or, as an alternative — and a mnemonic aid for the brand — the entrant may hand-letter the Pepsi-Cola name on six plain pieces of paper.

258 RKO General Broadcasting

A magazine's editorial features can provide inspiration for the copywriter. This particular ad is only a variation of a magazine photo quiz.

The magazine version showed only eyes or baby pictures of famous individuals and asked the reader to identify or match each photo with the personality.

Here, pictures appropriate to each subject, or station, are numbered to match the copy below. Beethoven (No. 3) represents WGMS — "programming classical music," two talking microphones (No. 9) literally stand for WNAC and WOR — "Talk Radio." "M$M" on a strip of film (No. 10) is for several stations' "Million Dollar Movie," and so on.

259 Nabisco

If the product can be used up faster in a game, invent one. While the game is being played, the selling story goes right on.

National Biscuit Co.

260

261

260 Falcon

This ad appeared in a publication for teenage boys, using a switch on the old game: "What's wrong with this picture?" This is in reverse, with the expected answer, the "all right" Falcon Hardtop.

The photo is an odd concoction of props, retouching, and a few zany shenanigans designed for a boy reader's careful scrutiny.

Ford Motor Co.

261 Volkswagen

"What is it? Glad you asked. It's a Volkswagen Station Wagon." And then the reader wades through all that selling copy for the answer he really wants. It's that intriguing photo that does it.

"It can carry nearly a ton of anything you can afford to buy...Or 8 people (plus luggage)... What's in the package? 8 pairs of skis, the complete works of Dickens, 98 lbs. of frozen spinach...80 Hollywood High gym sweaters..." ending up with "a full sized reproduction of the Winged Victory of Samothrace." In a word, you get the answer in its proper place — at the end of the copy.

©Volkswagen of America, Inc.

262 Young & Rubicam

If you still think that type is silent, just take a look at this screaming headline.

The first line tells the story: "Yelling doesn't equal selling." Pointed proof of this lies in the shouted proposal of marriage. It simply won't work. He cannot force her hand, or twist her arm to make her say "Yes," any more than an advertiser can do it to a reader.

The copy advances another saying to prove the point: "Namely, that the man who raises his voice is losing the argument." The layout, together with these analogies, conveys the message to the reader in the quickest possible terms. "The best advertising is persuasion through ideas. Ideas presented *persuasively* are what people buy."

"WILL YOU MARRY ME?"

Yelling doesn't equal selling.

Nobody likes the guy who backs you against the wall, hammers his finger through your chest, and bellows out his proposition.

Some advertising, unfortunately, is like that.

This brings to mind another saying we often hear. Namely, that the man who raises his voice is losing the argument.

The best advertising is persuasion through ideas.

Ideas presented *persuasively* are what people buy.

YOUNG & RUBICAM, INC., ADVERTISING

263

263   Jell-O

This ad takes a very popular game and visually paraphrases it. Instead of numbers, a mnemonic is used for the product.

Jell-O is trying to impress the reader with the idea that its flavors taste like fruit. On each package is a full-color photo of the particular fruit the contents is supposed to taste of.

Now, if the reader tears off those photos from the boxes he buys, he can match up the bingo card in four rows, mail in the label of any brand of canned fruit, and win $1.00.

General Foods

265   Imperial Margarine

Excellent use of an antiquated censorship decree. Few readers will pass up this challenge, which says, in effect, "We dare you to read this ad. You're forbidden to know what the blacked-out word is." The reader, without being seriously taxed, uses his imagination to figure out that the word is "butter."

Lever Brothers

266   Electric Auto-Lite Co.

Guessing games are always popular. In this case, Auto-Lite effectively compares famous look-alikes. The analogy is apt because spark plugs can look very much alike — just as an average person can look like a famous movie star — yet the performance of the two can be miles apart.

The copy doesn't tell you, until you're halfway through, that the real Joan Fontaine is on the left.

The "4 Star Benefits" of the product are listed separately in the box at right. An "X-ray view shows the Auto-Lite 10,000 Ohm Resistor."

264   Post Alpha-Bits

Copy ideas can come from any area of human activity. Here is an ad that will automatically ring a bell for crossword-puzzle fans.

Readers who do not work the puzzle will still get the idea. Each reader who does complete the forty-five-word puzzle will have been exposed to the ad forty-five separate times. Talk about getting more for your advertising dollar!

267   Sylvania

This was only a half-page ad, and that's all that was needed to bring home the idea of Halovision. An ad should be big enough to make the point.

When you are contrasting two ideas, it is wise to picture only the one idea you wish to bring home. In this case, if the TV picture had been different in each example it would have drawn some attention away from the idea of "Sylvania Halovision."

The cabinet is not shown in the comparison of the two screens, but down in the corner of the ad Sylvania is selling Halovision first; then a TV set.

General Telephone & Electronics

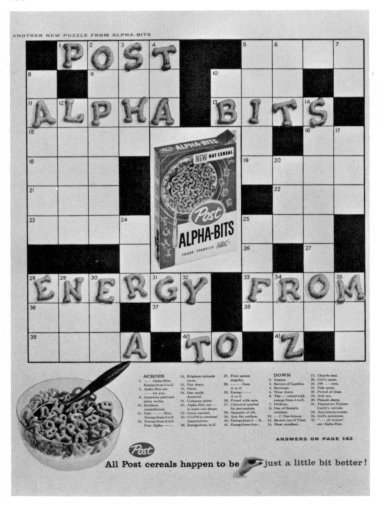

BEAUTYREST DAY at the Circus

"Hup," shouts the trainer—and "Big Mo," queen of the 9 herds of performing elephants under the big top hoists her five tons of weight up into the air, both rear feet firmly planted on a Beautyrest mattress. She did no damage to the mattress. What better proof of the durability of Beautyrest?

Next came M'Toto—all 460 pounds of her. She bounced and jostled on same Beautyrest when it was thrown into cage with her. When the Beautyrest mattress was cut open for inspection, not a coil spring was broken. No lumps or hollows. Because each of the 837 springs in Beautyrest is wrapped in its own pocket—absorbs tension separately. Gives natural, "Levelized Support."

Famous clown stretches out on same Beautyrest. Smiles, because Beautyrest is his favorite spot in Clown Alley. Matter of fact, all circus folk like Beautyrest, because no other mattress absorbs jolts and jiggles of circus caravan so gently. You'll like Beautyrest luxury-comfort, too. It's yours for about 2¢ a night. (Price is $69.50. There's a 10-year guarantee, which brings the price over 10-year period to about 2¢ a night.) At your dealer's.

Only SIMMONS makes BEAUTYREST*

*TRADE-MARK REG. U. S. PATENT OFFICE. COPR. 1961 BY SIMMONS CO., NOSE MART, CHICAGO, ILL.

268

Harry James proves it with a trumpet...

For a current TV commercial, Harry James tied a new Kleenex tissue on his trumpet, soaked it with water and blew! Even when he hit the high notes, the Kleenex tissue didn't break through!

you can prove it with a sneeze

New Kleenex is remarkably unlike any tissue you've ever seen or felt before! It has a brand new strength you'll discover with your first sneeze—and a new deep softness you'll feel the moment it touches your skin. Now all 3 Space-Saver boxes contain new Kleenex tissues.

KLEENEX, SPACE-SAVER and HI-COUNT are trademarks of Kimberly-Clark Corp.

New Kleenex tissues won't break through —much softer, too!

New!

---

268 Simmons

A test of your product, even if performed by circus animals, is still a test. An elephant, " 'Big Mo,' queen of the 9 herds of performing elephants" tests the mattress for durability — she "hoists her five tons of weight on it" with no damage to the mattress.

Gargantua's mate "M'Toto — all 460 pounds of her," tests the coil springs. After the mattress was cut open, not one coil spring was broken. The copy explains that "each of the 837 springs in Beautyrest is wrapped in its own pocket — absorbs tension separately." A famous clown ends the test at "his favorite spot in Clown Alley. Matter of fact, all circus folk like Beautyrest, because no other mattress absorbs jolts and jiggles of circus caravan so gently...yours for about 2¢ a night."

The clown and the girl add human interest to the animals' demonstration. This ad was in the Ringling Bros. Barnum & Bailey Circus program.

©Simmons Co.

270 Great Day

It is a rarely remembered premise that the human body is asymmetrical — and that this asymmetry gives the face a younger and an older side. This Clairol ad capitalizes on this phenomenon and, further, involves the reader in a personal demonstration.

By following the directions of the headline, the reader participates in a dramatic test from which he can immediately see results. The consumer is always his own best salesman and can convince himself to try the product if the facts are dramatically presented.

Clairol saw and opened up new marketing possibilities when it initiated hair coloring. The same marketing policy continues to be effective in pioneering this related men's product.

© Clairol

269 Kleenex

A famous personality dramatizes a test for a paper tissue that a reader also can try. As dramatic as it looks, a strong blast going through the tubing can only be dissipated when it comes out of a wide-mouth trumpet, no matter how loud the blast sounds.

A sneeze covers a smaller area and is of more concentrated intensity than even a high note on a trumpet. Still, if this tissue is stronger than another brand, this is one way of demonstrating it.

Kimberly-Clark Corp.

271 Xerox

Challenge and contrast are combined. The $2,800 price of a Picasso is contrasted with the 5¢ Xerox copy; the excellence of the Xerox copy is strongly implied.

Xerox has left hints as to which is the real Picasso and which the Xerox copy: the real Picasso, the one with the wallpaper in the background, on textured drawing paper, is on the left — or is it?

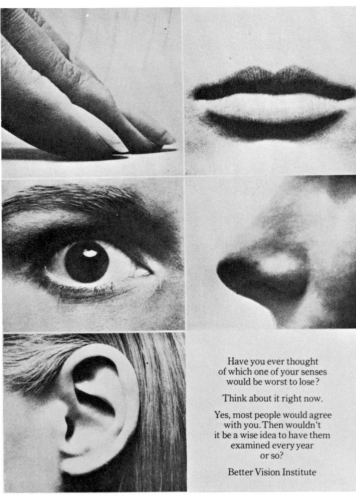

Have you ever thought
of which one of your senses
would be worst to lose?

Think about it right now.

Yes, most people would agree
with you. Then wouldn't
it be a wise idea to have them
examined every year
or so?

Better Vision Institute

272

Place your face here and go 'z-z-z-z-z-z-z.'

**NOW YOU KNOW HOW
IT FEELS TO SHAVE
WITH ROTARY BLADES THAT
SHAVE MORE THAN 18% CLOSER
THAN EVER BEFORE**

Norelco The Close Electric Shave

273

272 Better Vision Institute

This ad, without a headline, is straightforward and dramatic. The copy begins: "Have you ever thought of which one of your senses would be worst to lose?" And leaves you to your own conclusion.

The photographs depict the five senses, showing them from the most recognizable angles. The eye looking straight at you is both startling and essential in helping you to decide correctly. And to take action.

274 Remington

Explain what participation can mean to the reader who participates. Instructions are enumerated at every point of this ad. The copy states: "1. Sign this note and cut out. 2. Cut out picture of the cord/cordless REMINGTON 500 Selektronic shaver," and so on, leaving no doubts in the reader's mind as to what to do, even supplying dotted lines. A little selling copy in the note says: "It's the best shaving instrument ever...lets me dial a perfect shave everytime." Finally, the reader is told to cut out and assemble the envelope, put in the note and picture, address it "To the one I love the most" and give it to her. Down in the right-hand corner of the ad, the reader is reminded: "P.S. This is the way it looks in the store."

©Sperry Rand Corp.

275 Esterbrook

In the headline there is general appeal that the reader can personalize. Most readers will look for their particular style of writing or doodle. The bottom panel shows the various styles of nib.

In every copy block that analyzes a style of handwriting, Esterbrook is selling pens, either as a line or as a specific style, at a stated price. The selling copy relates well to each handwriting analysis.

273 Norelco

The shadow of the hand on the page gives the electric shaver a three-dimensional look, almost as though it were coming out of the page. The invitation to put your face on the shaver advertised is tempting.

The copy assumes you did what was asked: "You didn' feel anything? Good. Now you know how it feels to shave with the Norelco Speedshaver...we've shaved down our shaving heads 18% thinner...as thin as this sheet of paper." Thus, the feel of the thinness of the magazine paper is a further step in actual participation by the reader.

Tying in again with the headline, the ending gently spoofs the ad: "buy one before you have to explain what you're doing holding a magazine to your face and going z-z-z-z-z-z-z."

©North American Philips Co.

276 AMF

This was one of the first sing-along ads. The reader has a "voice" in his head that can "sing" to the tune in your copy.

The boy at the right, holding the ball, gives the reader the only quick cue that this is a unique sort of birthday party. It keeps older children occupied, out of trouble and, above all, out of the house. There is no mess left for mother to clean up.

American Machine and Foundry Company

277 Rice Krispies

Usually a reader holds a magazine in his lap or on a desk. The cereal bowl might have seemed to be in the reader's lap if the bowl had been placed at the bottom of the ad. Cross-lighting and a table setting would have suggested a more three-dimensional meal.

The copy says about the picture that "you can't hear their merry, morning talk...'Snap! Crackle! Pop!' which, in cereal language...spells out C-R-I-S-P...you've seen this page, why not bring it to life — at breakfast tomorrow?"

Kellogg Co.

How to get the REMINGTON 500 for Christmas.

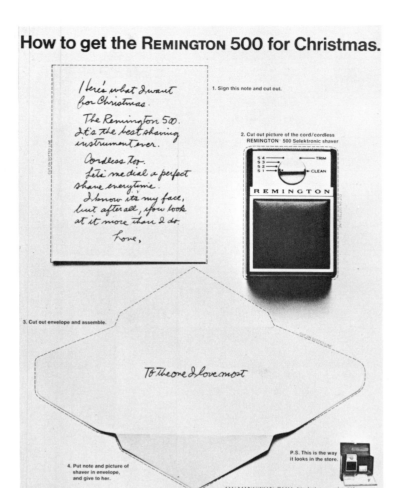

Here's what I want for Christmas.

The Remington 500. It's the best shaving instrument ever.

Cordless too.

Lets me dial a perfect shave everytime.

I know it's my face, but after all, you look at it more than I do.

Love,

1. Sign this note and cut out.

2. Cut out picture of the cord/cordless REMINGTON 500 Selektronic shaver

REMINGTON

3. Cut out envelope and assemble.

To the one I love most

4. Put note and picture of shaver in envelope, and give to her.

P.S. This is the way it looks in the store.

REMINGTON 500 Selektronic Shaver

274

What do your doodles reveal about you?

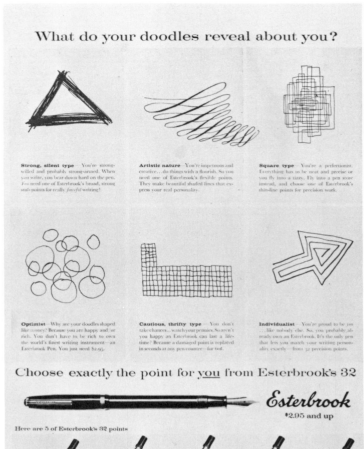

Strong, silent type — You're strong-willed and probably strong-armed. When you write, you bear down hard on the pen. You need one of Esterbrook's broad, strong stub points for really forceful writing!

Artistic nature — You're impetuous and creative... do things with a flourish. So you need one of Esterbrook's flexible points. They make beautiful shaded lines that express your real personality.

Square type — You're a perfectionist. Everything has to be neat and precise or you fly into a tizzy. Fly into a pen store instead, and choose one of Esterbrook's thin-line points for precision work.

Optimist — Why are your doodles shaped like money? Because you are happy and/or rich. You don't have to be rich to own the world's finest writing instrument—an Esterbrook Pen. You just need $2.95.

Cautious, thrifty type — You don't take chances... watch your pennies. So aren't you happy an Esterbrook can last a lifetime? Because a damaged point is replaced in seconds at any pen counter—for free!

Individualist — You're proud to be you... like nobody else. So, you probably already own an Esterbrook. It's the only pen that lets you match your writing personality exactly—from 32 precision points.

Choose exactly the point for you from Esterbrook's 32

Esterbrook
$2.95 and up

Here are 5 of Esterbrook's 32 points

student | Signature Stub | bookkeeping | fine writing | shaded writing

275

Happy birthday to you.
Happy birthday to you.
Happy birthday, dear Jackie-e-e-e.
Hap-py birth-day...to...you-u-u-u.
(It's your turn to bowl, Scotty.)

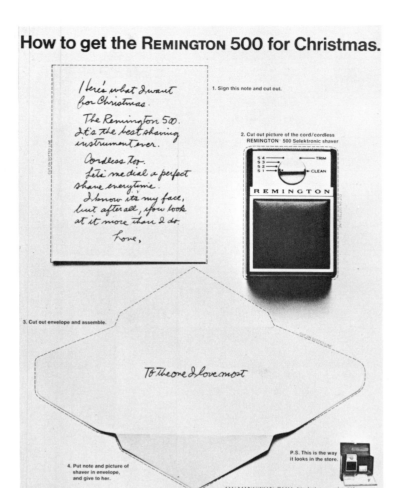

Jackie's 9th birthday was different.

It took place at a bowling center. Jackie and 8 of his closest friends bowled, cheered, giggled, ate cake and ice cream, laughed, screeched and even sang (see above).

The proprietor of the bowling center arranged everything from the birthday cake to party hats and soft drinks.

The thing Jackie's mother enjoyed the most was that the party didn't take place at home (and she's an avid bowler herself).

Perhaps your youngster would appreciate a bowling birthday party. It's easy to arrange. And the weather can't affect it.

For the best, always bowl where you see the Magic Triangle.

American Machine & Foundry Company

276

GOOD THINGS YOU CAN'T SEE IN THE PICTURE
Lots of energy generators, plus the natural rice values of thiamine (B₁), niacin and iron.

"snap!"

"crackle!"

"pop!"

Kellogg's RICE KRISPIES

HOLD THIS PAGE ON YOUR LAP
This picture was taken at an angle that would show you how wonderful Rice Krispies can look at breakfast. But even with the picture on your lap, you can't hear their merry, morning talk. They go "Snap! Crackle! Pop!" which, in cereal language, is a message that spells out C-R-I-S-P. That's why everybody calls KELLOGG'S RICE KRISPIES "the talking cereal." Now that you've seen this page, why not bring it to life -- at breakfast tomorrow?

277

Whether you decorate with Louis XV or Charles Eames, if your client has the electricity, Lightolier has the fixture.

And whether your next assignment is residential or architectural, you owe yourself a visit to a Lightolier showroom. That's where you'll find the newest and most creative innovations in lighting. Store or office building, private home or apartment house, motel or hotel—knowledgeable architects and designers have placed their confidence in Lightolier...for over 60 years the leader in skillfully engineered, well-designed lighting, fixed and portable. So whether your next project is an Evansville executive suite, Houston high-rise, Buffalo boutique or Manhattan manor house, Lightolier is your most logical single source for all your lighting needs—both decorative and functional.

P.S. Want something special for your "Inspiration File"? Write on your professional letterhead for our enlightening new catalogue. Lightolier, Jersey City 5, N.J.

LIGHTOLIER

Showrooms: 11 East 36th St., New York; 1362 Merchandise Mart, Chicago; 2515 South Broadway, Los Angeles; 1718 Hi-Line Drive, Dallas.

To emphasize the variety and versatility of lighting available to decorators, this Lightolier ad allows the reader an opportunity to interchange visually different styles of Lightolier lamps hanging above a selection of period pieces.

The individual pieces of furniture have been given character and warmth with props like books, knick-knacks, a bust on its pedestal, fern, sheet music and a recorder.

279 Mattel

How do you appear in a trade magazine for toys amidst hundreds of other advertisers and tell buyers that you have spectacular items? Put on a spectacular yourself!

This three-dimensional pop-up ad insert (see following right-hand page) is one of the most elaborate ever made. The array of die-cut shapes and bright colors backs up the theme: "Mattel-zapoppin." Noises "explode" from the ground as they shoot up to the theme name; loose-fitting and hanging shapes provide plenty of action in this exciting display."

Names of products are interspersed within the display, and a more detailed description of items is at the base of each dimensional projection. The back page of this insert gave details about $9,000,000 worth of advertising and promotional support for the dealer.

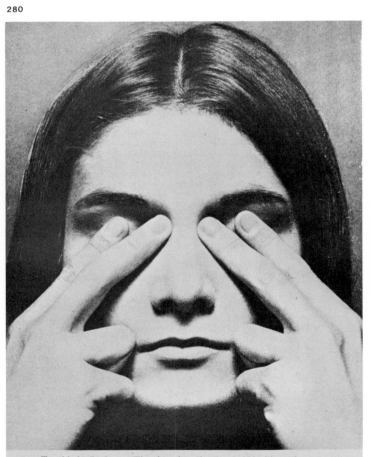

Stand Back About a Dozen Feet and look at the picture on this page. See the difference an optical correction makes? And so with Voigtlander cameras, the precision of the lens makes all the difference in the picture. But perfection also seeks innovation. That's why Voigtlander's VITRONA is the first and only 35 mm camera with built-in flash that doesn't need flash bulbs or cubes. If seeing is believing and you believe in seeing, turn this page upside down and look again. We'd like to make the point twice.

This is the Vitrona . . . with built-in electronic flash. Aperture and distance settings coupled for perfect flash exposures. 50 mm f/2.8 Lanthar lens. Shutter speeds from 1/30 to 1/250 sec. Flash operates from 2 "C" batteries in camera grip. Priced at $103.00.

Voigtländer Complete range of precision 35 mm, instant load and rapid cameras.

280

280   Voigtländer Vitrona

Here is a good idea that, visually, relates well to cameras. But the magazine reader may be in a confined office or commuting on a train where he can't possibly view the ad at the proper distance to achieve the "optical correction."

"If seeing is believing and you believe in seeing, turn this page upside down and look again. We'd like to make the point twice."

Zeiss-Ikon-Voigtländer of America

Try this for 5 minutes. Then imagine what it would be like . . . forever.
You have only one pair of eyes. When was the last time you had them examined?
Better Vision Institute.

281

281   Better Vision Institute

The ads in this excellent series are consistently related to vision. Whether the reader does or does not follow the activity suggested, he will still be struck by their visual impact. When he reads the ad he may not be in a position to participate, but he can sense what it would be like for a blind person.

"Try this for 5 minutes," the copy reads. "Then imagine what it would be like...forever."

WHAT
DIFFERENCE
DOES IT MAKE
WHICH
TYPGORAPHER
YOU USE?

LOTS. EVERYONE MAKES MISTAKES. BUT WE TRY HARD TO KEEP YOU FROM SEEING OURS.

FRANKLIN TYPOGRAPHERS   225 WEST 39TH STREET   NEW YORK N.Y. 10018   PENNSYLVANIA 6-4707

282

One sip and
you can write your own
Soft Whiskey ad.

283

282 Franklin Typographers

Read the headline again if you missed the ad's typgoraphical error.

The body copy follows the headline, in three short sentences: "Lots. Everyone makes mistakes. But we try hard to keep you from seeing ours." Another ad in this campaign had a headline which on close examination had nicks and broken type; a bottle of black ink and a touch-up brush were shown resting on the page.

284 Northwest Orient Airlines

This two-color newspaper ad was not meant merely to be read, but to be used. It helped wives who were interested in going to Hawaii try to convince their husbands to "Escape to Hawaii on Northwest."

The reader is given a way to make someone else aware of the problem (to get away) and the solution to that problem (escape to Hawaii). The copy beneath each promotion item identifies it and gives instructions on how to use it effectively.

"Pin-up. Tape to bathroom mirror. He'll get the message...Bumper sign. Fasten to the back of his car. Very sneaky. Looks like he's already decided...Place card. Set beside his dinner plate. You know the way to his heart..."

Each of these carries a little selling copy on special features of Northwest. The body copy gives free rein to the reader's own imagination: "Want to branch out on your own?" The copy says, "Try these ploys..."

283 Calvert

Here is a simple way to say one taste is worth a thousand words.

What if they had eliminated the hand-with-glass and just contrasted the dark product shot with the rest of the space in ruled lines?

© Calvert

285 Wallhide

Anyone can see the see-through difference, although it is slight — and, possibly for that reason, more credible. The "see through" of ordinary latex is contrasted with the covering properties of Wallhide.

The copy says that the "Zebra Test" proves that Wallhide "covers far better in just one coat!" But the copy only implies that Wallhide will hide the zebra stripes completely.

Pittsburgh Paints

286 Volkswagen

Here is participation — in two areas of the same ad. First it asks that the reader curve the panoramic window around himself like a Cinemascope screen. The ad gives the reader very definite, detailed instructions: "Hold this ad at eye level, 12 inches away. Curve it around like Cinemascope. You're in the Volkswagen Station Wagon." Or (in the cut-out) as simple as: "Cut. Fold. Paste. See? It's a box on wheels."

In other words, enough is said so the reader knows exactly what he is supposed to do. And by doing it, he is made more aware of the product's advantages.

©Volkswagen of America, Inc.

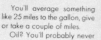

287 Detecto Scales

Probably no one stood on the page as the headline directs, but the imagination needs only a vivid presentation to grasp the idea and come to decisive action. It's a temptation to stand on that scale "and see how easily you can read the new Detecto bathroom scale...with the amazing new Magnif-eye dial."

288   Acousta-Pane

This ad was in two colors: black and red. When the reader detached the red cellophane "specs" and looked through them, the "noise" disappeared, visually; what he saw then is in the Acousta-Pane ad shown on the following right-hand page.

   The subhead adds that "instead of sheep, guests can count on a great night's sleep." If the "disappearing" picture, shown surprinted here, had been sheep instead of cars, you might have lost the idea of noise that passing motor vehicles suggest.

Amerada Glass Corp.

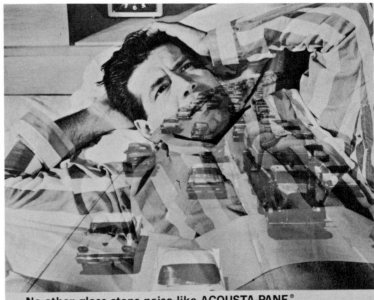

No other glass stops noise like ACOUSTA-PANE®... not plate, not spaced, not insulating glass!
Only Acousta-Pane keeps irritating noise <u>outside</u> your motel. Instead of sheep, guests can count on a great night's sleep.

Look! Acousta-Pane glass puts noise in its place!

Tear along perforated line and look through "specs" to see how the first and only true acoustical glass shuts out unwanted noise.

BUSINESS REPLY MAIL
No postage stamp necessary if mailed in the United States

Postage will be paid by:
AMERADA GLASS CORPORATION
3301 South Prairie Avenue
Chicago, Illinois 60616

Dept. AE 75

FIRST CLASS
Permit No. 60172
Chicago, Illinois

"Voilà de la publicité pour Berlitz."

See? You already know some French.

And in a matter of weeks you could be speaking it fluently.

Because the Berlitz method is the fastest and most effective way to learn any language.

Just as we did here, you start right in speaking. Each lesson is private, and your instructor won't speak a word of English to you.

He starts right in with "bonjour" and, through a process as natural as an infant learning to speak, you'll soon know the difference between une pipe and un cigare. In fact, within five minutes you'll be saying a sentence as complicated as "Je préfère la pipe au cigare."

With the aid of objects, pictures, and a lot of body English, your instructor will have you speaking fluent French before you can say Jacques Robinson.

Par exemple: A Paris there are many parcs where one may go for une promenade. And there are des chaises where one may sit and regarder les fontaines, or les enfants who play and les amoureux who kiss. And if you read this once again, you should comprendre every word.

We can have you speaking fluently in five weeks if you can spare your full time, or in three or four months if you can spare only lunch hours. (Or in ten to fifteen days, if you have the stamina.*)

We guarantee our method if you guarantee your diligence.

Now all you need do is téléphoner à l'école Berlitz de votre localité and make an appointment.

You've already started your first lesson.

Advertisements should not be secretive about the product they are selling. If the product has to do with words, that's all the more reason to part with a little knowledge rather than to part with the reader.

To show how simple it can be to learn another language, this ad gives a free lesson in French.

The secret is that just as the reader did with the headline, he starts right in reading, and "with the aid of objects, pictures, and a lot of body English" he can speak fluent French.

An entire paragraph is given with French words sprinkled throughout. The last line reads, "And if you read this once again, you should comprendre every word."

The sign-off says, "We guarantee our method if you guarantee your diligence."

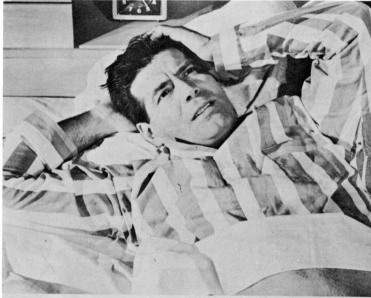

No other glass stops noise like ACOUSTA-PANE®... not plate, not spaced, not insulating glass!
Only Acousta-Pane keeps irritating noise <u>outside</u> your motel. Instead of sheep, guests can count on a great night's sleep.

Look! Acousta-Pane glass puts noise in its place!

Tear along perforated line and look through "specs" to see how the first and only true acoustical glass shuts out unwanted noise.

FIRST CLASS
Permit No. 60172
Chicago, Illinois

BUSINESS REPLY MAIL
No postage stamp necessary if mailed in the United States

Postage will be paid by:
AMERADA GLASS CORPORATION
3301 South Prairie Avenue
Chicago, Illinois 60616

Dept. AE 75

SEQUENCES

290 Booth's House of Lords

The repetition here is in the photographing of the same part of the face twelve times. Even though the features differ, the common factor is simply that they are average noses. Except the snifterini nose. "Do you have to have the right nose for the Snifterini? No. You have to have the right character." The copy calls the product "the non-conformist gin from England," and explains that the necessary qualification is "just to be a little different, and if you're willing to try one, you are."

An offer of four Snifterini glasses is made to any reader who wishes to send for them.

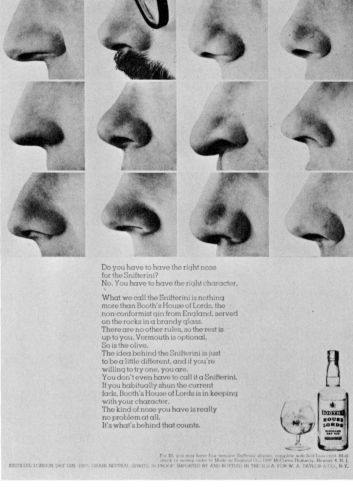

290

291 Lightolier

In the photo for this ad, the circle outline is constant while inside it is first a planet, then a sun, and finally a lighting fixture. The relationship among these lights is followed through from the headline: "night," then "day," and finally, "night and day."

The ad was in full color, the moon against a black background, the sun against an orange one, and the fixture against blue chroma.

THE CAT THAT MISCOUNTED

We were about to heave an old boot at this cat on the back fence. Then we remembered shoe rationing.

"Whatsa matter," we said instead, "why all the wailing?"

"Listen, chum, you'd wail, too," the cat complained. "I mislaid a *life!*"

Being pretty sleepy, that sort of shook us up. "One life. Mislaid. Hmmm," we said, "let's see, we know you had nine to start with. What happened to 'em all?"

"We-ell, when I was just a kit," said the cat, "I talked back to a police dog who caught me overparking. That was one. Then, I was curious to find out whether it's true about cats and curiosity. It is. That made two. . . ."

We let the cat run on, reminiscing. Suddenly he stopped, and started wailing again.

"Somewhere I got careless and lost count," he said, "and now I don't know whether this makes eight or m-m-maybe *nine*. It's a regular cat-astrophe, that's what it is!"

Like this cat, American business cannot afford to grow careless.

Business men consider accurate, up-to-the-minute figures an essential of good management. That's why, in their offices, you see Comptometer adding-calculating machines and modern Comptometer methods.

The Comptometer, made only by Felt & Tarrant Manufacturing Company, 1720 North Paulina Street, Chicago 22, Illinois, is sold exclusively by the Comptometer Company.

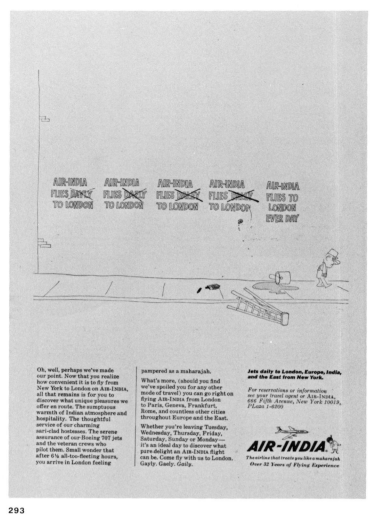

Oh, well, perhaps we've made our point. Now that you realize how convenient it is to fly from New York to London on AIR-INDIA, all that remains is for you to discover what unique pleasures we offer en route. The sumptuous warmth of Indian atmosphere and hospitality. The thoughtful service of our charming sari-clad hostesses. The serene assurance of our Boeing 707 jets and the veteran crews who pilot them. Small wonder that after 6½ all-too-fleeting hours, you arrive in London feeling pampered as a maharajah.

What's more, (should you find we've spoiled you for any other mode of travel) you can go right on flying AIR-INDIA from London to Paris, Geneva, Frankfurt, Rome, and countless other cities throughout Europe and the East.

Whether you're leaving Tuesday, Wednesday, Thursday, Friday, Saturday, Sunday or Monday—it's an ideal day to discover what pure delight an AIR-INDIA flight can be. Come fly with us to London. *Gayly. Gaely. Gaily.*

Jets daily to London, Europe, India, and the East from New York.

For reservations or information see your travel agent or AIR-INDIA, 666 Fifth Avenue, New York 10019, PLaza 1-6200

AIR-INDIA.

The airline that treats you like a maharajah.
Over 32 Years of Flying Experience

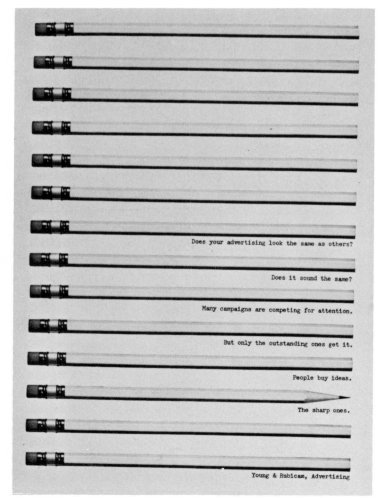

Does your advertising look the same as others?

Does it sound the same?

Many campaigns are competing for attention.

But only the outstanding ones get it.

People buy ideas.

The sharp ones.

Young & Rubicam, Advertising

When they grow up, will language still be a barrier?

As modern technology makes the world smaller, the need for understanding between peoples grows more pressing. But the barrier of language still hinders our efforts to communicate with each other. Even today, only a small fraction of the world's information ever passes beyond the frontiers of its original language.

How can we broaden the flow of information from one language to another? One answer may lie in the growing versatility of computer technology. For instance, a technique for automatic translation is now under development at IBM. Russian, French, and Chinese technical literature has already been translated into English at electronic speeds. The recent success in translating technical Chinese—a language that has no alphabet—indicates that all languages eventually may lend themselves to automatic translation.

Through new kinds of information systems, IBM is helping to meet the need for better communication in today's world. **IBM**

292 Comptometer

When an object or figure is repeated in an ad, one single image should stand out from the rest in some way — in size, color, art technique, or shape, perhaps. The photographs of cats in this ad are in negative, except for the one referred to, which is in positive, slightly larger, and separated from the others.

By abstracting the message intended (accuracy in counting), this ad provides human — or feline — interest in a conversation with the cat. "Whatsa matter...why all the wailing?" "Listen, chum, you'd wail too..I mislaid a *life!*"

Felt & Tarrant Manufacturing Co.

293 Air-India

In order not to bore the reader, this ad gives him a humorous drawing of a dejected sign painter who manages to spell the message correctly only after four failures.
But the painter's failure is the ad's success. Crossing out the key word "daily" rivets the the reader's attention on the repeated message which winds up, "Air-India flies to London ever day."

Plenty of white space makes a natural wall for the illustration, and allows nothing in the way of editorial matter or advertising to detract from the impact of the message.

"Oh, well, perhaps we've made our point," the copy says, as it describes services of the airline and concludes: "Come fly with us to London. Gayly, Gaely. *Gaily.*" The slogan is : "The airline that treats you like a maharajah."

294 Young & Rubicam

This ad is based on the premise that advertising consists of ideas and that it is the sharp ones that make consumers buy.

The pencil is a standard symbol of the writer of ideas and of ideas themselves. The blunt pencils are representative of routine ads and act as hurdles for the eye reading down the page. The reader must skip over the pencils and, literally, read the headlines between them. These pauses give the mind a moment's rest, as the line just read sinks in, and the eye follows to the next line.
The short bits of copy read this way: "Does your advertising look the same as others?" (Pause) "Does it sound the same?" (Pause) "Many campaigns are competing for attention." (Pause) "But only the outstanding ones get it." (Pause) "People buy ideas." (Pause) "The sharp ones."

296 Palm Beach

A few swallows don't make a summer but the right lines of copy and a little rain can make a winter. The first photo was taken at Coney Island on a sunny day. As seen on the following right-hand page, a short rain, with beach and boardwalk deserted and a change to winter wear converted this shot into a cold, bleak, wintry scene.

Goodall Sanford Inc.

295 IBM

Two children become symbols of different races, different languages. The Nordic child and the little Chinese boy in his kimono are shown each playing with blocks with lettering or stylized symbols of his own language. The headline acts as a visual barrier separating the two pictures and giving force to the headline.

The copy explains that "the barrier of language" hinders the understanding between peoples in a world made small by modern technology; "only a small fraction of...information ever passes beyond the frontiers of its original language...Through new kinds of information systems, IBM is helping to meet the need for better communication in today's world."

The people who uncrumpled the summer suit have ...

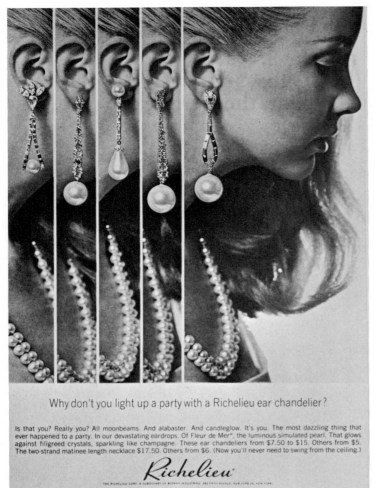

Why don't you light up a party with a Richelieu ear chandelier?

Is that you? Really you? All moonbeams. And alabaster. And candleglow. It's you. The most dazzling thing that ever happened to a party. In our devastating eardrops. Of Fleur de Mer*, the luminous simulated pearl. That glows against filigreed crystals, sparkling like champagne. These ear chandeliers from $7.50 to $15. Others from $5. The two-strand matinee length necklace $17.50. Others from $6. (Now you'll never need to swing from the ceiling.)

Richelieu

297

Majorca. Stromboli. Barbados. Corfu. Moorea, Skye. We've bottled a little of each.

Moorea
Skye
Corfu
Stromboli
Barbados
Majorca

MY ISLANDS COLOGNES STROMBOLI CORFU

We wish we could bottle the sunsets on Corfu. And the color of wildflowers on Majorca. And the wildness of Stromboli. And the lush foliage of Moorea. And the beaches of Barbados. And the sound of bagpipes through the mist on Skye. But we're not magicians.

Nevertheless, we are the first to take essences from each of these islands and put them in bottles. You'll find these essences in My Islands, a new collection of six colognes for women.

Now, depending on your mood and how far you want to go, you can open a bottle of any one of My Islands and splash it on.

Look for these colognes at most fine perfume counters. They're in the bottles that stack, one on top of the other. True, we only bring you a little of My Islands. But that's more than anyone else has done.

My Islands Colognes in selections of 2, 3, 4, and 6. From $8 to $20 In individual bottles or atomizers from $4 to $6.

298

Sherle Wagner has pulls in every period, for every purpose, to bring elegance and distinction to everything they adorn. All designed and crafted with the same care, skill and originality that have brought nationwide fame to Sherle Wagner's fixtures for the bath.
125 East 57th Street, New York 22, N.Y. PLaza 8-3300.

299

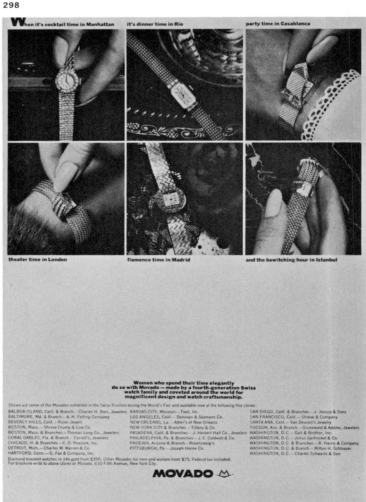

When it's cocktail time in Manhattan — it's dinner time in Rio — party time in Casablanca — theater time in London — flamenco time in Madrid — and the bewitching hour in Istanbul

Women who spend their time elegantly do so with Movado — made by a fourth-generation Swiss watch family and coveted around the world for magnificent design and watch craftsmanship.

Shown are some of the Movado exhibited in the Swiss Pavilion during the World's Fair and available now at the following fine stores.

BALBOA ISLAND, Calif. & Branch — Charles H. Barr, Jewelers
BALTIMORE, Md. & Branch — A. H. Fetting Company
BEVERLY HILLS, Calif. — Ruser Jewels
BOSTON, Mass. — Shreve Crump & Low Co.
BOSTON, Mass. & Branches — Thomas Long Co., Jewelers
CORAL GABLES, Fla. & Branch — Carroll's, Jewelers
CHICAGO, Ill. & Branches — C. D. Peacock, Inc.
DETROIT, Mich. — Charles W. Warren & Co.
HARTFORD, Conn. — G. Fox & Company, Inc.

KANSAS CITY, Missouri — Tivol, Inc.
LOS ANGELES, Calif. — Donovan & Seamans Co.
NEW ORLEANS, La. — Adler's of New Orleans
NEW YORK CITY & Branches — Tiffany & Co.
PASADENA, Calif. & Branch — J. Herbert Hall Co., Jewelers
PHILADELPHIA, Pa. & Branches — J. E. Caldwell & Co.
PHOENIX, Arizona & Branch — Rosenzweig's
PITTSBURGH, Pa. — Joseph Horne Co.

SAN DIEGO, Calif. & Branches — J. Jessop & Sons
SAN FRANCISCO, Calif. — Shreve & Company
SANTA ANA, Calif. — Van Deusen's Jewelry
TUCSON, Ariz. & Branch — Grunewald & Adams, Jewelers
WASHINGTON, D.C. — Galt & Brother, Inc.
WASHINGTON, D.C. — Julius Garfinckel & Co.
WASHINGTON, D.C. & Branches — R. Harris & Company
WASHINGTON, D.C. & Branch — Milton H. Schlosser
WASHINGTON, D.C. — Charles Schwartz & Son

Diamond bracelet watches in 14k gold from $395. Other Movado, for men and women from $75. Federal tax included. For brochure write to above stores or Movado, 610 Fifth Avenue, New York City.

MOVADO Ⓜ

300

297 Richelieu

Repetition of one section of photo is used here to good effect, showing five styles of earrings. The human element is not distracting because of the repetition, and the changing element — the earrings — increases in interest value.

This ad could easily have shown five more styles in similar strips across the page and still retained interest; accessories are rarely shown on a model, but against a plain background.

Botany Industries

298 My Islands Cologne

A cologne ad, in full color, features exotic sunsets reminiscent of six different islands — Majorca, Stromboli, Barbados, Corfu, Moorea, Skye — leaving a strong impression of the brand name, My Islands, on the consumer. Print advertising was colorfully backed up on TV.

The distinctive packaging concept, stacking six small bottles on top of one another, proved highly successful in the marketplace. The package was made flexible, too. It was possible to select one or more, in any combination, to suit every pocketbook.

© Colton Company

299 Sherle Wagner

Sherle Wagner has pulls in every period, for every purpose. When products are as distinctively styled as these, a common ground for displaying them should be found. Here that necessary unity is provided by having the pulls mounted on blocks of wood of different width and depth. As varied as these wood shapes are, they are all rectangular, a factor which relates them to each other while contrasting them with the ornate shapes of the metal fixtures.

With subtle shading, the blocks contrive to feature each separate fixture. The overall sepia tone of the ad adds warmth to the hard metal pulls.

300 Movado

Apparently the fashionable world moves by "Movado — made by a fourth-generation Swiss watch family and coveted around the world..."

The six divisions (in chronological order) are used in this ad to show six styles of dress watches for the elegant woman. The international gal starts out: "When it's cocktail time in Manhattan/ it's dinner time in Rio/party time in Casablanca/ theater time in London/Flamenco time in Madrid/ and the bewitching hour in Istanbul."

Synchronization of the watches with the far-flung locales is worked out. A few telltale symbols in each picture are all that is needed to indicate "foreign."

...engineered the perfect winter suit.

Anyone who discovered a summer suit fabric that wouldn't wilt, then tailored it so it went through the washer without looking as though it had been through the wringer, would find perfecting the winter suit a snap.

The same Palm Beach tailoring techniques that totally revolutionized the summer suit have been found to produce a vastly superior winter suit.

Palm Beach "engineered tailoring" cuts and sews fit into a suit forever, rather than pressing and molding it in for a while. The elimination of hand work makes tailoring more precise and fit more exact.

Palm Beach's "engineered" winter suits look superb, perform beyond your expectations, and because they are tailored through engineering rather than by hand labor, cost only 60.00 to 75.00.

Palm Beach

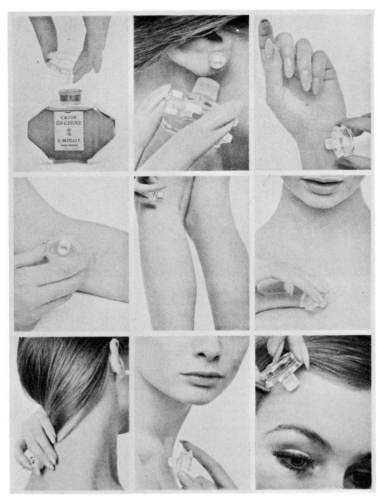

301

4:02 am   4:08 am   4:17 am

The meaningful pause. The energy it gives. The bright little lift. Coca-Cola with its never too sweet taste, refreshes best. Helps people meet the stress of the busy hours. This is why we say things go **better with Coke**

302

Gleneagles raincoats from $35. to $75. Illustrated: The Snowden of 65% DACRON® Polyester, 35% cotton. ®DuPont Trademark.

Will a Gleneagles protect you?

Good try, Officer O'Hallahan. We have boundless admiration for your sartorial sense. And it is true that Gleneagles specially selects its fabrics to defy the elements. And uses an exclusive Dri-Zone Shelter construction. And adds extra protection against rain and stains with DuPont **ZE PEL®** fabric fluoridizer. But let's face it. When you're directing traffic in a drenching downpour, the official heavy-duty slicker is *de rigueur.* But don't feel bad, O'Hallahan. With your enterprising spirit, we expect you to be upped to detective status any minute now. **Then you'll** be able to wear your Gleneagles day and night...just like in the movies. Gleneagles, at well-informed stores, or write **Gleneagles**, 1290 Ave. of the Americas, N.Y.C.

303

301 Crepe de Chine

The different shots in this ad are a how-to on applying scent. The little perfume stopper travels over the page with its magic, directing the reader's eyes to the effective spots of application. The photographs (medium, close-up and extra close-up) are cropped to a minimum, just enough to to identify the spot.

Warm but delicate skin tones, in full color, cover most of the page. The pale green perfume bottle at the top of the page attracts attention to itself without marring ,the ad.

No headline. No copy. No logo. None of the standard musts for an effective ad.

304 Jantzen

The technique of presentation in this ad is pleasantly startling to the reader. The answer (see following right-hand page) is part of the headline and strikingly simple.

Sunglasses give just enough of the undercover-agent look to the girl without overdoing it. Simple clues such as these are all that are needed to help the reader in placing, or identifying, a situation.

302 Coca-Cola

The same subject matter can be made to differ if shots are spaced through timed intervals, as with this 15-minute Coke break.

The stethoscope indicates an important pause; the finished puzzle, a relaxing pause. The copy follows through, "The meaningful pause. The energy it gives. The bright little lift." (The headline could have been lost here.) "Helps people meet the stress of the busy hours." Then the slogan: "This is why we say things go better with Coke."

© The Coca-Cola Company. Coca-Cola and Coke are the registered trademarks which identify only the products of The Coca-Cola Company.

305 Mead Papers

A black-and-white photograph of the back of a head stares you right in the face. But just turn to the next right-hand page and a shocking, formidable face, in full color, demands your attention.

The face of the man, who had turned his back, has green eyebrows, yellow nose and chin, and ruby-red lips — splashes of color enough to shock the most phlegmatic reader.

When you show two sides of an object — and costs are not prohibitive — show one side on one page and the other side on another page It's particularly good technique to use with pictures of people. The model comes alive when the reader turns the page. The four-color impact adds immensely to the effectiveness by contrast with the preceding image in black and white.

303 Gleneagles

A policeman is a symbol of protection. Yet it is the repetition, and the sudden contrast, that make the Gleneagles raincoat stand out. Set a pattern, then interrupt it with an idea that will make the product conspicuous.

The copy is personal and specific: "Good try, Officer O'Hallahan. We have boundless admiration for your sartorial sense." Then it itemizes the protection afforded by Gleneagles in the fabric's construction and DuPont ZePel against rain and stain. However, it ends quite candidly: "But let's face it. When you're directing traffic in a drenching downpour, the official heavy-duty slicker is *de rigueur.*"

Who rules the underworld?

304 a

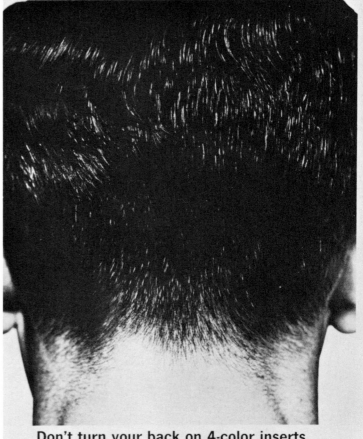

Don't turn your back on 4-color inserts...

305 a

Who says you must decide on just one pair of Miles Boots?

Have a closetful! Why not? Have high boots with high heels ... low boots with high heels. Boots to wear with stretch pants ... warm Hi 'n' Dri boots to take you out in style ... 100% waterproof boots to weather the wildest storm. So the question isn't which. It's more like "How many?"

Left, "Knee-Hi" in leather **7.99** Right, "Sabat" in suede **4.99**

OVER 300 SHOE CENTERS ... SEE YOUR DIRECTORY **MILES**

1. FOOD
costs Mary Ann Forsman $198 a month.

2. CLOTHING
costs the Forsmans $80 a month.

3. SHELTER
costs David Forsman $173 a month.

4. THE FOURTH NECESSITY
guarantees the family the other three, yet it costs less than any of them.

"We spend almost $5,500 a year just for the three necessities," says Dave Forsman, who sells paper products in the San Francisco area.

"You can imagine how long my $10,000 of group insurance would last Mary Ann and the boys. My own personal life insurance is what will make the difference." Dave realizes that in addition to food, clothing and shelter there is a Fourth Necessity: enough life insurance to guarantee his family the first three necessities at their present level.

"Now, if anything happens to me," Dave says, "Mary Ann will get a generous income every month for eighteen years — on top of the cash from my company policy — to raise the kids on. And, in addition, there will be money to start the boys' college education.

"What surprised me was how little it all costs — just $39 a month, about half of what we spend on clothing. I expect to live, of course. At age 65 I'll get $12,000 to buy an annuity for a lifetime monthly income." Have you figured out what your family would need? How much should *you* be putting into the Fourth Necessity? **Metropolitan's Family Security Check-Up will give you the answer.**

At no charge, a specially trained Metropolitan man will add up your savings, property, Social Security and present insurance. Then he'll estimate your family's needs, and figure what's needed to secure their future and the most economical way to do it. Like Dave Forsman, you'll probably find the Fourth Necessity — enough life insurance — costs much less than any of the other three. Find out from your Metropolitan man. There's no obligation ... *except to those you love.*

Metropolitan Life
INSURANCE COMPANY

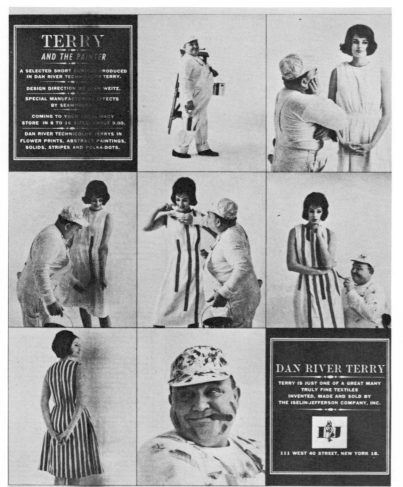

TERRY
AND THE PAINTER

A SELECTED SHORT SUBJECT PRODUCED IN DAN RIVER TECHNICOLOR TERRY.

DESIGN DIRECTION BY JOHN WEITZ.

SPECIAL MANUFACTURING EFFECTS BY SEAMPRUFE.

COMING TO YOUR LOCAL MACY STORE IN 8 TO 16 SIZES. ABOUT 9.00.

DAN RIVER TECHNICOLOR TERRYS IN FLOWER PRINTS, ABSTRACT PAINTINGS, SOLIDS, STRIPES AND POLKA-DOTS.

DAN RIVER TERRY

TERRY IS JUST ONE OF A GREAT MANY TRULY FINE TEXTILES INVENTED, MADE AND SOLD BY THE ISELIN-JEFFERSON COMPANY, INC.

111 WEST 40 STREET, NEW YORK 18.

1. Can you identify this city?

2. Clue: It's the hub of the nation's Eighth Market -- and booming!

3. Home Building Gains Reported
(SFX: BOOM)
Residential construction up 12% in '64!

4. Store Sales Are Higher
(SFX: BOOM)
Retail sales up 8%

5. Want to reach the families who are building and buying?

6. take TAE and see WTAE CHANNEL 4
Clue: Take the "homes-reached" station! Take TAE.
Swell. But you forgot to mention PITTSBURGH.

306 Miles

This was a newspaper ad that ran on two separate half pages. The ad straddled editorial and advertising matter, "walking" across a double-page spread, thus visually increasing its space. All the space between the two halves of the ad "belonged" to the advertiser without his having to pay for it.

The headline was incomplete until the reader reached the second half of the spread. If the sentence had been completed in the first half, the reader might have missed the other half and been left in the dark about what the incomplete half-page ad was trying to say.

This distribution of space is well utilized, tying in with the headline, to show two different styles of Miles boots.

307 Metropolitan Life Insurance Company

The whole is equal to the sum of its parts; the "fourth necessity (insurance) guarantees the family the other three, yet it costs less than any of them."

Insurance companies have presented few innovations in advertising concepts because their products are intangible ones. The usual ad puffs up the name of the logo. Here a new way of presenting insurance — not as a luxury, but as a necessity as great as any of the three basic needs — guarantees the continuation of the necessities in case of the insured's death. And it guarantees them at their present level.

To this end the copy gives a case history so that the reader can make a personal application of the ad that is wholly credible. Quotes from the insured are used liberally.

308 Dan River

The idea of painting the stripes on a dress is inspired. Dan River designs a simple dress in terry cloth. Instead of taking the reader to the factory to show routine production, Terry and the Painter put on a step-by-step show, completing a blue-and-white striped dress.

The painter comes on in his sparkling white outfit. He carries a ladder — a simple, identifying prop — and two cans of paint. Like a typical painter, he stands sizing up the job. Then, carefully, painstakingly, he applies the stripes to the terry-cloth dress. At the end, he leaves the scene with paint authentically spattered all over his clothes and face and dripping down the sides of the can.

Iselin-Jefferson Co.

309 WTAE

Since this appeal is made to agency media buyers, the format of a familiar art director's TV storyboard is used. The numbered panels give sequence to the frames. A couple of push-pins, rings from the bottom of a glass, and a few marginal notes give verisimilitude to the setup. Low-cost typewritten copy also is appropriately used here as it would also be used on a TV storyboard.

The No. 1 panel starts the reader off, asking, "Can you identify this city?" This, indirectly, leads up to the question of how to reach these families (who are building and buying) with your advertising message.

The last panel shows a teacup and makes a pun from a Lipton Tea ad phrase: "take TAE (TV Channel 4) and see." A handwritten footnote adds, "Swell. But you forgot to mention Pittsburgh!"

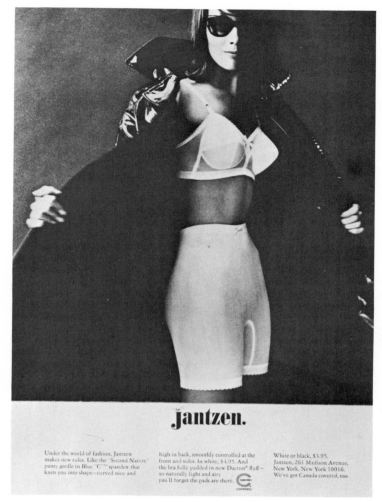

304 b

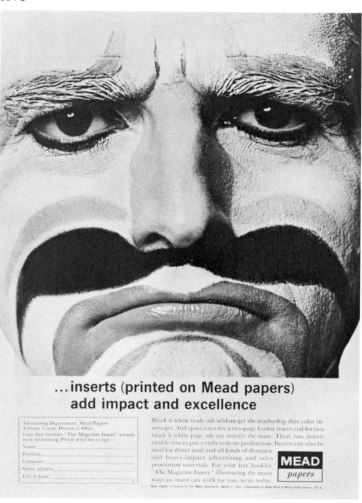

305 b

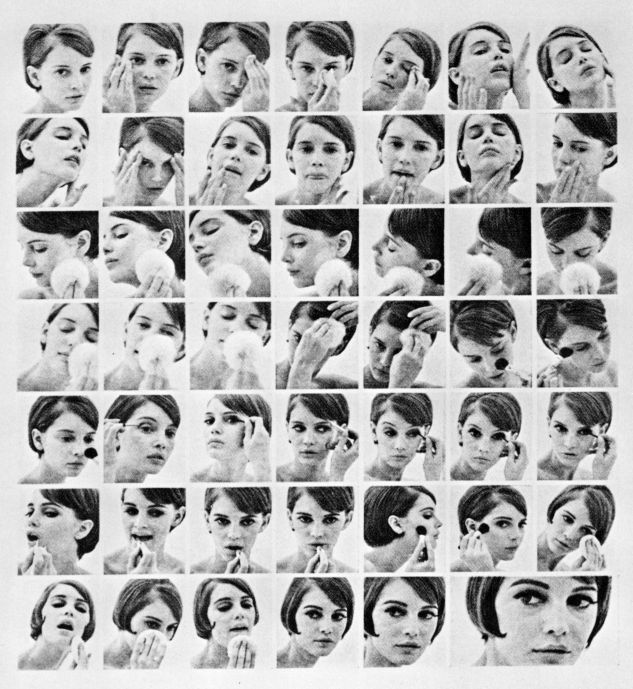

We know of nothing that gives makeup a smoother finish than loose powder. And who knows better than Charles of the Ritz?

Charles of the Ritz

In this slow-motion sequence the model's makeup goes on right before the reader's eyes from left to right, through the seven horizontal strips of photographs. The model actually seems to pick up a certain "live" motion of her own.

It becomes clear now why it takes a woman so long to get ready. Wouldn't it you, if you had someone to pamper you? Even if it's only yourself?

The final photo takes up two units of space, providing a subtle but startling contrast with the plain Jane of the first photo. Lots of picture, and very little copy.

311 Van Heusen

In this brochure ad (see following right-hand pages), you see the beard "growing" before your very eyes. The turning of each fold serves as a pause between takes.

Your eyes rest for a moment and, when you turn the page, you are surprised. Not that you hadn't expected more to follow. But all that...? Finally, at the last unfolding — with a full-grown, grandfather beard — the headline is completed: "and wears...up to twice as long as other cotton wash and wear shirts."

Announcing! Van Heusen's new Century Vanaplus that wears

311 a

312

312 Camels

Appearing in a circus magazine, this ad was geared specifically to circus-goers. It featured the top-billing star of that season, the sequence following the actual stunts in the performance, in the hope that the cigarette would subsequently be associated with the act.

The copy begins to tie in specifically with the product near the last panel, when a Camel is offered as a reward for an outstanding performance. The performer is featured with the famous "T-Zone" mnemonic, graphically pinpointing his throat area. "T-Zone...T for Taste...T for Throat..."

A footnote tells the reader that "More doctors smoke Camels than any other cigarette."

R. J. Reynolds

313 Schlitz

There is a paraphrase here of "I came, I saw, I conquered." The picture is arranged to allow a pause for the eye between phrases: "I was curious... I tasted it...Now I know..."

In the first panel, actors are rehearsing for *Romeo and Juliet.* Next, from the balcony, Romeo sees a tray with beer and glasses on it. He comes down, tastes the beer for the first time, out of curiosity, and is convinced. A bottle and a can are shown in the right-hand corner below, with a blow-up of the bottle's label.

© Jos. Schlitz Brewing Co.

and wears

311 b

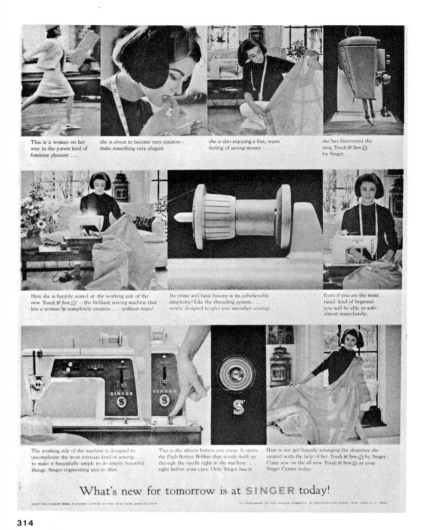

314 Singer

In six pictures, interspersed with product features, is a complete story about a woman making draperies for the house. Close-ups, middle-distance and long shots create variety. The white river running between the bands of photos serves as a reading channel that isolates the copy from the photographs. These are cropped and closely connected to make less white in the ad.

The copy, which is pleasantly rhythmic, leads from picture to picture, telling about the utter simplicity of the new Touch & Sew Singer machine. "This is a woman on her way...Here she is happily seated..." Benefits of the machine and early rewards for the buyer are noted: "a fine warm feeling of saving money...even if you are the most timid kind of beginner you will be able to solo almost immediately...Push-Button Bobbin that winds itself up."

314

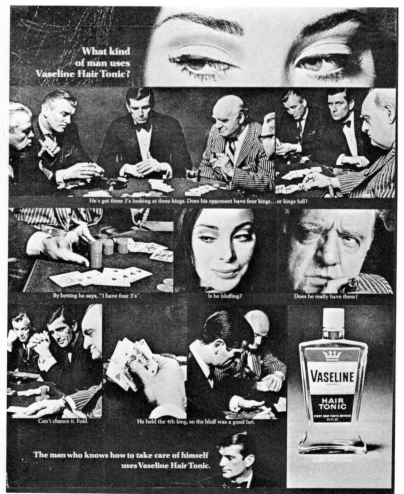

315 Vaseline

If a product is not inherently dramatic, it can be made to seem so by placing its user in an exciting situation. Our hero is playing poker and the chips are piling high. He puts in a stack and bluffs his way out, forcing his opponent to fold.

The strip panels go from distance shots to medium, to close-up to extra close-up, ending with the bottle of tonic in the last panel.

The slogan is: "The man who knows how to take care of himself uses Vaseline Hair Tonic."

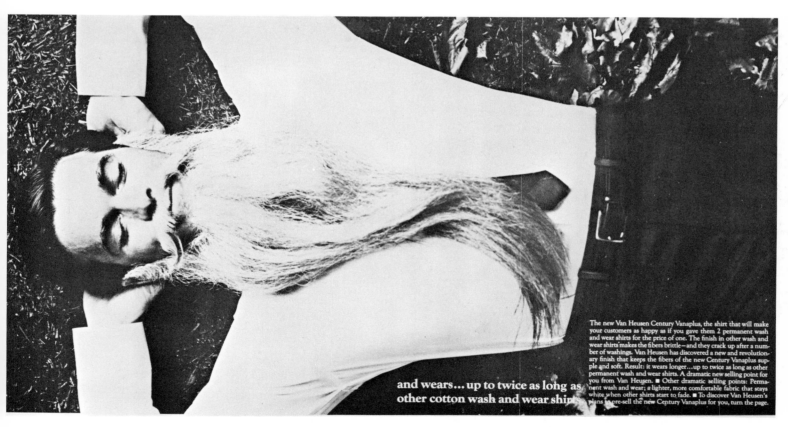

and wears...up to twice as long as other cotton wash and wear shirts.

The new Van Heusen Century Vanaplus, the shirt that will make your customers as happy as if you gave them 2 permanent wash and wear shirts for the price of one. The finish in other wash and wear shirts makes the fibers brittle—and they crack up after a number of washings. Van Heusen has discovered a new and revolutionary finish that keeps the fibers of the new Century Vanaplus supple and soft. Result: it wears longer...up to twice as long as other permanent wash and wear shirts. A dramatic new selling point for you from Van Heusen. ■ Other dramatic selling points: Permanent wash and wear; a lighter, more comfortable fabric that stays white when other shirts start to fade. ■ To discover Van Heusen's plans to pre-sell the new Century Vanaplus for you, turn the page.

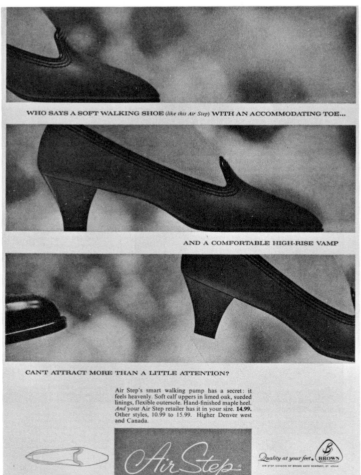

316 Wildroot

Charlie Wild, in name, is the exact opposite of what the product does to his hair: it makes it neat.

In this comic-strip ad, Taja, the beautiful snake charmer, is fatally poisoned by a "harmless" snake. Our man Charlie is on the scene to expose Kahab, her jealous, murdering assistant. Charlie has a moral for Kahab, who substituted a venomous snake for Taja's harmless one. "He should've used less snake-oil and more Wildroot Cream-Oil!"

© United Feature Syndicate

317 Wildroot

That famous arm of the law, Fearless Fosdick, is the hero of this comic-strip ad. In this episode a lion is on the loose, but our boy Fosdick, although he riddles the lion with bullets, knows very well that this is really "Anyface, — master of disguise!!" Fosdick was not fooled, he says: "No self-respecting lion would ever have such messy hair!!"

He pronounces the slogan; "Get Wildroot Cream-Oil, Charlie!!" and gets the response, "But, that would be illegal! My name is Leonard!" "No matter what your name is, get Wildroot Cream-Oil today!"

318 Air Step

Since the photograph of the shoe itself must dominate the ad, the problem is how to introduce a little human interest without distracting the reader's attention from the product.

Obviously, the girl is walking across the page in order to show the three special features of the shoe: first, the accommodating toe; second, the comfortable high-rise vamp; and third, the sensible heel. As she completes her short walk, the toe of a man's shoe comes into the picture to prove that she has attracted more than a little attention.

The slogan: "Quality at your feet."

Brown Shoe Co.

320 Ciro

This is the first of a sequence of four quarter-pages (see following right-hand pages), which build up to the finale — a half-pager that says, "Oh la la ... for those black lace moods!" It turns out that the garter motif is the same used in the design on the perfume package.

319 Old Grand-Dad

Progression unfolds with the same subject as he advances through life. The same father model ages from picture to picture, on that great holiday for giving, Father's Day. In the hands of a competent make-up man, a new Dad can age very rapidly indeed.

Repetition of the same pose increases the illusion of the changing face, the most interesting element in the picture. The clothes change, too, along with the make-up, the suit becoming more somber.

320 a

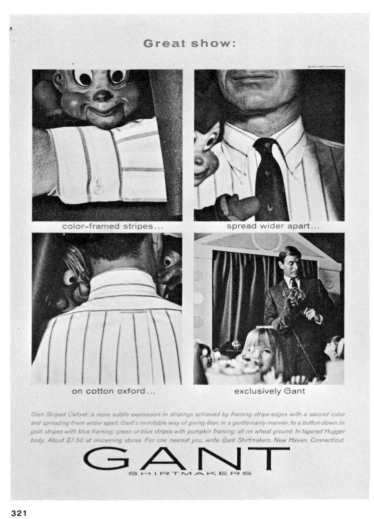

Great show:

color-framed stripes...   spread wider apart...

on cotton oxford...   exclusively Gant

Glen Striped Oxford: a more subtle expression in stripings achieved by framing stripe-edges with a second color and spreading them wider apart. Gant's inimitable way of giving élan, in a gentlemanly manner, to a button-down. In gold stripes with blue framing; green or blue stripes with pumpkin framing; all on wheat ground. In tapered Hugger body. About $7.50 at discerning stores. For one nearest you, write Gant Shirtmakers, New Haven, Connecticut.

GANT
SHIRTMAKERS

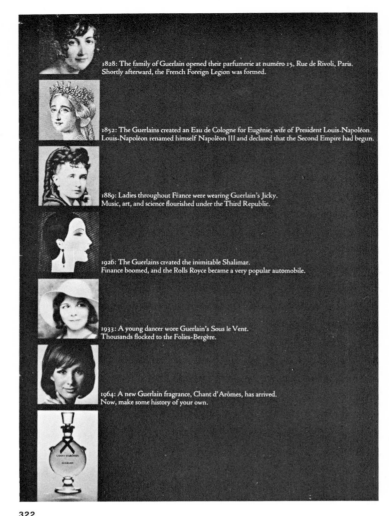

1828: The family of Guerlain opened their parfumerie at numéro 15, Rue de Rivoli, Paris. Shortly afterward, the French Foreign Legion was formed.

1852: The Guerlains created an Eau de Cologne for Eugénie, wife of President Louis-Napoléon. Louis-Napoléon renamed himself Napoléon III and declared that the Second Empire had begun.

1889: Ladies throughout France were wearing Guerlain's Jicky. Music, art, and science flourished under the Third Republic.

1926: The Guerlains created the inimitable Shalimar. Finance boomed, and the Rolls Royce became a very popular automobile.

1933: A young dancer wore Guerlain's Sous le Vent. Thousands flocked to the Folies-Bergère.

1964: A new Guerlain fragrance, Chant d'Arômes, has arrived. Now, make some history of your own.

people

who
know

buy
Bigelow
RUGS CARPETS SINCE 1825

Give your home the climate of luxury with Bigelow's Richmead —a lush, deep, all-wool face Wilton. Subtle chevron effect gives surface interest. 10 contemporary multi-color combinations.

Drink
Coca-Cola

Thirst knows no season

COPYRIGHT 1958, THE COCA-COLA COMPANY

321 Gant Shirtmakers

Extreme close-up photography, showing the fabric and stripe of the shirt, gets stepped-up attention when the puppet peeks into the picture.

The camera angles around the scene and finally lets us in on the locale of the great show, explaining the preceding shots. This is a puppet show and the puppeteer is wearing the shirt. Since this is a very exclusive party, the implication is that the shirt also is exclusive.

© Gant

322 Chant d'Arômes

If a product is linked with historical events, it can be dramatized in a chronological sequence. In this ad dates and events from 1828, when the Guerlain family founded the *parfumerie* in the rue de Rivoli, shortly before the French Foreign Legion was formed, lead up to the present.

In 1852 Guerlain created an *eau de cologne* for Eugénie, wife of Louis Napoleon, who that year renamed himself Napoleon III and announced the Second Empire. 1889: French ladies were using Guerlain's *Jicky*. Science and the arts flourished under the Third Republic. 1926: Guerlain's *Shalimar* appeared, France boomed, the Rolls-Royce became very popular. 1964 (year ad appeared): "A new Guerlain fragrance, *Chant d'Arômes* has arrived. Now, make some history of your own."

Guerlain

323 Bigelow

This series has. been running for ages. The theme is consistently one of luxurious living that goes with lush carpeting, rich in texture and color. (Imagine the same room shown without carpet or rugs.)

In this three-part setup, the camera spotlights the carpet throughout. The sunlit patio blacks out in a sudden thunderstorm, forcing the party-goers indoors. We sense the sheltering comfort of the room with the warmth of the rug transferring itself to the party. That's what a rug is for. The slogan is the headline, too: "People who know buy Bigelow."

324 Coca-Cola

Showing or saying a lot in a single space is difficult unless there is a unifying factor. Here the job is particularly exacting because both the product and a logo have to be shown.

The solution is good. We are looking out of a window while an entire year passes before our eyes: spring, summer, fall and winter, night and day, in all kinds of weather. The telegram headline is the only thing that is necessary to get the idea across.

© The Coca-Cola Company, 1952. Coca-Cola and Coke are the registered trademarks which identify only the product of The Coca-Cola Company.

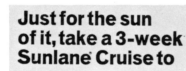

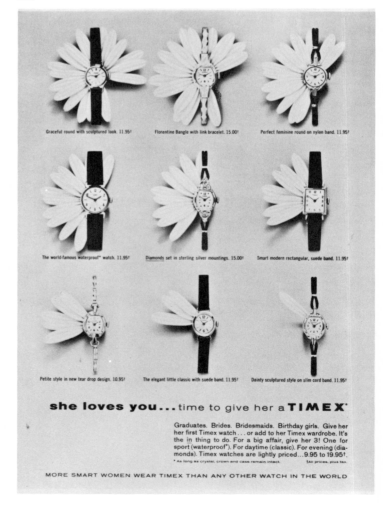

325 Ivory

The message in this ad is twofold. One, that for
young-looking skin, Ivory is equally good be it for
grandmothers, mothers, or babies; two, by implication,
that Ivory has been around a long time and therefore is time tested. The "snapshot" of three gener-
ations raiding the bag of groceries for Ivory Soap
is convincing on both counts. Below the three blocks
of copy, the thought is reiterated: "Three gener-
ations prove: Young-looking skin runs in an Ivory
Soap family."
   The famous old slogan: "99 44/100% pure...it
floats."

Procter & Gamble

326 Ballantine

The three-ring sign is used here to epitomize the
qualities of Ballantine ale. It is appropriately accompanied by a visual/verbal aid which explains that
symbol. Even such visual aids as graphs or charts are
useless unless the reader is given copy to interpret
them.
   In a step-by-step sequence, the Ballantine cowboy
with his rope throws rings — first one, then two, then
three — to symbolize "purity," "body," and "flavor."
He accomplishes this feat in a far more fascinating
way than any graph or chart ever could.

327 American Export Isbrandtsen Lines

A shape can be repeated and telling little changes
made, provided an ad's basic idea is not over-
shadowed by its props.
   A decorative face made with the sun adjusts itself to the various climates and headgear typical of
the natives. The copy sells the reader on the attractions of each country: "Spain, land of castanets
and bullfights...France, laughing country of pretty
girls...Africa, mysterious, teeming continent... Italy,
cradle of civilization..."

328 Timex

The old daisy game — "she loves me, she loves me
not" — is used here as a springboard for the message: She loves you — you should give her a Timex
watch.
   The daisy is pulled apart, in nine progressive
stages, until only the last petal remains. Nine different watches, related in a pleasant way, have had
their showing. The diffused cast shadow of the daisy
helps to feature each style. Captions describe each
one separately while relating them to the overall
picture.

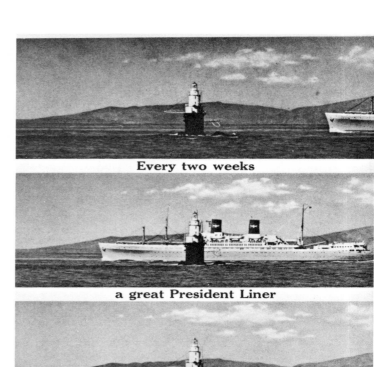

329 Panagra

This ad demonstrates how easily progression in space can be handled with one piece of art work. The outlined shape of the plane makes it easily identifiable as the same object while it grows progressively larger.

The plane is coming closer to us as we read downwards from the top. The placement of type between illustrations helps the reader to take in an intelligible sequence.

Pan American-Grace Airways

330 American President Lines

As the reader takes in the first line, the ship's prow appears from the east. Almost before he can take in the second line, the hull of the ship is nearly halfway past "Mile Rock Lighthouse. Ahead: the open sea." The last shot shows the stern of the liner, disappearing toward the Orient. There is a kind of breathlessness for the reader in this swift sequence.

Many full-page ads lose some of their impact when they are reproduced at less than full size. This, unfortunately, is one of them.

331 Irvington Place

The series of photos gives the complete race. It progresses smoothly because of the usual left-to-right movement of the eyes, reading across and down the page.

The camera is in a fixed position as the subjects move towards it, while the perspective of receding white lines corresponds with the increasing size of the figures. This makes for the illusion of great depth.

The girls in white suits become a background that repeats itself over and over, in contrast with the girl in a dark dress. The color of the brand name in the headline matches that of the dress. The copy begins: "On your mark! Get set! Go with Irvington Place! Win every time in this three-piece denim..."

332 Sir Pendleton

The model is casually, correctly posed. He becomes more and more like a manikin as the camera gets in closer to him. The copy and progressively closer shots invite the reader to "note the correct casual look of fashion...handsome at a distance, better the closer you approach."

When the reader is close enough to perceive the weave, the actual structure of the cloth, the switch is made to the brand-name label.

© Pendleton Woolen Mills

320 d

333 Talon

This company sells zippers, zippers and more zippers. Its advertising gets zippier each time. This soft-sell sequence is almost the equivalent of a Peanuts comic strip in photographs.

The pitcher is going great and the catcher calls time out. He thinks quickly: "What's he coming out here for...He'll say my fast ball is losing its zip and he'll rattle me. I just know he's going to say something to rattle me."

He's right. But the rattling is not what he, or the reader, expected. The catcher whispers to him, "Your fly is open!" and walks away. The visual pause is there, before the last panel, showing the discomposure of the pitcher who is now about to break his own winning streak — by losing.

The slogan: "Talon makes the zipper that always remembers to stay up."

© Talon

334 Straw Hat (See following pages)

In full color, spread across two pages, this "commercial" with its rhyme and rhythm gives the reader a visual happening. The astonishing variety of shots, taken at varying distances, reflects the excitement — and the practical applications — of the whole line of Straw Hat products. No doubt the background music for the actual TV commercial provided unity for so heterogeneous an assortment of electronic impressions.

Fabergé

This is a TV commercial for perspicacious people

presented for your diversion
by tongue-in-chic Fabergé,

who created STRAW HAT,
that going-places scent

for the young-at-heart
on pleasure bent.

it tells the world
STRAW HAT's in the air!

Purty, flirty STRAW HAT
— fashioned for fun

any place
under the sun...

Frolicky, rollicky
STRAW HAT

keeps you young
in the sun

...and it's fun!
Cool Tanning Gelée.

new STRAW HAT 65
Oval Lipstick...Nail Glacé

— toetips too! It's the
smartest shade to be under.

Small wonder! And so, dear
barefoot girl with chic,

334

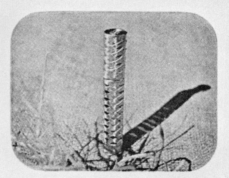

Here the abrupt change between picture one and picture two jolts you; you get the feeling of instantaneous motion. At the same time you have the visual/verbal answer to the question in the headline. (You don't need the subhead.)

The photo at the top is sharp and close-up. But below it, the car that is accelerating on the stretch of wooded road seems slightly out of focus. The light haze of smoke from the exhaust is the visual clincher as to the pick-up of a V-8 in a Chevy II.

The copy tells you what the additional effects are, too. *"Hills don't seem half so hilly. And even when you've got every nook and cranny of cargo space filled, still there's no holding you back."*

General Motors

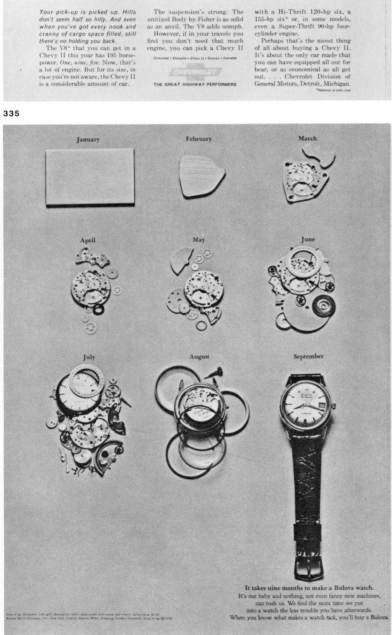

Just as it takes nine months for a baby to develop, so it does to make a Bulova watch. The evolution of the watch is shown in stages, from the metal plate to the finished watch, labelled by months from January through September. The last line of copy reads: "When you know what makes a watch tick, you'll buy a Bulova."

By the time the reader has been led past the world-shaking inventions of the past in this ad, he is convinced that the final product is as much of an innovation as the others, particularly as it is shown in full color in contrast to the sepia-toned photographs of the items preceding it.

The copy tells how people laughed at the first wheel, the first light bulb, the telephone, automobile, steamboat, and airplane. The square, homely VW Station Wagon also was laughed at when it was introduced in America. The copy winds up: "The VW Wagon is still a pretty funny sight. And people are still laughing. But the laughter is dying down."

© Volkswagen of America, Inc.

They laughed.

3000 B.C. Somebody invented the wheel. It was round and funny. And since the road wasn't invented yet, everybody laughed.

1879. The electric light bulb. It was so dim, people had to use a gas lamp to see it. They laughed.

1875. The telephone. Who'd want to stand and talk to a box full of wires? They laughed.

1877. The automobile sputtered down the road. The horse and buggy passed it like it was standing still. And it usually was.

1807. The first steamboat in America made it from New York to Albany in 32 hours. A small boy could've beat it in a rowboat. They laughed.

1903. The airplane. Off it soared into the wild blue yonder; down it came 59 seconds later. They laughed.

1950. The Volkswagen Station Wagon. It was square and homely. But it held almost twice as much as un-funny wagons, took 4 feet less space to park, never froze up or boiled over, and cost about half as much to run.

The VW Wagon is still a pretty funny sight. And people are still laughing. But the laughter is dying down.

337

SYMBOLISM

338 Canoe

The flag symbols spell out C-A-N-O-E, telling part of the story. The curlicue wire of the chair's back and the French sailor hat tell the rest — this is a French perfume. The flag charade is fun for nautically minded viewers.

Dana

338

339 Onyx

A few props evoke an image for the product: oak paneling, a bowler hat and rolled umbrella; the London Times, symbolizing the typical Britisher, representative of the "scent that Englishmen created for Englishmen...Newly in America, for those immaculate men who will settle for nothing less than an air of effortless elegance."

Lenthéric

The sponsors are sports-happy too!

We have a program that covers the world of sports like no other. It's called Worldwide Sports and it breaks the mold. Leading advertisers—for whom the name of the game is sales—love it, and the results it chalks up.

Worldwide Sports, with pivotman Frank Gifford, goes where the action is, across the country, around the world. Worldwide Sports tracks late news and scores time zone by time zone. It's on every week night at 7:15-7:30 PM local time* with a new edition for each zone so no one gets part-time scores when

games are all over.

This kind of diligence and completeness indeed wins the fans. And the sponsors. In 1964 some two dozen advertisers—among them Armour, Pepsi-Cola, Alcoa, Barbasol, Mars, and Millers Falls—sold everything from soap to soda-pop to power tools on Worldwide Sports. The Millers Falls Company uses Worldwide Sports as a major effort. They can pinpoint sales results. And President Jack Owen says this:

"Last year our Worldwide Sports campaign helped significantly in increasing

consumer acceptance of our line of tools. This was reflected in substantial sales growth, so naturally we are continuing with Worldwide Sports on the CBS Radio Network."

Millers Falls found out first-hand: there's exceptional consumer loyalty for this exceptional CBS Radio sports coverage.

Want a piece of the action? Give us a call. We've got a sporting proposition for you.

The CBS Radio Network

340

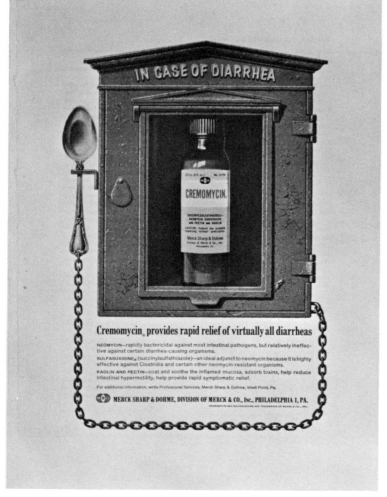

Cremomycin provides rapid relief of virtually all diarrheas

NEOMYCIN—rapidly bactericidal against most intestinal pathogens, but relatively ineffective against certain diarrhea-causing organisms.

SULFASUXIDINE₄ (succinylsulfathiazole)—an ideal adjunct to neomycin because it is highly effective against Clostridia and certain other neomycin-resistant organisms.

KAOLIN AND PECTIN—coat and soothe the inflamed mucosa, adsorb toxins, help reduce intestinal hypermotility, help provide rapid symptomatic relief.

For additional information, write Professional Services, Merck Sharp & Dohme, West Point, Pa.

MERCK SHARP & DOHME, DIVISION OF MERCK & CO., Inc., PHILADELPHIA 1, PA.

342

Premenstrual tension?

Premenstrual tension with edema can cause many and diffuse psychic and somatic symptoms. It can complicate diagnosis and treatment of other disorders. Yet, all too frequently, women accept these difficulties as inevitable. Fortunately, premenstrual tension is not inevitable. Once identified, it can often be helped with CYCLEX. CYCLEX relieves symptoms, but does not interfere with hormonal balance. The effects are direct...excess fluid is eliminated by the action of hydrochlorothiazide; the psychic component is minimized by meprobamate. CYCLEX may be given from the onset of premenstrual symptoms until the end of the menses.

INDICATIONS: Premenstrual tension with edema; hypertension; congestive heart failure.

CONTRAINDICATIONS: Hydrochlorothiazide: Anuria. Meprobamate: History of allergic reaction to meprobamate.

PRECAUTIONS: Hydrochlorothiazide: Reduce dosage of coadministered antihypertensive agents by at least 50 percent. Use caution during intensive or prolonged diuresis, in dietary inadequacy or salt restriction, impaired renal function, hepatic disease, rising level of BUN, hyperuricemia or history of gout, patients receiving other antihypertensive agents, surgical patients. Avoid hypokalemia especially during digitalis administration and in myocardial ischemia. Meprobamate: Use only in recommended dosage to minimize habituation or addiction potential.

SIDE EFFECTS: Hydrochlorothiazide: Electrolyte imbalance with hypokalemia or hypochloremic alkalosis may occur. A low-salt syndrome may be precipitated. Other possible reactions: hepatic coma, azotemia, decreased glucose tolerance, hyperuricemia and gout, blood dyscrasias, nausea, vomiting, diarrhea, dizziness, paresthesias, rash, photosensitivity. Meprobamate: Possible side effects include drowsiness, fatigue, allergic reactions (death reported), blood dyscrasias (death reported), visual disturbances, hypotensive crises, withdrawal symptoms. Large or suicidal doses may result in cardiovascular and respiratory collapse, shock, absent reflexes, coma, and death. Tolerance to alcohol may be reduced. Tendency to convulsions may be increased. Grand-mal seizures may be precipitated.

Before prescribing or administering, read product circular with package or available on request.

SUPPLIED: Tablets, bottles of 100. Each tablet contains 25 mg. of hydrochlorothiazide and 200 mg. of meprobamate.

CYCLEX DIURETIC-TRANQUILIZER

MERCK SHARP & DOHME | where today's theory is tomorrow's therapy

343

340 CBS Radio Network

On one model are shown many different sports out-fits, ideal symbols of each game, and all clearly visible. Golf clubs and hockey stick are jutting out behind the figure. He wears a catcher's mask and skis. Bowling ball and tennis racket are easily identifiable.

The copy reveals that the program, Worldwide Sports, will broadcast on the CBS Radio Network all successful sports shows. Many of the advertisers who have been successful with the program are listed. One case history of a satisfied customer, Miller Falls Company (tools), is thrown in for good measure.

341 El Al Israel Airlines

Talk about wearing many hats! These hats, and the zany but telling faces the model is pulling, inform you that the versatile travel agent can do almost anything for you, that he is the man for you. The ad sells both agent and customer, thereby winning the love of both traveler and agent for this helpful bit of advice.

342 Cremomycin

This familiar alarm box gives the reader a visual telegram, pinpointing what the product is and for what emergency. Three elements contribute to its impact, first, the headline; second, the medicine bottle sealed behind glass; third, the spoon-hammer for breaking the glass to get at the bottle. The copy, enclosed within the hanging chain, all about "intestinal pathogens" and "neomycin-resistant organisms," is presumably to be read at leisure.

Merck, Sharp & Dohme

344 Jell-O.

The reverse side of the cut-outs on the upper part of the ad (see following right-hand page) was a coupon that could be redeemed for a five-cent saving on any purchase of the product.

The fruit cut-outs, if properly matched to the three separate packages, would be worth $25,000 in groceries (or cash). The cornucopia of fruits coming out of the one-armed bandit is intermixed with Jell-O boxes of different fruit flavors.

343 Cyclex

Photo-graffiti are here to stay, even in ads. The idea is simple — a woman can act like the devil because of premenstrual tension. Without a profusion of props, which would distract the reader's attention from the copy below, the idea is put over with a few deft red strokes of the brush on the photograph. The whimsical expression of the model adds to the light tone of this ad; the tail and pitchfork leave no doubt as to the identity of the dark one of whom she is possessed.

Merck, Sharpe & Dohme

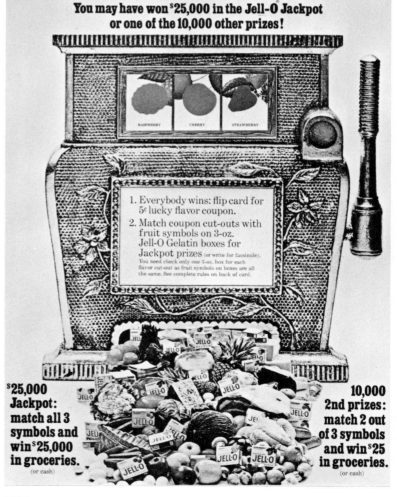

344 a

The complete picnic kit? Not with just one bottle of Coca-Cola. Things (like picnics) go better with Coke after Coke after Coke. After all, Coke has the taste you never get tired of.

Coca-Cola

KING SIZE

Coke

SPEAK TO NO DOCTOR   SEE NO DOCTOR   HEAR NO DOCTOR

This man is his own worst enemy! Yet most of us can sympathize with him—for most of us don't "run to the doctor" every time we have an ache or pain.

We're much more likely to say: "Oh, I'm all right. It's really nothing." Or to tell ourselves: "I'm too busy . . . haven't time to bother with doctors."

Yet, the man (or woman) who ignores seemingly minor symptoms often runs the risk of inviting much more serious ailments. That's because most diseases thrive on neglect; the worst thing we can do is to ignore warning symptoms until it may be too late for the doctor to help.

Medical research in America today is writing one of the most heart-warming chapters in the story of man-

Copyright 1955—Parke, Davis & Company

kind. Our great laboratories, our hospitals, universities, and a host of governmental and private organizations are cooperating as never before to improve our chances of living a longer, healthier life.

Your own doctor has at his disposal all of the discoveries, all of the knowledge, of modern medical science. But you are the only one who can put these vast resources to work to help *you*.

So next time you are tempted to ignore warning symptoms, remember that your *greatest danger* lies in neglect and delay. Remember—in your physician's hands, you're in *good* hands. But only by acting promptly can you take advantage of the help he can give you *now*.

This message is published in the public interest by Parke, Davis & Company.
Since 1866, physicians have prescribed and pharmacists have dispensed medicines bearing the Parke-Davis label.

PARKE, DAVIS & CO.
Research and Manufacturing Laboratories, Detroit 32, Michigan

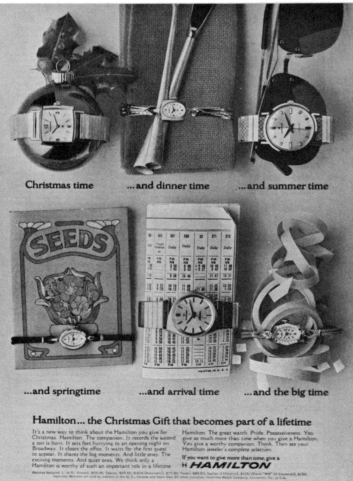

Christmas time   ...and dinner time   ...and summer time

SEEDS

...and springtime   ...and arrival time   ...and the big time

Hamilton... the Christmas Gift that becomes part of a lifetime

It's a new way to think about the Hamilton you give for Christmas. Hamilton. The companion. It records the second a son is born. It sets feet hurrying to an opening night on Broadway. It closes the office. It waits for the first guest to appear. It shares the big moments. And little ones. The exciting moments. And quiet ones. We think only a Hamilton is worthy of such an important role in a lifetime.

Hamilton. The great watch. Pride. Possessiveness. You give so much more than time when you give a Hamilton. You give a worthy companion. Think. Then see your Hamilton jeweler's complete selection.

If you want to give more than time, give a

H HAMILTON

Watches featured: L. to R.: Vincell, $59.95; Edwae, $69.50; A-606 (Automatic), $79.50; Tindel, $125; Chiron "NN" (4 Diamonds), $150.
Hamilton Watches are sold by jewelers in the U. S., Canada and more than 50 other countries. Hamilton Watch Company, Lancaster, Pa., U.S.A.

If you have more than one policy to cover all these business risks, you could be paying up to 25% too much.

Stop wasting your money. One Continental policy can cover all your property, liability and fidelity risks.

At savings up to 25%.

You'll also save a lot of headaches. Such as handling a lot of different policies. With a lot of different premiums. And a lot of different renewal dates. From a lot of different companies. With a lot of different agents.

Had enough?

Call your Continental agent. (He's

listed in the Yellow Pages.)

He'll help you decide what kind and how much protection you need. (Based upon your business. He doesn't have to fit you into some inflexible package plan.)

Then, he'll put it into one Comprehensive Business Policy. With one premium. One renewal date. No duplicate coverage. And less chance of an uninsured loss.

Now—can you afford more than one policy?

The Continental Insurance Companies

Continental Insurance Co. · Fidelity and Casualty · Fireman's of Newark · Commercial of Newark · Seaboard Fire and Marine · National Fire Insurance Co. · Boston Old Colony Co. · Buckeye Union ·
HOME OFFICES: 80 MAIDEN LANE, N.Y., N.Y. 4
20 PARK PL., NEWARK, N.J.

345 Coca-Cola

A symbol need not be elaborate. Few and simple props serve to hold the spotlight on the product. Instead of showing a picnic scene, or the cliché of the picnic basket, a Coke carry-carton is substituted. At that, the idea of carrying the picnic in a Coke case might be successfully adapted for a small picnic.

The copy says that it can't be a complete picnic with only one Coke, even if it is King size. As their slogan goes: "Things (like picnics) go better with Coke after Coke after Coke...the taste you never get tired of."

© The Coca-Cola Company, 1966. Coca-Cola and Coke are the registered trademarks which identify only the product of The Coca-Cola Company.

346 Parke, Davis & Co.

The symbolism of the three monkeys' speak-no-evil, see-no-evil, hear-no-evil has, at one stroke, been humanized and paraphrased in the headline.

Without directly accusing the reader of negligence, the copy implies that he may well be the one imitating the monkeys. "This man is his own worst enemy! Yet most of us can sympathize with him — for most of us don't 'run to the doctor' every time we have an ache or pain."

© Parke, Davis & Co.

347 Hamilton Watch Co.

This ad is aimed at selling Hamilton watches as Christmas gifts. At the same time it relates watches to other seasons and occasions — "dinner time... and summer time...and springtime...and arrival time..." It builds up the Hamilton watch as a companion for life, recording "the second a son is born. It sets feet hurrying to an opening night...It closes the office...It shares the big moments. And little ones."

The inanimate symbols of each occasion are well chosen. The slogan, "If you want to give more than time, give a Hamilton," ties in well, too, with the headline and copy.

348 Continental Insurance

The more complicated the idea, the more simply it should be communicated visually. In a business of intangibles, some very specific applications are shown for the types of risk for which this company will insure a business.

A splattered brick wall stands for vandalism, a hand reaching into an open cash register for employee liability, a gavel for general liability, and jets flying in formation for sonic boom.

"Stop wasting your money," the copy exhorts, explaining how to get a policy covering property, liability, fidelity risks, "At savings up to 25%. You'll also save a lot of headaches. Such as handling a lot of different policies...premiums...different companies...renewal dates...and different agents."

The company's name is literally represented by a soldier of the Continental army in the 1770's.

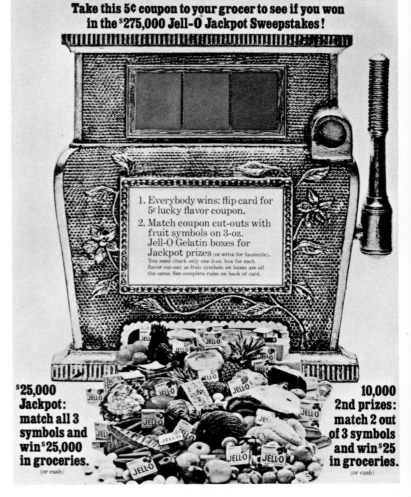

349 Ford Motor Co.

The V - 8 engine is represented by geese flying in V-formation; the straight-six engine by a string of ducks flying in a straight line.

"Parks anywhere" is symbolized by the possum who sleeps most anywhere, even hanging by his tail. A turtle's hard shell stands for the body, "59% more rigid with 'Lifeguard' body of heavy gauge steel." A frog on a lily-pad croaks: "You float on Ford's new springs."

Other "feel" features are praised by the cat: "Feel its purring power!"; by the squirrel: "Room for everything in the 'Deep Deck' Luggage Locker;" by the lamb: "Feel the wool in Ford's upholstery." The butterfly adds "10 Wonderful new colors," and the daisy: "You'll feel fresh, too!"

On a signboard, a crystal ball held in the palm of a hand has the slogan: "There's a New Ford in your future."

350 Lady Esquire

These shoes are drawn in animated situations; they are symbols of the different types of shoe that can be colored. Whimsical drawings depict shoe materials — alligator, straw, leather, fabric — and use a pair of sneakers to make the Indian's canvas tent.

The copy explains that 120 shades "are now yours…Exciting new Mix & Match, the color multiplier…Match any color. Change the color in a wink."

The sign-off is a familiar analogy: "It's as easy as coloring your nails."

350

351 Budweiser.

The use of a cliché as a symbol is necessarily accepted when there is no substitute. The representatives of various countries from "the world over," sampling Budweiser, symbolize the enjoyment this beer gives around the world. To make the concept more tangible, a revolving globe has been thrown in.

The package and the glass of beer serve to provide a pictorial mnemonic. The slogan is: "King of bottled beer."

Anheuser-Busch

351

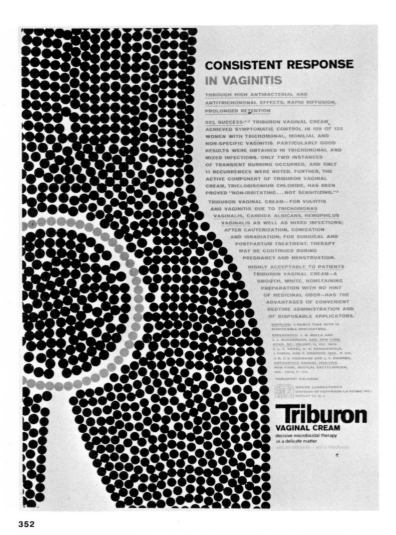

CONSISTENT RESPONSE
IN VAGINITIS

THROUGH HIGH ANTIBACTERIAL AND
ANTITRICHOMONAL EFFECTS, RAPID DIFFUSION,
PROLONGED RETENTION

85% SUCCESS[1,2] TRIBURON VAGINAL CREAM
ACHIEVED SYMPTOMATIC CONTROL IN 109 OF 128
WOMEN WITH TRICHOMONAL, MONILIAL AND
NON-SPECIFIC VAGINITIS. PARTICULARLY GOOD
RESULTS WERE OBTAINED IN TRICHOMONAL AND
MIXED INFECTIONS. ONLY TWO INSTANCES
OF TRANSIENT BURNING OCCURRED, AND ONLY
11 RECURRENCES WERE NOTED. FURTHER, THE
ACTIVE COMPONENT OF TRIBURON VAGINAL
CREAM, TRICLOBISONIUM CHLORIDE, HAS BEEN
PROVED "NON-IRRITATING ... NOT SENSITIZING."[3]

TRIBURON VAGINAL CREAM—FOR VULVITIS
AND VAGINITIS DUE TO TRICHOMONAS
VAGINALIS, CANDIDA ALBICANS, HEMOPHILUS
VAGINALIS AS WELL AS MIXED INFECTIONS;
AFTER CAUTERIZATION, CONIZATION
AND IRRADIATION; FOR SURGICAL AND
POSTPARTUM TREATMENT. THERAPY
MAY BE CONTINUED DURING
PREGNANCY AND MENSTRUATION.

HIGHLY ACCEPTABLE TO PATIENTS
TRIBURON VAGINAL CREAM—A
SMOOTH, WHITE, NONSTAINING
PREPARATION WITH NO HINT
OF MEDICINAL ODOR—HAS THE
ADVANTAGES OF CONVENIENT
BEDTIME ADMINISTRATION AND
OF DISPOSABLE APPLICATORS.

SUPPLIED: 3-OUNCE TUBE WITH 18
DISPOSABLE APPLICATORS.

REFERENCES: 1. N. MULLA AND
A. J. McDONOUGH, AM. NEW YORK
ACAD. SC., STUART, EL 910, 1959.
2. L. E. SAVEL, D. H. GERSHENFELD,
3. FINKEL AND F. DRUCKER, PHIL., P. 166.
3. R. C. V. ROBINSON AND L. C. HARMON,
ANTIBIOTICS ANNUAL 1955-1956,
NEW YORK, MEDICAL ENCYCLOPEDIA,
INC., 1956, P. 112.

TRIBURON CHLORIDE

ROCHE LABORATORIES
DIVISION OF HOFFMANN-LA ROCHE INC.
NUTLEY 10, N.J.

Triburon
VAGINAL CREAM
decisive microbicidal therapy
in a delicate matter

not an irritant... not a sensitizer

`352`

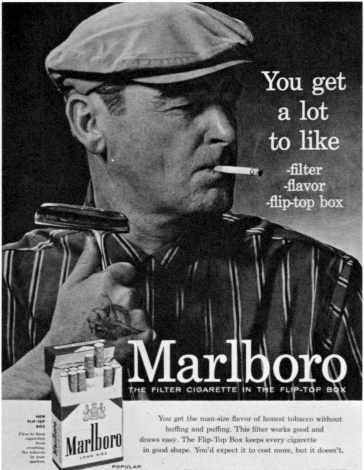

352 Triburon

Symbolism is invaluable for showing a normally "censored" part of the body. It provides detachment for the viewer while, at the same time, spelling out the necessary information in a practical, accurate way.

Here a mosaic of hundreds of outsize black spots has been put together to indicate the shape of a woman, with a circle of red spots outlining the specific area in question. This is an original approach; it might spur other advertisers in medical journals (and consumer media) to devise visuals equally clinical and inoffensive.

Roche Laboratories

356 Mitsouko

Comment as brief as the ad: The girl is Oriental. The perfume is, too.

Guerlain

353 Revlon Moon Drops

The sepia tones of the photograph give flesh tints to the girl's skin. We know she is in a bath even without the headline clues: her hair is wet and water droplets are beaded all over her.

The copy confirms these impressions — "Here's Revlon's 'dew-it-yourself' recipe." Then, as for any recipe, instructions follow: "Let yourself settle in, stirring gently from time to time. While the luxury laps around you…let the rest of the world go dry. You go fill the tub."

354 Marlboro

The sudden switch, to men, of a product preferred by women was brought about by the simple device of tattooing the hand of the model in the ad. The same basic idea could have been expressed by showing an outdoors type chopping down a tree. But this suave, masculine-looking golfer puts it over with dignity — with the suggestion of an interesting, tattooed past.

This new image tends to obliterate the old one — that Marlboro is a woman's cigarette. Indeed, in the last line, the copy assures the reader of a material change: "Made in Richmond, Virginia, from a new Marlboro recipe." In other words, this is not the same cigarette that appealed to women, even though they may continue to smoke Marlboros. The headline is used as a mnemonic, to drive home the special features of cigarette and package.

357 Hathaway

The man with the eye-patch has broken out of his Madison Avenue circuit and emerged in "the hometown of a certain British singing group," putting on a tie with his favorite shirt in a refreshing new shade of blue.

This is a casual, almost a candid, shot. The headline and copy read a bit to the right to counterbalance the leaning model. The eye-patch stays with these ads; it has become a natural member of the. Hathaway mnemonic family.

Warner Bros.

355 Knorr

A nice variation from straight food shots, these enrich that European flavor with pleasing, picturesque backgrounds from Switzerland, Austria, Denmark, Sweden, France, and Norway.

Mitsouko by Guerlain

356

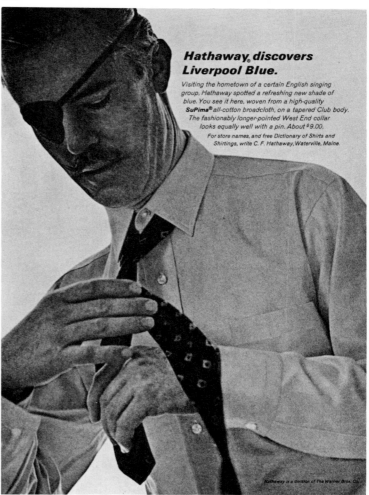

Hathaway discovers Liverpool Blue.

Visiting the hometown of a certain English singing group, Hathaway spotted a refreshing new shade of blue. You see it here, woven from a high-quality **SuPima®** *all-cotton broadcloth, on a tapered Club body. The fashionably longer-pointed West End collar looks equally well with a pin. About $9.00.*

For store names, and free Dictionary of Shirts and Shirtings, write C. F. Hathaway, Waterville, Maine.

357

The elasticity of air and the compliancy of water are associated for your comfort in Citroen's Hydropneumatic Suspension. In effect, as illustrated in the diagram, each wheel is linked to the chassis by a piston. This piston displaces a liquid which more or less compresses a cushion of air contained within the suspension sphere. The reciprocal action of these two elements absorbs shock to a degree unattainable by conventional leaf spring, coil spring or torsion bar suspensions. The ride it affords is as unique as the concept. Flattening bumps, reducing fatigue, giving the utmost roadability at all speeds, on any surface; as if Citroen were rolling out its own magic carpet. Words can't make you feel it, but a test drive will.

CITROËN

Sold and Serviced by Citroen dealers throughout U.S.A. For brochures and Overseas Delivery information, write: Citroen Cars Corporation, 300 Park Avenue, New York, New York. Or, 8623 Wilshire Boulevard, Beverly Hills, Calif.

358

358 Citroën

Believe it or not, this is an automobile ad. It sets out to sell one idea, an important one in driving comfort — Citroën's Hydropneumatic Suspension.

Most standard solutions have evolved from "torsion bar suspension," leaf or coil springs. You can look underneath the average American car and see the similarity to baby carriage springs.

In this French-built car, as indicated in the diagram above the picture, "each wheel is linked to the chassis by a piston. This piston displaces a liquid which more or less compresses a cushion of air contained within the suspension sphere...flattening bumps, reducing fatigue, giving the utmost roadability at all speeds...as if Citroën were rolling out its own magic carpet..."

Then the punch line: "Words can't make you feel it, but a test drive will."

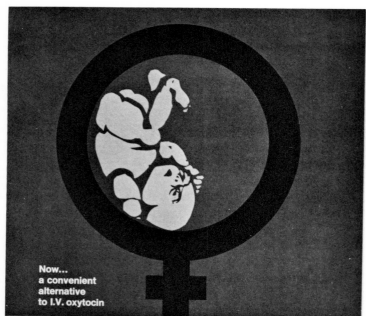

Now...
a convenient
alternative
to I.V. oxytocin

new
PITOCIN® CITRATE, BUCCAL TABLETS
(OXYTOCIN CITRATE) PARKE-DAVIS

In selected obstetric cases, PITOCIN CITRATE, BUCCAL Tablets offer a number of advantages over other dosage forms. Action is comparable to I.V. oxytocin, but pain or discomfort of parenteral or intranasal dosage is eliminated. Moreover, the rate of absorption from the buccal mucosa tends to prevent overdosage. Tablets can simply be removed from the mouth if signs of overstimulation should occur. Under proper supervision, PITOCIN CITRATE, BUCCAL can thus provide ease of administration and control in induction or stimulation of labor.

Indications: Induction or stimulation of labor in selected cases.
Precautions: Pelvic adequacy and maternal and fetal condition should be considered. Oxytocin should not be used simultaneously by more than one route. Intended for use only in hospitals under adequate medical supervision.
Contraindications: Severe toxemia; cephalopelvic disproportion; malpresentation of fetus; prematurity or unripe cervix; hypertonic labor patterns; abruptio placentae, unconscious patient; predisposition to uterine rupture as in patients with great parity (4 or more) or overdistention of uterus; other serious obstetric complications such as fetal distress or previous cesarean section; prolonged use in uterine inertia.

Side Effects: Tetanic contraction of the uterus has been reported. Nausea, vomiting, premature ventricular contractions, fetal brachycardia and cardiac arrhythmias, including tachycardia have also been reported.
How Supplied: Package of 10 tablets each containing 200 units of synthetic oxytocin.

PARKE-DAVIS

For more facts circle 135 on reply card

359 Pitocin Citrate

The fetus is as important in this ad as the woman about to bear him. The product, Pitocin tablets, works for the welfare of both. This new dosage "under proper supervision...can thus provide ease of administration and control in induction or stimulation of labor."

Raw umber was used as a second color for the square picture area. This was changed to a lighter tone for the baby's skin, lending warmth in contrast to the stark, cold sans-serif type used throughout the ad.

Parke, Davis

SMALL
ADVERTISEMENTS

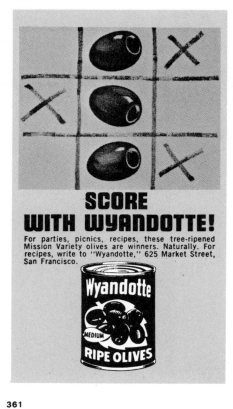

360 Hoffritz

The familiar eye chart is used as a basis for this headline set-up. It is well related to the contact-lens case being advertised. Posing a question, with diminishing type size, leads the eye line by line down to the lens case and the answer.

364 Stieff

Small ads present special problems. First, because the space is so small, it must be adroitly exploited to get all possible attention for the visual/verbal content.

Instead of showing a whole spoon, including the shaft — and so losing important details of the pattern — Stieff shows both ends close up.

The name of the silverware pattern is given prominence for instant impression. And the small headline whispers to those who stay with the ad, "If you weren't born to Royalty, acquire it."

361 Wyandotte

Participation in a small ad can be effective. As in this case, the reader can take part, scoring the tick-tack-toe, with the product as winner. The simpler the game — both graphically and in concept — the more quickly it communicates with the audience.

362 Brut

For quick identity, the product is shown as large as possible, while the minimum amount of copy is used so that nothing gets crowded in the small space.

The copy is headed, "Et tu Brut?" — a mnemonical word play on the product name.

Fabergé

365 American Cancer Society

The unusual photograph of a baby rat cuddled up in a human hand is a visual stopper. The use of a hand, in that small space, is a valuable asset because it captures instant human interest. The close-up photo together with the headline — variations of which you have seen before — take full advantage of a very small space.

363 Tower Suite

Talk about personalizing an ad! This headline makes sure you get the idea by repeating it three times. It shows the butler's face and lets him introduce himself to you.

This tiny ad has been running continuously, overpowering the "shout'em, sock'em, knock'em down" school of advertising which frequently appears on the same newspaper pages.

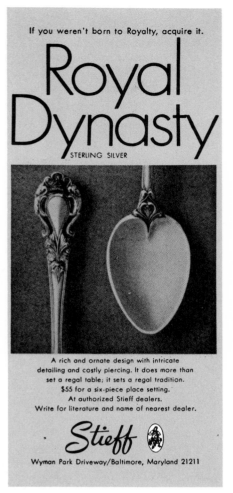

If you weren't born to Royalty, acquire it.

Royal Dynasty
STERLING SILVER

A rich and ornate design with intricate detailing and costly piercing. It does more than set a regal table; it sets a regal tradition. $55 for a six-piece place setting. At authorized Stieff dealers. Write for literature and name of nearest dealer.

Stieff

Wyman Park Driveway/Baltimore, Maryland 21211

364

Some of your best friends are rats.

They could help save your life through research—in the laboratories where the unceasing war against cancer is fought. Like all wars, it is expensive to wage.

Last year the American Cancer Society spent $12,000,000 on research. Send your check to "Cancer," c/o Postmaster. To cure more, give more.

AMERICAN CANCER SOCIETY

365

366 huk-a-poo sportswear

By using large type and crowding everything except the picture area, you can squeeze in a lot of easy-to-read copy.

    The white space to the right and left of the "head" makes a relaxing break for the eyes, and the absence of human form focuses the reader's attention on the garment itself.

    Since the whole object of this ad was to inform the reader about what huk-a-poo does, dictionary and format (including the thumb-index "H" at left margin) were justified.

366

367 Sterling

Attention-getting gimmicks are often necessary in small ads. They should always come out of the product idea or be related to it.

    Since a majority of sports fans are beer drinkers (and bars are aware of this when they pre-tune their TV sets), a listing of the ten best players in the field of sports would interest them.

    The cartoon characters add human interest to the scoreboard. Hiding the figures behind the scoreboard conveys their presence without the use of additional space.

    The rhyming slogan supports the sports theme, "With fans around here, it's Sterling Beer."

367

368 Dobbs

A face distracts the eye from the hat above it. Here, the face has been pretty well dropped out and is replaced by a scene of doubtful interest — a couple going places. The man, presumably, wears a Dobbs hat.

    The hat is aggressively three-dimensional, especially against the flat "DOBBS" lettering. The scene beneath it is also, by contrast, a flat-looking shot.

Hat Corp. of America

368

369 Jacqueline Cochran

Since eyes get circles under them, what could be more natural than to offer a woman this "Opaque Touch-Up, in a half-dollar size case that goes out with you"? The white space around the little circle draws attention to it very conspicuously.

369

370 Witty Brothers

To familiarize readers with a unique fabric, "Blue Shark, glinted with silk," an extreme close-up is shown. To show a full figure would detract from the texture shot and block out a large part of it.

The solution — to use a line drawing of the figure and let the enlarged texture-pattern serve as a background for the suit — keeps the identity of the fabric clear while providing a little human interest.

370

371 Pennsylvania Bureau of Travel Development

This was a very successful small-space newspaper ad. It has a short message and says it quickly. It singles out the traveler on his way to the World's Fair and invites him to send for information about Pennsylvania as a stopping point. Space on both sides of the headline keeps it isolated from surrounding ads on the page.

371

372 Cybis Porcelain

The pages of a partly open book accomplish two purposes here: they give a clue as to the relative height of the Peter Pan figure and serve as a relatively neutral background for the shiny figurine.

372

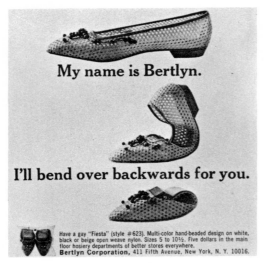

373

373 Bertlyn

The flexibility of the Bertlyn shoe is graphically demonstrated by this amusing sequence of pictures and words in which the shoe assumes an engaging personality of its own. Informative body copy provides the necessary details.

374

374 Aziza

It's amazing to find how many things can be related to the concept of a puzzle. Starting with the head-line, "Puzzled about eye make-up?" the name of the product is featured in a crossword puzzle, with an eye substituted for the letter *I* . Three things are thus related: an eye, a brand name, and the puzzle. Two products are thrown in: an eyebrow and lid liner, and an eye-shadow stick.

The terse subhead answers the headline: "Aziza has all the answers."

Prince Matchabelli

375

375 Bermuda Shop

The text, "Sailors and landlubbers alike will want our...pants from the island" gets the message over by using a symbol of the water — a rowboat.

Turning the boat on end and posing the model in it provides a compact unit and an unusual symbol photograph. The two vertical oars emphasize the girl's narrow build and make it easy for the reader to identify the rowboat as such

376 Worumbo

Contrast in photo size works well for showing up specific details in a product. Attention is first riveted on the coat itself and then turned to the detail of collar and seaming, and the fabric, enormously enlarged. This is used as an overall background for the ad. A woman might prefer to study the style of the coat before examining the fabric.

J. P. Stevens & Co.

376

377 Wurlitzer

By good placement, this small ad encourages the reader to participate and supplies him with the tools for filling in and cutting out the coupon, along with step-by-step instructions.

The headline, "Rent-a-Piano," is within the coupon.

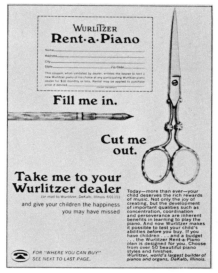

377

378 Paper Mate

Repetition of the same kind of object provides uniformity of pattern, as in this ad. The different hands are posed in the same profile position, neatly forming a diagonal that leads to the copy.

The pens were developed for hands of different character, and are shown close to each other for quick comparison. The name, Profile-Trio, may have been the starter for this visual.

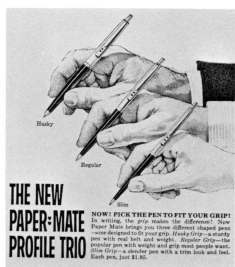

378

379

379 Art Instruction Schools

Readers have been participating in this ad for years. The average reader believes that, as against other occupations — the law, medicine, even plumbing — he has hidden talent when it comes to art. It's just that he's never had a chance to develop it, but he's got it. Another correspondence school lets a famous illustrator talk about the "natural talent" of the reader. It's one of the school's most successful ads.

A pen or pencil is always handy. If possible, the reader should be encouraged to reach in his pocket and use it on the ad.

380

380 Topaz Hosiery Mills

There's no need to contrive an artificial situation to have an attention-getting ad. For stockings, especially, think up an occasion when legs may quite normally be seen, and use that for your stocking ad, as has been done in this case.

Another stocking ad showed a phone booth on a street corner. Seated inside, and not shown, was a girl whose legs were sticking out of the phone booth door.

381

381 Plaza Sunglasses

If you have a product of unusual shape, such as eyeglasses, break it down to a simple, identifiable part of its shape and then insert the entire object within it, as has been done here.

With the enlarged shape serving for background, a girl is shown wearing the sunglasses, adding human interest. We know, by the repetition of the glasses' shapes, that they, not the earrings, are being sold.

382 Thos. Cook & Son

A world map is bait for making interesting travel plans. It's a provocative prop over a good headline. The reader not only is told to participate but is given the pencil with which to do so.

Notice how far the pencil can be whittled down to fill the small space without losing its identity. If a pen were used, it would have to be reduced in size or, perhaps, might cover up a part of the world where the reader has a yen to go.

Plot your own course

That's the way Cook's Independent Travel works. You decide where you want to go, when, with whom, and exactly how much or how little you want to spend. Cook's, the world's largest and most experienced travel organization—with over 400 offices in 60 countries—will take care of the rest . . . transportation, reservations, accommodations, every detail is pre-confirmed. Travelling the Cook's Independent way, you're on your own — yet completely free of the uncertainties of unplanned travel. For information, stop by your nearest Thos. Cook & Son office.

COOK'S

382

383 Tonette

Take an adult happening, or custom, and use a child for it to attract attention.

This two-part ad (each one-third of a page on facing pages of a spread) actually appeared in a true-story type of magazine. The readers were familiar with the story, but not with seeing a little girl in the lead role.

MY TRUE STORY

I was a plain Jane. A failure. Then I got to thinking . . .

I needed a Tonette! But how could I convince my mommie?

"Tonette," I told her, "is the home permanent made with the younger woman in mind."

And you know what? She promised me a Tonette! SEE?

383 a

Yep, that's me. See my new curls? They're soft and bouncy, too. And Tonette is gentle and easy to use. And fun! Mommie and me had a lot of laughs. Give your little girl a Tonette, okay? Promise? Soon?

FREE

Tonette

383 b

384　Nuit de Noël

Repetition of the Caron name is one good point for this ad; so is the boldness of the name in diagonal, which leads the reader's eye straight to the bottle. A reader gives your ad many exposures if he repeats a word or phrase you have repeated in your ad.

Caron

384

385　Barton's

TV Munch, the new candy by Barton's, plays a literal role in this ad as it rests temptingly on top of the TV set. The character on the screen who can't resist it is munching the candy and reaching for more. The reader is surprised at the incongruity of the flat image reaching out, three-dimensionally, into the room.

　This ad could have been even smaller if a portable TV, without a stand, had been used.

385

386　Hotel Bar Butter

This is one of a series, all in the same casual style and format, with an ingenious little word game. The package is shown as large as possible, the copy space surrounded by a black frame, the paper clip to make the message informal, to invite reading. Initials in the signature add a personal touch.

386

387 American Home Cook Book and Herald Tribune

These two small ads point up the fact that good ones don't have to be elaborate. The use of the oval and the words "Cook Book" in large type are quick stoppers for cooks. The rest of the information, in smaller type, can be read by those who are interested.

The thick-and-thin, round-cornered box makes a simple, attractive border; the typewritten copy simplifies this one-sentence ad even more.

387 a

387 b

388 Campbell's

This was one of a series appearing in comic strips of daily newspapers as a regular feature, "Good Cook's Corner." The reader's only clue to the advertiser's name is in the recipe itself. When this calls for a can of Campbell's soup, the reader begins to wonder about the objectivity of the "column." The headline fills the space boldly; the ruled-in fish attracts the eye.

388

389 9 Brothers Slipcover Co.

If there's a great deal to be said in a very small space, it's a good idea to imitate the appearance of editorial matter in the medium used. An attention-getting headline with shock value, but related to what is being said about the product, is almost a must. The mandatory word, "Advertisement," above the story will not turn the reader away if the headline is interesting enough.

389

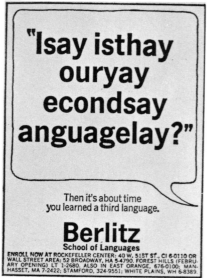

390

390 Berlitz School of Languages

An invitation to participate is a feature of this company's campaign. The query in quotes, for a headline, and the balloon around it give life to this all-type ad. Readers rusty in their pig-Latin may have difficulty in catching on.

391

391 Golden Blossom Honey

Three bees symbolize three different kinds of honey for the jar below. The simple drawing of the bees suffices to put over the selling point visually — "3 great honeys make one great flavor." A fourth bee points out the jar to make sure you're sold.

392

392 Ralph Allen, Inc.

A participation gimmick should relate directly to the product — flowers, here — especially in a small ad. This one does just that.

Flowers smell. Therefore the reader is asked to smell the ad. "Smells just like paper, doesn't it? Maybe you thought you'd smell moonlight and roses..." Then the copy tells you that you can come close to moonlight and roses by ordering fresh flowers from Ralph Allen, Inc.

393

393 Chock full o' Nuts

When an image has been established for a product, it is frequently possible to include related products within that image. In this ad, for example, the "instant" version of a famous brand becomes "The almost heavenly coffee."

Pepsi-Cola, when it introduced a new diet soda, carried the Pepsi name and image. In the mad scramble for this new market, Pepsi-Diet had a headstart because the name was familiar as compared with new brand names.

394 K & F Productions

If you can combine two or more elements within
a small space — no easy feat — it will allow you
to increase the copy or the size of type; or let
you reduce the space allotted.

In the center of this ad, the initials of well-
known musicians appear together with their pro-
files in silhouette.

394

395 Time Magazine

This ad is directed to advertising men, and features
Time magazine readership statistics of interest to
those considering the magazine as a vehicle for
their advertising. These ads appeared regularly on
the business page of major metropolitan newspapers and featured the current week's *Time* cover.

395

396 Oppenheimer Fund

A familiar gambit is this four-handed seat, used to
carry someone. The hands are used here as a
symbol of unity and mutuality — a very powerful
symbol, too.

396

397 Dannon Yogurt

Yogurt has always been thought of as a low-calorie
food for dieters. To help weight-losers, Dannon ran
this headline announcement in the newspapers and
on window stickers which were distributed to food
stores. When the reader dialed the number, he
was gently told not to go off his diet. This led
into the sales pitch — what a good low-calorie
food Dannon is and how it makes a diet more
flavorful and satisfying.

The diagonal placement of type is a good attention-getting device for a small space.

397

398 Monkees

Believe it or not, this ad drew a very considerable
response. It ran, in the size shown here, to call
attention to the premiere of "The Monkees," a
singing group. The reader was asked to send 25¢
for a 10¢ picture; some teenagers actually filled out
the coupon.

398

COUPONS

399 Hidden Magic

One factor of interest in a coupon is the illustrative matter it contains — line drawing, photograph, or some sort of decorative device. Wanda the Witch, dispenser of hair goods, attracts the eye by putting a pretty girl under the peaked hat of an old witch.

399

400 U. S. Plywood

In this ad the dotted line has been thrown around the figure adjacent to the coupon. Obviously, the reader is not going to cut out the coupon to the shape outlined, but the coupon has become more interesting and attention-getting because of its unusual shape.

400

401 Scott Paper

This ad offers a dress made of paper for $1 (plus 25¢ for handling). There is not space enough to show the style of the dress, but a choice of patterns is reproduced in miniature on the coupon with four check-off boxes covering eight basic dress sizes. A coupon should be designed not only for the item advertised but also for instructions on filling in styles and sizes, on correct dispatching, to facilitate matters for the advertiser so that when he receives the coupon he can respond with all speed.

401

402 Armour

In the Armour coupon the talking turkey tells the reader that if he will mail the order form, with a seal "from the lid of any new Armour Boneless Turkey Roast," he will receive in return a coupon worth "59¢ on a carton of any low calorie soft drinks."

402

403 Texas Tourist Development Agency

The Texas Tourist coupon is a full-color picture, with the information on what services the Texas Tourist Development Agency can supply to the reader surprinted right on the picture. There may be a problem in trying this technique if, as in some cases, the picture is too dark and the type is hard to read.

403

I have enclosed the top flap only from a package of _Metrecal_ Cookies. (Note: The top flap says "To open, pull flap up.") And have purchased a carton of TAB: One of the numbers from the bottom of the carton of TAB is

Name_____

Address_____

City_____

State_____ Zip Code_____

Mail to: Metrecal, Mead Johnson & Company, Evansville, Indiana 47721. This offer good except where prohibited, taxed or regulated by law and only in the U.S.A. Limit one refund per family. Offer expires January 1st, 1967.

25¢ refund
on a carton of TAB
with purchase of a box of Metrecal®Cookies.

404

Feed me more!

Videotape Productions, Inc. TR 3-5800
101 West 67th Street, N.Y.C.

Name_____ Title_____

Company_____

Address_____

Videotape Productions, Inc. 3M
A SUBSIDIARY OF 3M COMPANY

405

AUDIOVISUAL SALES DEPT.
EASTMAN KODAK COMPANY
ROCHESTER, N.Y. 14650   Kodak
☐ Please send details on the KODAK PAGEANT
   16mm Sound Projector, Model AV-126-TR.
☐ Please arrange a personal demonstration
   without cost or obligation to me.

NAME_____

ORGANIZATION_____

ADDRESS_____

CITY   STATE   ZIP CODE
                                        6-119

406

407

---

404 Metrecal

If the coupon offers a booklet or brochure, show it. If it offers a refund, show the coin, as in this ad: "25¢ refund on a carton of TAB with purchase of a box of _Metrecal_ Cookies."

Mead Johnson & Co.

405 Videotape Productions

The ad for Videotape gave recipes for a good TV commercial. That was followed by the recipe-shaped card coupon with the line: "Feed me more!"

3M Co.

406 Eastman Kodak

In the Kodak coupon, the mnemonic aid, the turned-down corner of a page, is used as always, revealing the familiar logo. Two simple boxes are supplied for the reader to check off what he wants.

407 Wishing Spoons

Coupons can be as decorative as one has time and money for. In the Wishing Spoons ad, birds, cupids, hearts and flowers, in charming color, are intertwined to make a wide border. It almost seems a pity to part with it by mailing it back to the advertiser.

408 Allied Chemical

The shape of coupons need not be restricted. In fact, an odd shape may attract more attention, as in this Allied Chemical coupon. Here the product seems caught in the web of the dotted line. A sort of facsimile of its technical brochure also is suggested at the bottom of the coupon.

Gentlemen:

I'd like to know more about the complete line of Plaskon epoxy molding compounds. Please send me your technical brochure.

E-9

Name_____

Company_____

Address_____

City_____State_____

PLASTICS DIVISION
POST OFFICE BOX 365
MORRISTOWN, N. J.

Allied Chemical

408

409 Fisher Radio

The Fisher postcard coupon is ready for mailing out. The reader simply fills in his name, affixes a stamp, and he's all set for his free copy of the *New Fisher Handbook* valued at $2.00.

FREE! $2.00 VALUE! Send for your free copy of *The New Fisher Handbook.* This entirely new, revised and enlarged edition of the famous Fisher high fidelity reference guide is a magnificent 76-page book. Detailed information on all Fisher components is included.

THE NEW FISHER HANDBOOK

Name_____

Address_____

City_____State_____

PLACE 4¢ STAMP HERE

FISHER RADIO CORPORATION
21-40 44th Drive
Long Island City, N. Y. 11101

409

410 Syroco

A triangular shape can be used to increase the depth of the space taken, as Syroco has done with this coupon. The most natural way to tear a right-hand page coupon is on a diagonal. A rectangular shape has to be torn or cut out at two angles.

Syroco, Syracuse, N. Y. 13201

Lady Syroco, ma'am:

Enclosed please find 25¢ in coin for your new booklet, "Wall to Wall Decorating" with Syroco Accessories.

NAME

ADDRESS

CITY

STATE   ZIP CODE

410

POSTERS

411 New York City

The trick of leading the eyes around a layout may be passé, but a small revival might be in the making. Leading the reader's eye around the page is an artificial device; but not to make use of it, when the concept lends itself, is foolish.

This poster made good use of the device. The eye follows the up-hill direction of the hand, where the girl's eyes are turned, and then the natural fall of the wastepaper into the basket, where the headline is.

412 Ford Motor Co.

The illustration is the headline and the logo. This is among the best of posters. It delivers the message in the simplest terms.

The four-letter logo is seen from the inside of a Ford dealer's window and, naturally, is seen in reverse. The excited family is looking into the window at the exciting new Ford.

413 Ford Motor Co.

A very youthful audience stands agape while a magician, with one mystic word, works a miracle before its eyes.

The new Ford convertible, with open trunk and hardtop halted midway, leaves it to the viewer to determine whether the top is coming up and out, or going down.

412

413

414 Milady's Blintzes

The headline in this poster has used the title of a familiar old song. The row of fresh fruit above symbolizes the quality of the preserves used in making the blintzes. Certainly, no bananas in Milady's Blintzes.

415 Falcon

Next to faces, hands are the most expressive members of the human anatomy. And this picture of them cleverly replaces words.

The key chain is obviously being pulled at, the motion indicated by the two flying keys. This exciting shot of two hands follows a diagonal line, adding to the hidden drama of a clash between two individuals. You know, of course, who gets the keys to the car.

Ford Motor Co.

414

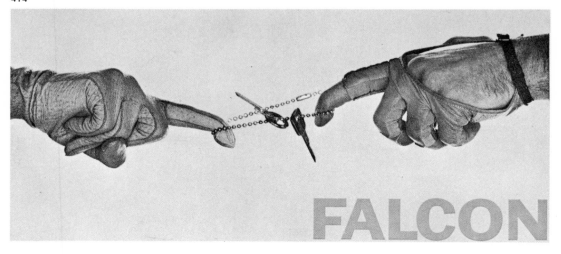

415

416 Public Service Ad

This car card appealed to students to stay in school.
Contrary to some comment — that this ad was aimed
at the very students who wouldn't recognize the
mistake, thus rendering the poster ineffectual —
the error is simple enough for most high school
students to notice. It isn't necessarily the illiterate
who are dropouts, but students who may not realize
the importance of a good education.

417 Falcon

Here is another sharp, clearly outlined picture that
speaks faster than words. It communicates instantly
the high mileage to be gotten out of a gallon of
gas with a Falcon. The woman's hand declining
unneeded gasoline is perpendicular to the logo.
These two elements serve as a frame for the hand
which holds the nozzle.

Ford Motor Co.

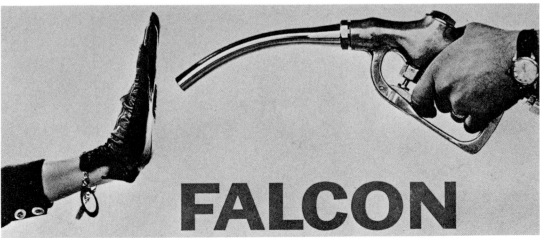

"I quit school
when I were sixteen."

416

FALCON

417

418 Wiedemann

The quick, cogent message is all that outdoor
posters aim for. Therefore, the fewer elements that
make up the poster, the better. The illustration, the
headline, the logo or package should require a minimum of effort to interpret. If any one element is
hard to grasp, communication is lost.

One symbol of fresh beer is the draught-beer tap.
In this poster it is fastened to the neck of the
bottle from which the beer is flowing — with no sign
of a normal spout. The logo or label on the bottle,
"Wiedemann Fine Beer," is none too easy to read at
best; laying the bottle on its side doesn't make it
any easier. Some beer drinkers may recognize the
bottle, but the poster may not be speaking to new
customers.

Repeating the name of the product in the headline, or in the right-hand corner, will assure its
being read at a glance.

419 Rice Krispies

Here is a rule breaker, but with good reason. A
delicious bowl of cereal with raspberries and cream
has every right to be shown. And it is. The very
distinctive logo spread across the full width of the
billboard is recognizable to millions of households;
the readability gap is not as considerable as it might
seem. Besides, "Rice Krispies" is in clear type at the
right, and this is the name of the product, anyway —
Kellogg's is the brand name.

Kellogg Co.

Fresh-from-the-barrel taste

418

RICE
KRISPIES

419

420 Life Savers

The animated moon is really enjoying his Life Saver,
which is very clearly defined in the picture. A
decorative illustration such as this is unusual in a
poster. But any treatment is acceptable, providing
the art work adheres to a few basic rules, such as
having one subject, keeping it simple, and showing
it in at least one-third of the overall space.

421   Chooz

A literal interpretation of the headline shows the
fire raging in the stomach of the cartoon character
reaching for a piece of gum.
   This approach is unusual in the United States, but
is typical of European posters. While the dark background is heavy looking, the light-colored package
and the funny little man contrast well with it.

420

421

422 Esso

When four Esso gas dealers are shown on a billboard, singing joyously at the top of their lungs,
they become stoppers. The members of the chorus
in this painting have been posed naturally. The
placement of the headline on their song sheets
breaks it easily into two short phrases.

Humble Oil & Refining

423 Wrigley's

After long years of showing heads of people having
fun, Wrigley's came up with this excellent concept,
based on a familiar office routine: the coffee break.
To prolong that interlude once a person is back at
his desk is not practicable. One way to extend the
coffee break, however, is to chew gum. Although
thousands of school teachers have reprimanded
millions of students over the years for chewing gum,
and the practice is frowned upon in polite society,
it can offer a break in the monotony of most office
life, this ad points out.

422

424 Genesee Beer

A natural situation in a familiar setting can provide
ideas for posters. This neon-sign poster is one of the
break-aways from the rules on making an effective
poster.

No Gothic lettering is used against a white background, no separate picture with a distinctive
silhouette. New rules have been established. The
name is encircled by an oval of light, the neon-
Gothic lettering is large and smack in the center of
the poster. In the photo, the man is drinking beer
while the girl admires him; she is holding up her
stein in the last stop-over for the moving eye — the
right-hand corner.

425 Birds Eye

The Campbell kids have competition here. In this
poster the animated Birds Eye kids are repeating
the slogan and bringing the brand name into sharper
focus. The alliteration of "Better buy Birds Eye"
makes it easy to remember. Slicing up the slogan
into small bits and putting them in the ballons may
make it easier for the fast motorists to digest. (This,
of course, would have to be researched; breaking
up the phrase into fragments might have the op-
posite effect.)

It is easy to recognize the children as triplets
because of their height, head shape, and fat cheeks.

424

426 Chevrolet

A familiar phrase is taken up and used quite literally for a new twist in a car poster. For boiling down a headline, there's nothing like letting the picture do some of the talking. Here it has been cut to two words.

Since a barrel of monkeys is a symbol of fun, the longer subhead below is for those who have time to read it. Poster ideas are best telegraphed to the viewer in a few words.

General Motors

427 Simmons

The idea of using a diagram here grew into an entire poster. The side view cut-away shows visually how the mattress supports the relaxed frame.

In the six seconds or so allotted to a driver going 30 miles an hour, he must be given enough visual/verbal information. to communicate the meaning of a poster. The headline has grasped the urgency of quick communication, putting Simmons and Beautyrest in caps. The distorted copy on the cut-away section below may not be read by all because it's not in a straight line. Only "Head to Toe" may get through.

426

428 Chase Manhattan

This bank ad amply fulfills the demands made on posters. It tells the story fast, bringing the image of a financial giant down to earth in the most homely and human terms with amusing drawings. The rough-edged texture of the grease pencil makes these simple drawings interesting and suitable to the subject matter.

429 Drake's

The headline gives the "double" art work meaning; the twins interpret it literally. The drawings are as simple as they are cute. The two-word headline is bouncy, with plenty of white space around it, and alliterative when read into the logo: "Double delicious Drake's."

428

429

430 Ford Motor Co.

This is one of the most popular, most talked-about posters ever made. A great deal of thoughtful planning went into making it a success. It went through various visual changes — there was a baby in it, no baby, a watchdog just sitting, then straining at his leash.

The idea was to spotlight the leader in the low price field. Research yielded the information that Ford sold about one out of every five convertibles in the U.S.A. The copywriter sought a popular symbol for another kind of convertible: hence the baby carriage. Ford actually received three orders for the baby carriage.

431 Jell-O

Most posters show heads, or perhaps the whole subject, but it's best to make your point with an absolute minimum of props, as in this poster, a pair of plump legs on a telltale scale. This telegraphs the message quickly.

There are four elements here, a lot for any poster — headline, illustration, package, and product shot. Confusion is avoided by making two groups of them, separated by a respectable amount of white space.

430

431

432 Ford Motor Co.

The public has always associated a quiet car with
a costly one. Ford presented this concept dramatically in a print campaign using the headline,
"Quieter than a Rolls-Royce." When they adapted
it to a poster campaign, they adhered rigidly to
the content but not the form.

A poster would have had to show a Ford car — a
cliché; it would have had to name another car —
a risk, in the quick glance a poster gets, since
the Rolls-Royce name might have registered before
the Ford name; and, finally, Rolls might not be a
familiar name to the poster-reading market — as
opposed to the magazine market. The animated
mouse, with a finger to his lips, assures you that a
ride in a Ford is as quiet as he is.

433 Mrs. Wagner's

Rarely used in posters, the sequence in this poster
is not only justified but most effective.

In the first place, the circular shape of the pie is
a basically simple one; the only change that takes
place is on the inside of the shape, not on the outside contour. The problem in using this technique
with a model is that the outline is not only complicated but, unless artificially posed, the human
outline changes with even the slightest change of
posture.

The two-word headline is long and drawn out,
carrying the viewer from picture to picture. The
long row of "M's" in the "Mrs." tells more than any
explanatory line of copy.

432

433

BIBLIOGRAPHY

Creativity

Baker, Stephen. *Visual Persuasion:* McGraw-Hill, 1961.
Chase, Stuart. *Guides to Straight Thinking:* Harper & Row, 1956.
Flesch, Rudolph. *The Art of Plain Talk:* Harper & Row, 1960.
Hodnett, Edward. *The Art of Problem Solving:* Harper & Row, 1955.
Keyes, Kenneth S. *How to Develop Your Thinking Ability:*
     McGraw-Hill, 1950.
Koestler, Arthur. *The Act of Creation:* Macmillan, 1964.
Mathieu, Aron M., editor. *The Creative Writer:* Writer's Digest,
     Cincinnati, Ohio, 1961. (See chapter, "Man Against
     White Space.")
Osborn, Alexander F. *Applied Imagination:*
     Charles Scribner's Sons, 1953.
_____. *Wake Up Your Mind:* Charles Scribner's Sons, 1952.
_____. *Your Creative Power:* Charles Scribner's Sons, 1949.
Reiss, Otto S. *How to Develop Profitable Ideas:*
     Prentice-Hall, 1945.
Samson, Richard W. *The Mind Builder:* E. P. Dutton, 1965.
Wheeler, Elmer. *How to Sell Yourself to Others:*
     Prentice-Hall, 1947.

Idea Starters

Esar's *Comic Dictionary.* Crown, 1960.
Ripley, Robert. *Believe It or Not:* Simon & Schuster, 1934.
Shipley, Joseph T. *Playing with Words:* Prentice-Hall, 1960.

Psychology

James, William. *The Principles of Psychology:* Fawcett, 1963.
Wolff, Janet. *What Makes Women Buy:* McGraw-Hill, 1958.

Copy Writing

Burton, Philip Ward and G. Bowman Kreer.
     Advertising Copywriting: Prentice-Hall, 1962.
Caples, John. *Making Ads Pay:* Harper & Row, 1957.
_____. *Tested Advertising Methods:* Harper & Row, 1961.
French, Elbrun Rochford. *The Copywriter's Guide:*
     Harper & Row, 1959.
Glim, Aesop. *Copy, The Core of Advertising:* McGraw-Hill, 1949.
Metzger, George P. *Copy:* Doubleday, 1926.
Schwab, Victor O. *How to Write a Good Advertisement:*
     Harper & Row, 1962.

General

Grosbeck, Kenneth. *Invitation to Advertising:*
     Simon & Schuster, 1951.
Hopkins, Claude C. *Scientific Advertising:* Moore Publishing Co.
     (reprint), 1952.
Klepner, Otto. *Advertising Procedure:* Prentice-Hall,
     (revised), 1948.
Ogilvy, David. *Confessions of An Advertising Man:*
     Atheneum, 1966.
Reeves, Rosser. *Reality in Advertising:* Alfred A. Knopf, 1961.
Whittier, Charles L. *Creative Advertising:* Henry Holt, 1955.

Reference

Barzun, Jacques, and Graff, Henry F. *The Modern Researcher:*
     Harcourt, Brace & World, 1962.
Copeland, Lewis. *High School Subjects Self-Taught:*
     Garden City Books, 1967.
Copeland, Lewis and Faye. *10,000 Jokes, Toasts, and Stories:*
     Garden City Books, 1940.
Eaton, Helen S. *Word Frequency Dictionary:* Dover, 1961.
Editors of *Year, Pictorial History of The World:*
     Year, Inc., Wilton, Conn., 1956.
Leslie, Louis A. *20,000 Words:* McGraw-Hill, 1959.
Roget's *Thesaurus of Words and Phrases:* Grosset & Dunlap, 1947.
Sickles, Evelyn R. and Sayers, Frances C.
     Anthology of Children's Literature: Houghton Mifflin, 1959.
Strunk, William, Jr., *The Elements of Style:* Macmillan, 1959.

INDEX OF ADS

INDEX OF PRODUCTS